REFORMATION CHRISTIANITY

A PEOPLE'S HISTORY OF CHRISTIANITY

Denis R. Janz
General Editor

Volume 1
CHRISTIAN ORIGINS
Richard Horsley, editor

Volume 2
LATE ANCIENT CHRISTIANITY
Virginia Burrus, editor

Volume 3
BYZANTINE CHRISTIANITY
Derek Krueger, editor

Volume 4
MEDIEVAL CHRISTIANITY
Daniel E. Bornstein, editor

Volume 5
REFORMATION CHRISTIANITY
Peter Matheson, editor

Volume 6
MODERN CHRISTIANITY TO 1900
Amanda Porterfield, editor

Volume 7
TWENTIETH-CENTURY GLOBAL CHRISTIANITY
Mary Farrell Bednarowski, editor

A PEOPLE'S HISTORY OF CHRISTIANITY

Volume 5

REFORMATION CHRISTIANITY

PETER MATHESON

Editor

FORTRESS PRESS
Minneapolis

REFORMATION CHRISTIANITY
A People's History of Christianity, Volume 5

Cover art: *Jakob Muffel* (1451–1526) by Albrecht Dürer, 1526. Photo by Bildarchiv Preussischer Kulturbesitz / Art Resource, NY. Used by permission.
Cover design: Laurie Ingram
Book design: James Korsmo / Trio Bookworks / Timothy W. Larson

Further materials on this volume and the entire series can be found online at www.peopleshistoryofchristianity.com.

Library of Congress Cataloging-in-Publication Data

Reformation Christianity / Peter Matheson, editor.
    p. cm. — (A people's history of Christianity ; v. 5)
  Includes bibliographical references and index.
  ISBN–13: 978–0–8006–3415–5 (alk. paper)
  ISBN–10: 0–8006–3415–2 (alk. paper)
  1. Reformation. I. Matheson, Peter.
BR305.3.R44 2006
270.6—dc22   2006032701

Manufactured in Canada
10   09   08   07   06   1   2   3   4   5   6   7   8   9   10

CONTENTS

Part 3. Finding Their Voice

CONTRIBUTORS

Susan R. Boettcher is Assistant Professor of History and Religious Studies at the University of Texas at Austin (USA). She has published numerous articles on the attitudes of Lutherans toward their origins, history, and contemporary confessional situation in the second half of the sixteenth century, particularly as these are reflected in confessional preaching. She is working on a book on the commemoration of Martin Luther in the same time period.

David Cressy, Professor of History at the Ohio State University, is a world authority on the intersection of elite and popular cultures in the early modern period. He is the recipient of countless distinctions. His many books include *England on Edge: Crisis and Revolution 1640–1642* (Oxford, 2006). Currently he is researching the relationship between governors and governed.

Keith P. Luria is Professor of History at North Carolina State University. He is the author of *Territories of Grace: Cultural Change in the Seventeenth-Century Diocese of Grenoble* (1991) and *Sacred Boundaries: Religious Coexistence and Conflict in Early-Modern France* (2005). He is currently working on early-modern religious coexistence.

Peter Marshall is an Orcadian, educated at Kirkwall Grammar School and University College Oxford. Between 1990 and 1994 he taught history at Ampleforth College, York, and since 1994 has done so at the University of Warwick, where he is now Professor. His books include *The Catholic Priesthood and the English Reformation* (1994), *Beliefs* *and the Dead in Reformation England* (2002), *Reformation England 1480–1642* (2003), and *Religious Identities in Henry VIII's England* (2006). His current project is a seventeenth-century ghost story called *Mother Leakey and the Bishop* to be published by Oxford University Press in 2007.

Peter Matheson has taught at Edinburgh University and Otago University; he is Principal Emeritus of the Uniting Church Theological College in Melbourne. His publications include writing on New Zealand and Third Reich history but focus mainly on the German Reformation, including *The Collected Works of Thomas Müntzer, The Rhetoric of the Reformation,* and *The Imaginative World of the Reformation.* His current research is on Argula von Grumbach.

Elsie McKee is Archibald Alexander Professor of Reformation Studies and the History of Worship at Princeton Theological Seminary. Her research has focused on exegetical history, the historical understanding of the church, and ethics, with particular attention to the Reformed tradition in the sixteenth century, especially John Calvin and Katharina Schütz Zell. Recent books include *Katharina Schütz Zell: The Life and Thought of a Sixteenth Century Reformer* (1999). Translations of Zell's writings can be found in *Church Mother: The Writings of a Protestant Reformer in Sixteenth Century Germany* (2006). Her current research focuses on the practice of pastoral ministry in Calvin's Geneva.

Raymond A. Mentzer holds the Daniel J. Krumm Family Chair in Reformation Studies in the Department of Religious Studies at the University of Iowa. His publications include *Blood and Belief: Family Survival and Confessional Identity among the Provincial Huguenot Nobility* (1994), *Society and Culture in the Huguenot World, 1559–1685* (edited with Andrew Spicer, 2002), and *La construction de l'identité réformée aux XVIᵉ et XVIIᵉ siècles: Le rôle des consistoires* (2006). His current research focuses on Reformed ecclesiastical discipline in early modern France.

Karen E. Spierling is Assistant Professor of Early Modern European History at the University of Louisville. Her publications have focused on Reformed baptismal practices and children in the Reformation, including *Infant Baptism in Reformation Geneva: The Shaping of a Community, 1536–1564* (2005) and articles in *The Archive for Reformation History* and *Sixteenth Century Journal*. Her current research explores the perpetuation of Protestant–Catholic relationships in and around Reformed Geneva.

James M. Stayer most recently taught at Queen's University in Ontario before retiring in 2000. He has been associated with the postconfessional trend in the study of the German Reformation, particularly with a secular approach to Reformation radicalism; his published works include *Martin Luther, German Saviour: German Evangelical Theological Factions and the Interpretation of Luther, 1917–1933* (2000). Currently he is researching Anabaptism and Spiritualism.

Margo Todd is the Walter H. Annenberg Professor of British History at the University of Pennsylvania. Her books include *Christian Humanism and the Puritan Social Order* and *The Culture of Protestantism in Early Modern Scotland*, and she has published numerous articles on puritans in England and Ireland and on Scottish religious history. Her current research is divided between the urban history of sixteenth-century Scotland and a history of religious anxiety in the Calvinist traditions of the British Isles and Anglo-America. She is also editing the sixteenth-century volumes of the Perth Kirk Session minutes for the Scottish History Society.

Merry E. Wiesner-Hanks is Professor of History at the University of Wisconsin-Milwaukee. She is the coeditor of the *Sixteenth Century Journal* and the author or editor of many articles and books, including *Christianity and Sexuality in the Early Modern World* (2000) and (with Susan Karant-Nunn) *Luther's Writings on Women: A Sourcebook* (2003). She is currently working on a book of readings about sixteenth-century reformations in many world religions.

ILLUSTRATIONS

Color Plates (following page 160)

FOREWORD

This seven-volume series breaks new ground by looking at Christianity's past from the vantage point of a people's history. It is church history, yes, but church history with a difference: "church," we insist, is not to be understood first and foremost as the hierarchical-institutional-bureaucratic corporation; rather, above all, it is the laity, the ordinary faithful, the people. Their religious lives, their pious practices, their self-understandings as Christians, and the way all of this grew and changed over the last two millennia—*this* is the unexplored territory in which we are here setting foot.

To be sure, the undertaking known as people's history, as it is applied to secular themes, is hardly a new one among academic historians. Referred to sometimes as history from below, or grassroots history, or popular history, it was born about a century ago, in conscious opposition to the elitism of conventional (some call it Rankean) historical investigation, fixated as this was on the "great" deeds of "great" men, and little else. What had always been left out of the story, of course, was the vast majority of human beings: almost all women, obviously, but then too all those who could be counted among the socially inferior, the economically distressed, the politically marginalized, the educationally deprived, or the culturally unrefined. Had not various elites always despised "the people"? Cicero, in first-century BCE Rome, referred to them as "urban filth and dung"; Edmund Burke, in eighteenth-century London, called them "the swinish multitude"; and in between, this loathing of "the meaner sort" was almost universal among the privileged. When the discipline called "history" was professionalized in the nineteenth century, traditional gentlemen historians perpetuated this contempt, if not by outright vilification, then at least by keeping the masses invisible. Thus when people's history came on the scene, it was not only a means for uncovering an unknown dimension of the past but also in some sense an instrument for righting an injustice. Today its cumulative contribution is enormous, and its home in the academic world is assured.

Only quite recently has the discipline formerly called "church history" and now more often "the history of Christianity" begun to open itself up to this approach. Its agenda over the last two centuries has been dominated by other facets of this religion's past such as theology, dogma, institutions, and ecclesio-political relations. Each of these has in fact long since evolved into its own subdiscipline. Thus the history of theology has concentrated on the self-understandings of Christian intellectuals. Historians of dogma have examined the way in which church leaders came to formulate teachings that they then pronounced normative for all Christians. Experts on institutional history have researched the formation, growth, and functioning of leadership offices, bureaucratic structures, official decision-making processes, and so forth. And specialists in the history of church–state relations have worked to fathom the complexities of the institution's interface with its sociopolitical context, above all by studying leaders on both sides.

Collectively, these conventional kinds of church history have yielded enough specialized literature to fill a very large library, and those who read in this library will readily testify to its amazing treasures. Erudite as it is, however, the Achilles' heel of this scholarship, taken as a whole, is that it has told the history of Christianity as the story of one small segment of those who have claimed the name "Christian." What has been studied almost exclusively until now is the religion of various elites, whether spiritual elites, or intellectual elites, or power elites. Without a doubt, mystics and theologians, pastors, priests, bishops and popes are worth studying. But at best they all together constitute perhaps 5 percent of all Christians over two millennia. What about the rest? Does not a balanced history of Christianity, not to mention our sense of historical justice, require that attention be paid to them?

Around the mid-twentieth century a handful of scholars began, hesitantly and yet insistently, to press this question on the international guild of church historians. Since that time, the study of the other 95 percent has gained momentum: ever more ambitious research projects have been launched; innovative scholarly methods have been developed, critiqued, and refined; and a growing public interest has greeted the results. Academics and nonacademics alike want to know about this aspect of Christianity's past. Who were these people—the voiceless, the ordinary faithful who wrote no theological treatises, whose statues adorn no basilica, who negotiated no concordats, whose very names themselves are largely lost to historical memory? What can we know about their religious consciousness, their devotional practice, their understanding of the faith, their values, beliefs, feelings, habits, attitudes, their deepest fears, hopes, loves, hatreds, and so forth? And what about the troublemakers, the excluded, the heretics, those defined by conventional history as the losers? Can a face be put on any of them?

Today, even after half a century of study, answers are still in short supply. It must be conceded that the field is in its infancy, both methodologically and in terms of what remains to be investigated. Very often historians now find themselves no longer interrogating literary texts but rather artifacts, the remains of material culture, court records, wills, popular art, graffiti, and so forth. What is already clear is that many traditional assumptions, timeworn clichés, and well-loved nuggets of conventional wisdom about Christianity's past will have to be abandoned. When the Christian masses are made the leading protagonists of the story, we begin to glimpse a plot with dramatically new contours. In fact, a rewriting of this history is now getting under way, and this may well be the discipline's larger task for the twenty-first century.

A People's History of Christianity is our contribution to this enterprise. In it we gather up the early harvest of this new approach, showcase the current state of the discipline, and plot a trajectory into the future. Essentially what we offer here is a preliminary attempt at a new and more adequate version of the Christian story—one that features the people. Is it comprehensive? Impossible. Definitive? Hardly. A responsible, suggestive, interesting base to build on? We are confident that it is.

Close to a hundred historians of Christianity have generously applied their various types of expertise to this project, whether as advisers or editors or contributors. They have in common no universally agreed-on methodology, nor do they even concur on how precisely to define problematic terms such as "popular religion." What they do share is a conviction that rescuing the Christian people from their historic anonymity is important, that reworking the story's plot with lay piety as the central narrative will be a contribution of lasting value, and that reversing the condescension, not to say contempt, that all too often has marred elite views of the people is long overdue. If progress is made on these fronts, we believe, the groundwork for a new history of Christianity will have been prepared.

Historians of Christianity have traditionally given the sixteenth century privileged treatment as a unique period of crisis, disintegration, and new beginnings. Here, it seemed, a rare historical constellation of dramatic event, unquestionable genius, and dynamic personality could make for riveting narrative. Over the last century this realization has resulted in an almost endless retelling, overburdening library shelves and devolving, by today, into tired convention. The volume before us intends to offer something decidedly different. In it the likes of Luther, Calvin, Leo X, Henry VIII, and Charles V recede into the wings, taking on supporting roles. Supplanting them at center stage are "the people"—the quite average

Christian laity immersed as ever in their ordinary, everyday laughing and crying, living and dying. What difference did "the Reformation" make for them? Volume editor Peter Matheson has assembled a remarkable team of experts to explore the various facets of this question. I am enormously grateful to him for lending his extraordinary talents—as historian, writer, and editor—to this project. Who better than him to show us the contours of a new narrative, a drama perhaps in its own way as riveting as the old?

Denis R. Janz, General Editor

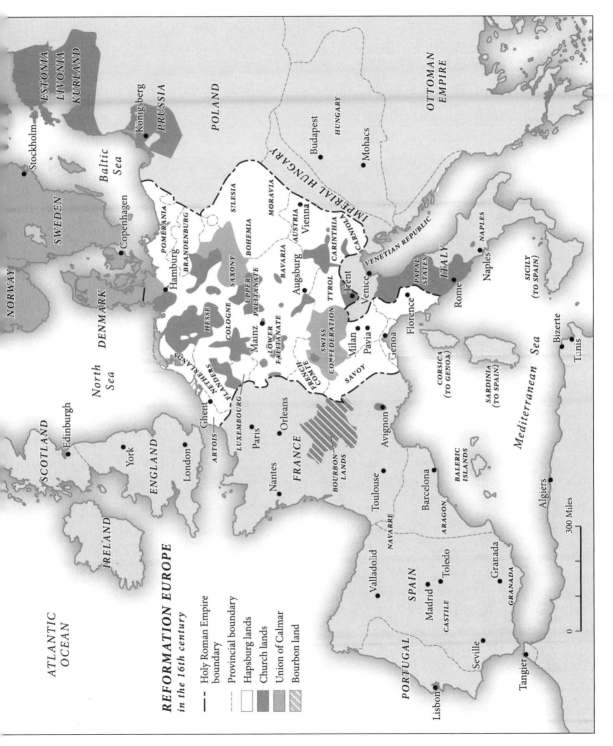

REFORMATION EUROPE
in the 16th century

- – - Holy Roman Empire boundary
- – – Provincial boundary
- Hapsburg lands
- Church lands
- Union of Calmar
- Bourbon land

Fig. 0.1. Map by Lucidity Information Design.

Fig. 0.2. Looming high above the town of Eisenach, the Wartburg castle was a refuge for Luther in his time of need. Symbolically, it has personified the endangered but defiant "fortress" of the Lutheran faith and Lutheran believers. Yet it was also a prison for those who dissented from that faith. This impressive image from the first part of the twentieth century captures something of that ambivalence. From *Views of Germany*, Library of Congress Photochrom print collection, 1905.

REFORMING FROM BELOW

PETER MATHESON

INTRODUCTION

High above the town of Eisenach in Saxony towers the imposing Wartburg castle. With its great halls, its superb museum, and its Renaissance façade, the Wartburg is one of those rare, haunting places a visitor can never forget. It became famous as the refuge of Martin Luther when he was smuggled there after the dramatic gathering of the German princes at Worms in 1521. Luther had already been excommunicated by the papacy. By the time he left Worms, he was also under the ban of the empire. He had had the audacity to defy the assembled might of church and state. He was now the ultimate outsider, both heretic and outlaw. His marvelous hymn "A Mighty Fortress Is Our God," which still inspires people today, recalls this time of crisis and yet confidence. Luther's productivity in the Wartburg was remarkable. Despite the threats he was under and his inner turmoil, he succeeded in translating the New Testament into pulsing, vivid German in the unbelievably short period of eleven weeks. Just imagine it!

This, then, is the familiar, glory side of the Reformation. On the southern tower of the Wartburg, however, one notices a bronze plaque that alerts us to a much darker side. It records the solitary confinement there of Fritz Erbe, a peasant arrested in 1533 for his refusal to have his child baptized. Though by all accounts he had been a gentle, good-living man, the Wittenberg theologians and the Saxon Elector wanted him beheaded for what they regarded as a blasphemous act. The Protestant leader, Landgrave Philip of Hesse, however, hoping that Erbe might still be persuaded to recant, succeeded in commuting his sentence to life imprisonment. At first, Fritz Erbe was imprisoned in the "Stork Tower" in Eisenach, but courageous supporters were able to reach him there and give him some encouragement, so he was transferred to the dark, freezing cold underground dungeon in the South Tower of the Wartburg. He was let down into it by the "terror hole" in the floor, and he remained there until his death in 1548, sixteen years later. He remained firm in his faith to the end, despite the appalling conditions he had to endure and the arguments of the Lutheran preachers who were sent to convince him of the error of his ways.

Martin Luther and Fritz Erbe. Which represents the reality of the Reformation? This latest in a long succession of books about the Reformation has no interest in making either heroes or demons out of Luther and leaders like him, but it will seek to transform the way in which we approach this vast religious upheaval by directing the center of interest away from princes and popes and professors to ordinary people like Fritz Erbe. How did the Reformation, or rather the Reformations—for there were many—affect laypeople, children, the rhythms of day-to-day life? Whose Reformation was it, anyway? Who gave it its momentum? What part did the ordinary urban or village dweller have in shaping it? What about the role of parents or of the great majority of the population that was illiterate or semi-literate? One glance at the table of contents of this book may give some indication of its perspective: it approaches the religious history of the early modern period "from below," in a grounded and down-to-earth way.

A generation ago, the central focus of a volume such as this one would have been on Martin Luther, John Calvin, and other major reformers. It would have traced in detail the controversy about indulgences (certificates of pardon), the rupture with the papacy, and the breakthrough to a new theology—justification by faith and the supremacy of scripture. It would have proceeded to detail the Catholic response to Lutheranism and Calvinism: the great Council of Trent in the middle of the sixteenth century, the emergence of the Jesuits and other new orders, the programs of Catholic reform. The bookends holding the narrative together would have been the prolonged hostilities between the Holy Roman Empire of Charles V and the new nation-states of France, Spain, and England, and the educational and cultural renewal we call the Renaissance.

There remains much, of course, to be said for such an approach. There will always be a need for the history of doctrine and religious concepts, for an account of institutional reform and high politics and the fascinating interplay between them. There will always be a place, too, for grand narrative and for the color and sparkle of towering personalities, with which our period is particularly abundant. It is a dull soul who cannot thrill to that. This book, however, will traverse a different path. Its aim is to alert the reader to quite new streams of research and perspective that are redressing an imbalance—one that has existed for far too long. Academic historians in the past have tended to focus on what is familiar to them: on ideas and political movements and the cultural elite. Moreover, all too often it has been male historians talking about male thinkers, politicians,

Fig. 0.3. Here peasants swear an oath of allegiance as they prepare to rise up against their masters. Note the central Christian symbolism of the flag under which they will fight. The woodcut by Pamphilus Gengenbach (c. 1480–1525) dates from 1524.

and clergy. The aim of this book is to open up some new ground, especially for those who have not had the advantage of access to the discussions in learned journals and advanced scholarship, by focusing on the aspirations and frustrations of ordinary folk. How did they react to the religious, social, and cultural upheavals around them? Were they simply swept along, or did they themselves contribute to and modify them?

A NEW DAWN

As we set out on this journey, we have to remember, of course, that the period we are entering was a highly optimistic, utopian one, at an almost infinite remove from our contemporary Western one, with its pluralism and cynicism and disillusionment with all grand narratives and heroic solutions. The literary deposit of this optimism is to be found everywhere, from Thomas More's famous *Utopia* to Campanella's *City of the Sun*, or Martin Bucer's blueprint for a godly society, the *Kingdom of Christ*. Ordinary people, too, had their own fervent dreams of a New Jerusalem, based on stubborn memories as well as ardent hopes. As we will see, many of them had no intention of sitting down passively when they found their rights and freedoms endangered, of letting things take their course. Others did follow the immemorial path of resignation, but what is so distinctive about this age is that a significant minority dared to blaze a new trail.

Indeed, the stirring of spirits was so extraordinary that to make sense of it, people reached back not only to dimly remembered events in their corporate memory but to texts from prophetic and visionary books from the Bible such as Joel and Revelation. The young would again see visions, and the old would dream dreams. Nothing seemed impossible anymore. A new age was dawning, and it was time to lasso the future. The New Jerusalem would come to pass in their own "green and pleasant land." A good and godly society was in its birth pangs.

After all, were not new lands with unheard-of wealth and wondrous plants and animals being discovered? Signs and portents in the sky were eagerly studied for evidence that changes in church and society were imminent. The whole world, it seemed, was to be turned upside down. In this highly charged atmosphere premonitions of doom mingled with hopes for the return of a Golden Age and for liberation from oppression and corruption. It was as if one were eavesdropping on the awesome battles of the legions of angels and devils in the heavens, of the Archangel Michael with Satan, of Christ with Antichrist. As the infidel Turks banged at the eastern door of Europe, as wars and rumors of wars abounded, it seemed that a cosmic battle was about to be joined, one that would be above all a spiritual battle. Therefore, you had better know which side you were on. Woodcuts, vividly colored broadsheets, popular poems, and songs and ballads set these apocalyptic ideas circulating among ordinary people. Sensational preachers such as Savonarola in Florence and still more fantastic rumors swept through homes and marketplaces. Above all, the printing press had put the vernacular Bible into laypeople's hands, and the message of the ancient prophets and apostles, raw and relevant and relentless was released. It seemed that Jeremiah was knocking at the gates of the cities and the apostle Paul was once again opening up people's minds and hearts to the great themes of the crucified and resurrected Lord. It was a time, then, for great hopes and expectations and for incandescent rage, too.

> What is the evil brew from which all usury, theft and robbery spring but the assumption of our lords and princes that all creatures are their property? The fish in the water, the birds in the air, the plants on the face of the earth—it all has to belong to them. Isaiah 5. To add insult to injury, they have God's commandment proclaimed to the poor: God has commanded that you should not steal. But it avails them nothing. For while they do violence to everyone, flay and fleece the poor farm worker, tradesman and everything that breathes, Micah 3, yet should any of the latter commit the pettiest crime, he must hang. And Doctor Liar [Luther] responds, Amen. It is the lords themselves who make the poor man their enemy. If they refuse to do away with the causes of insurrection how can trouble be avoided in the long run? If saying that makes me an inciter to insurrection, so be it![1]

This quotation is taken from the fiery pamphlet *Vindication and Refutation*, written in 1524 by the preacher Thomas Müntzer. It reminds us that religious enthusiasm could easily slip at this time into social and political radicalism. Those who ministered to the poor on a day-to-day basis saw the oppressive conditions of their lives and could not neatly separate the religious world from the secular one. Müntzer, a conscientious pastor and creative liturgist, wrote, long before Luther, a German Mass for his congregation of tradespeople and peasants in the little town of Allstedt; he went on to play a leading role in the peasant rebellions in Thuringia. Eventually he was to die, after torture, by the sword of the avenging princes. Lutheran and Catholic historians alike have tended to dismiss him in the past as a bloodthirsty terrorist. Yet he was very much part of the whole Reformation movement. He pioneered a mystical theology for ordinary people and sought to open up the scriptures to simple, rough-hewn folk.

THE RADICAL REFORMATION AND THE PEASANTS' WAR

How, then, do we incorporate the whole spectrum of religious concerns into our treatment of the period? How do we free the Reformation from a false intellectualization and spiritualization? Over the past decades there has been a gradual move away from the previous confessional and largely doctrinal and institutional approach. One important step was that from the middle of the twentieth century, historians in the United States in particular began to draw attention to the "left wing" of the Reformation. Mennonites had a special interest in the bitterly persecuted groups of believers who emphasized their simple discipleship of Christ and who became known as the Anabaptists. Up to this time, Lutheran and Calvinist historians from Europe had tended to categorize such radicals either as naive idealists or as bloodthirsty maniacs. Historians such as G. H. Williams, however, have demonstrated that the so-called Radical Reformation needed to be taken seriously as a significant theological and social movement. Williams showed that it embraced a wide variety of groups, from the quietist Anabaptists, who turned their back on all coercion and violence, state-sponsored or not, to the millenarian militants who, for example, attempted to set up a new communal kingdom in the city of Münster in 1534–1535. The emphasis of the radicals on lay leadership and on communal forms of worship and lifestyle commended them to American readers in particular. Their critique of Christendom and their frequent advocacy of tolerance appeared to put them well ahead of their time. Their bravery under persecution also seemed quite inspiring. Though a minority group, they were far from an insignificant one.

Closely associated with this new scholarly appreciation for the Anabaptists and other radicals has been the growing attention paid to the conflagration of the Peasants' War, which spread across most of central Europe in the mid-1520s. Many other peasant revolts preceded it, such as the Peasant Revolt in fourteenth-century England, and many other insurrections were to follow it; nevertheless, until the French and American Revolutions in the eighteenth century, there was to be nothing to rival it in creativity and scope and impact. Marxist historians hailed the Peasants' War as part of the early bourgeois revolution, and their research on its origins and development contributed considerably to our knowledge of it. As with the Radical Reformation, superb editions of new source material became more readily available, and these editions now sit side by side with those on the "official" or "magisterial" Reformation. The crude, smudgy pamphlets of the period have been painstakingly collected and published in readily available microfiche form.

As a result of this work and because of excellent collections of woodcuts and broadsheets, we are now much better equipped to see what the common folk thought and believed—although caution is warranted. By no means, for example, were all the pamphlets attributed to the stereotypical "simple peasant" written by them! While most Western historians in the late twentieth century were unable to accept the historical-materialist analysis of the Marxists, the importance of the Peasants' War was beginning to be recognized. By 1975, the 450th anniversary of the rebellion, serious theologians and church historians were noting its intimate relationship to the Reformation. After all, the peasants and tradesfolk who marched under the rebel flag were often advised, counseled, and led by Christian preachers. Their flags themselves featured Christian symbols such as the rainbow, and the articles they drew up to negotiate with the authorities began with a call for proper preaching, quoted scripture, and were inspired by a thirst for divine justice. They saw Christ as their captain, as the Christ of the poor, and they denounced the oppressive princes, bishops, and magistrates because they had, according to the rebels, acted contrary to "law, honor, and God."

REFORMATIONS, NOT REFORMATION

At the same time, however, as Mennonites and Marxists alerted us to the Radical Reformation and the crucial significance of the Peasants' War, we were also coming to recognize the plurality and diversity of the Reformation movements. From the 1950s, there had been a renaissance of Catholic scholarship that reminded us of the breadth and depth of humanist and Catholic reformers such as Lefèvre in France or the cosmopolitan Erasmus, who had long been offering their own programs of educational reform and creating their own lay networks, wanting to take a very different path from a Luther or a Zwingli.

The guild of twentieth-century historians came to recognize that there was not one Reformation. There were many: humanist, Catholic, communal, Zwinglian, Calvinist, Radical. Few were centered like Luther's on universities such as Wittenberg. While not denying the astonishing brilliance of Martin Luther as translator and interpreter of scripture, as hymn writer and reformer, we began to pay attention to the small army of other reformers and opinion makers, of teachers and city clerks, civic counselors and lawyers. We noted the prevalence of urban sodalities (we would call them book clubs today) and well-staffed professional academies, and the way in which monasteries often harbored alternative opinions.

The reformations were quite varied. Under Cranmer England went its own distinctive way. François de Sales initiated very attractive and popular forms of Catholic reform in Savoy. In Scotland and the Netherlands grassroots elements worked alongside an insurrectionist nobility. First we began to pay attention to the civic-centered reforms with their focus on the "common weal." Studies appeared on one city after another. But then this was complemented by some remarkable work on rural movements. It became clear that in some areas discontent had been simmering right down to the village level, where new initiatives were being launched to secure resident pastors, their own local church building, and accountable pastoral care. In this "communal reformation," in both town and country, the emphasis was not on the finer points of doctrine or on restructuring the church's institutions but on the rights and liberties of the common folk based on divine justice.

Some historians suggested that urban reform in southwest Germany and Switzerland had a distinctive "republican" profile. A reformer such as Martin Bucer, for example, in the bustling trading city of Strasbourg had firsthand awareness of laypeople's

---

**Erasmus to Archbishop Warham
1521**

The condition of things is extremely dangerous. I have to steer my own course, so as not to desert the truth of Christ through fear of man, and to avoid unnecessary risks. Luther has been sent into the world by the genius of discord. Every corner of it has been disturbed by him. All admit that the corruptions of the Church required a drastic medicine. But drugs wrongly given make the sick man worse.... For myself I am a man of peace, and hate quarrels. Luther's movement was not connected with learning, but it has brought learning into ill-repute, and the lean, and barren dogmatists, who used to be my enemies, have now fastened on Luther, like the Greeks on Hector.[2]

concerns for the "common good," while the wealthier patricians, guild members, and even women such as Katharina Schütz Zell began to make their voice heard. Anticlericalism was another particular focus of research. Its opposition to the channeling of power and wealth to the clergy bound together theological and social concerns, the interests of city leaders and the urban poor, including impoverished clerics. Traditional foci of spirituality, such as monasteries or the revered Franciscan and Dominican friars, found themselves being scrutinized by disenchanted lay eyes and often found wanting. This anticlericalism combined with the apocalyptic excitement we have already noticed to sweep aside centuries-old devotional practices such as pilgrimages and the adoration of the saints. Ritual processions were caricatured in the streets, while in pamphlets long processions of derisory words mocked traditions: worshipers brought to the shrines "bread, wine, beer, along with chicken, goose, and horse"; hoping for healing, they offered wax images "in the shape of your diseased legs, arms, eyes, head, feet, hands, cows, calves, oxen, sheep."[3] This focus on anticlericalism points to the popular roots of the Reformation.

What fired anticlericalism? As important as the sermons or tracts of the new generation of reformers was the sense of injustice and exploitation that they were able to tap into. Reformations need fertile social soil if their proposals are to grow roots. Countless early sermons and pamphlets raised very concrete socioeconomic issues, and since they regarded Holy Scripture as an infallible mirror of God's will for justice, they possessed divine justification for their passionate concern for social justice and at the same time a uniquely authoritative blueprint for a better society.[4] We have to remember, of course, that in this period no one regarded religion as an individual matter. The Christian gospel, a good individual conscience, and social harmony were seen as quite inseparable.

SOCIAL HISTORY

Perhaps the most groundbreaking change in our understanding of the Reformation in recent times has come from the contribution of social historians. Church historians had tended to work within theological faculties. Social historians operated within secular history or economics or sociology departments. While not necessarily unsympathetic to theological and religious issues, they have naturally been much more interested in social dynamics and outcomes than in ideas for their own sake. Their researches, too, were based on very different source materials. Most people in our period could not read—perhaps as few as 5 percent, though literacy could be much higher in the towns. Social historians, therefore, have drawn the obvious conclusion that if we are to do justice to the great majority, we should turn our gaze from theological tomes and sermons and institutional records to humble tax records, wills, domestic accounts, marriage contracts, family chronicles. Since wills were crafted for public effect, they throw light on communal as well as individual concerns.

Thus social historians have given us the tools to get closer to the lifestyles and relationships of the vast majority of the population. They have demonstrated the inadequacy of relying upon the aspirational teachings and literature of the preachers, intellectuals, and theologians, which certainly tell us what the latter believed but give little clue as to how much of this fell on fertile ground. A careful analysis, for example, of the reception of the Reformation in Strasbourg "suggests the social specificity of the various forms of Reformation religion." The upper classes embraced the Lutheran distinction between spiritual and secular freedom; among the tradesfolk, on the other hand, a more radical communitarian Christianity commended itself.[5] It is not just that people accepted or rejected the new teachings according to where they stood in society: they did not even register what was being said unless it spoke to their own situation.

Social historians also introduced a different interpretive grid, which involves asking a variety of questions, sometimes borrowed from the related field of social anthropology. They have asked questions about kinship and social relationships, marriage and family property, patronage, civic and rural pressure groups. English historians have been particularly helpful in pointing to the role of the local parish, for example, in building community and reconciling feuds.

The perspectives of social historians enable us, therefore, to view reality through another lens to view, for example, bishops or monasteries or their anticlerical opponents in terms of their social role in society as well as their spiritual capacity. We have become conscious that the same theological ideas could be quite differently understood by the aristocracy, the lesser nobility, wealthy townsfolk, guildsmen and artisans in the town, and the destitute. Economic historians have also reminded us that much if not most history is made not by startling cataclysmic events such as Henry VIII's break with the papacy but in long, slow movements of change in agricultural practice or commercial innovation or even in climate. The chapters in this book, therefore, rest on a host of unbelievably patient, qualitative and quantitative studies in regional and national archives across Europe.

CULTURAL HISTORIANS

Cultural history has been another rich vein that has increased in value in recent Reformation studies. Our lives, including our religious lives, are framed and informed much less by formal credos or confessions of faith, or by papal or synodical pronouncements than by the songs we sing, the illustrations we hang on our walls, the daily rhythms of our lives, the feasts and festivities we celebrate, and perhaps above all our "rites of passage"—how we mark birth and death, growing up into adulthood, forming lifelong relationships, facing illness and death. How do we celebrate and mourn, how do we distinguish between our private and public life, and how are these practices reflected in the spatial design of our homes and streets and city squares and plazas? These days historians of the Reformation work cheek by jowl with historians of art and music, of architecture and language, not to mention historians of food and costume. Material evidence, such as that provided by architecture, funeral monuments, and inscriptions, has also been paid increasing attention. All these contribute to building up some sense of the texture of the lives of ordinary people.

We have learned, too, from the cultural historian that we may understand a church or a society best when we view it not from the centers of power but from the margins. Accordingly, cultural historians have turned our attention to how urban and rural societies treated their "outsiders": the unclean trades, for example, such as the butchers; nonsedentary groups such as the mercenaries, Gypsies, and wandering players; feared or despised groups such as the Jews and the "witches." The role that the church has played thus appears in a new light.

The quest, of course, for the "ordinary" or average person can be something of a chimera and can sometimes lead to a false dichotomy between popular and elite culture. Rather fringy outsiders, such as the miller Menocchio with his homespun theories of the universe,[6] have sometimes been taken to represent popular religion, while entire swaths of Catholic and Lutheran rural and urban dwellers have been labeled submissive pew-fodder and therefore quite uninteresting.

Unlike today's world, however, the "high culture" in the early modern period was not hermetically separated from the "popular culture" of the majority of the population. With one or two exceptions, such as court and university life, people of all classes mixed quite freely. Gradations, of course, were respected, even to the shape and color of the clothes one was allowed to wear. But everyone attended the same church, went to the feasts and festivals together, mixed and mingled in the street and the marketplace. Shakespeare's dramas remind us how philosophical monologues and buffoonery succeeded and complemented one another.

No small part of the challenge of the religious Reformations, therefore, was that they altered life for everyone, not just for the nuns and the monks who were forced out of their monasteries. The changes impinged on every dimension of life. It is true that many of the fundamental patterns of family relationships, with their intimate connection to property rights, proved remarkably resistant to change, but what is astonishing is how many of the subtle textures of daily life were transformed: the intimate discourse and gestures of divine and human love, the practice of prayer and almsgiving, the central metaphors in which God and Christ, church and spirit, individual and communal life were expressed, were transmuted and transfigured. It was not just the furniture of church buildings that changed but, much more fundamental, the furniture of people's minds and hearts. Where such changes took firm root in the imagination, the Reformation was most profound.

REFORMATION AND WOMEN

At long last, too, historians have come to ask a question so obvious that it was universally ignored: Was there a Reformation for women? Within the last generation or so, we have finally woken up to the fact that 50 percent of the people living, thinking, and working in our period were women. Unsurprisingly, much of this is attributable to the relatively new phenomenon of women historians. It is, however, remarkable how long it has taken to "rediscover" the perspectives and contribution of women in this period, whether as mothers or nuns, wives or single women, and to investigate how they crafted their lives, formed their children, and influenced their menfolk. I can still remember my delight at finding a very useful biographical index at a splendid German library but then my growing mortification as it dawned on me that it listed not a single woman.

The role women have played, however, is only one issue. Interest has moved well beyond casting them as either heroine or victim. As scholars have reviewed gender perspectives, they have discovered that virtually all our previous presuppositions about piety and worship, the fashioning of theology, the reading of scripture, the life of children, the realities of home and public life need to be comprehensively revisited. Issues of male honor, for example, impinged hugely on how women were regarded and treated. Historians are beginning, therefore, to look at understandings of masculinity, and as this is addressed, it has become quite clear that the way in which men viewed themselves varied greatly from one region to another and from one time to another. Once the questions were posed, it all seemed so obvious, but why has it taken us so long to get there?

> **Argula von Grumbach challenging the Ingolstadt theologians to a debate:**
>
> I do not flinch from appearing before you, from listening to you, from discussing with you. For by the grace of God I, too, can ask questions, hear answers and read in German. There are of course German Bibles which Martin [Luther] has not translated. You yourselves have one which was printed forty-one years ago, when Luther's was never even thought of. . . .
>
> God grant that I may speak with you in the presence of our three princes and of the whole community. It is my desire to be instructed by everyone. . . .
>
> I have no Latin; but you have German, being born and brought up in this tongue. What I have written to you is no woman's chit-chat, but the word of God; and [I write] as a member of the Christian Church, against which the gates of Hell cannot prevail.[7]

HOTLY DEBATED ISSUES

Many issues remain wide open as this book goes to press. That is good, because it illustrates that there has never been such an exciting time to study Reformation history as now. At virtually every gathering of early modern historians, for example, there is a debate about periodization: How should we carve up the course of Christian history? This is far from being just a typical academic infight. If, for example, we set a starting point around 1520, this suggests a view of the Reformation as an abrupt break from the past, which begins and ends with Luther. It has become increasingly clear, however, as we work through a whole raft of issues—from popular piety to biblical interpretation to institutional reform—that there is substantial continuity with the late medieval period. If, on the other hand, we were to see the Reformation or Reformations as a subset of a much wider Renaissance movement, that could set the starting point far back in the fifteenth century or even earlier. There are economic, social, political, and cultural arguments for a whole host of different positions. In this volume we are opting for the "long sixteenth century" option, which assumes that the early modern period stretches back into the medieval period and extends well into the seventeenth. Again there are unmistakable signs of a revolt against a narrowly European view of this period, recognizing that the new religious movements were already beginning to have an impact on North and South America and Asia.

Another highly controversial area is that of confessionalization. To what extent should we see this whole period as one in which the real motor and determiner of events was the early modern state, with its agendas of centralized control, standardization, and repression of dissenting views? Were theological and religious considerations at best secondary to state propaganda and indoctrination, especially as religious conflict became identified with political rivalry and military confrontation between nation-states? What degree of popular or personal support did the various Reformations really enjoy? This is, of course, a crucial question for a book such as this one, which focuses on the views of the ordinary person.

Ultimately, the answer given may be dependent not only on the evidence available but on the historian's understanding of what constitutes human nature and human society. As the carefully choreographed Catholic processions wound their way through the streets, however, it is hard to doubt that most people must have felt a heightened sense of solidarity with the earthly community as well as the heavenly community that the processions were prefiguring. On the other hand, the plurality of religious options and the trend toward interiorization of the faith encouraged what the irenic Catholic theologian George Cassander (1513–1566) called "a sort of third type of people," who found good and bad in both sides and longed for a mediating position. Should we assume, from a patronizing position in the present, that communal identity and personal freedom are necessarily opposed to one another? Recent research has certainly shown that the old distinction between a bourgeois, republicanizing Protestantism and a submissive, politically absolutist Catholicism can no longer be maintained.

Finally, how are we to do justice to the "cross-pollination" that took place in people's hearts and minds as well as in institutions at this time? How can we represent appropriately the interplay of biblical themes with social unrest, of theological motifs with cultural or nationalist considerations, of personal inclinations with the whole matrix of economic and social determinants? If the traditional style of doing church history sometimes suggested that nothing mattered except ideas and institutions, doctrine and churchmanship, the new can go to the other extreme, with an overwhelming preponderance of social or gender analysis. There has been, of late, something of a revolt against too analytical and determinist readings of this period. It has been suggested that we have permitted the intrusion of anachronistic categories. Do modern political terms such as "liberal," "conservative," "radical," and "reactionary" really help us to understand this period?

It has been emphasized, therefore, that it would be good to treat the language and values of sixteenth-century men and women with the utmost seriousness and not to read them from our perspectives. We need to avoid using "shopworn" modern categories for the time and place we are studying and "patiently seek conceptions better suited to bring out [their] character." We have to guard against assuming that common folk were only interested in social outcomes and were not passionately engaged with faith in God and love of their neighbor. Countless men and women, after all, risked the loss of property, security, and lifelong friendships, put witnessing to their faith above family or marriage, bought forbidden books, harbored fugitive preachers, and stood firm under all manner of threats. Women faced the risk of being shut away for life. Many believers died a ghastly death by beheading or by drowning or at the stake. It seems inappropriate not to take this seriously.

There are undeniable problems of interpretation here. We can never wholly escape from our own vantage point. The task of fusing the horizons of early modern people with our own will always be a challenging one. At the very least, however, their language and thought, their spirituality, their courage and timorousness have to be allowed to appear in their own alien forms. The great sobering corrective for all of us historians is that we are driven back again and again to the sources, social as well as personal. Analysis and smooth synthesis must always be held to ransom by the discordant testimony of the evidence, textual and nontextual. We have to attempt to create from that testimony and the questions of other historians a rich, textured picture of what faith, discipleship, martyrdom meant for ordinary people. We always have to remember that, as Robert Scribner put it, "the ways in which they sought to relate their religious and secular aspects were more varied and complicated than the neat compartmentalizations 'religious' and 'social' imply."[10]

Behind the simplest hymn or prayer or action or protest lies a whole raft of factors, associations, hopes, and visions that no individual or team of people can hope to uncover or recover. The past is in the past, and it is forever lost to us. Yet its allure and challenge remain. As in all human relationships, we may need both to preserve the courtesies and to move beyond them. A respect or even reverence for the people of the past can spur us to stretch our imaginations, to deploy a comprehensive palette

---

Wilhelm Rem's Augsburg Chronicle of 1524

Then on 15 September the Council had two weavers beheaded furtively; the alarm bells were not rung. The first was called Speiser, a good follower of the Gospel with a good reputation. When they struck off his leg-irons and brought him to the front of the Council Chambers he asked where they were taking him, and they said to him, they intended to execute him. . . . He said, the Council was dealing with him unjustly and violently. . . . It was because of the word of God that he had to die, and he was quite ready to die. He had a good reputation and was a God-fearing man. Then they chopped his head off on the marketplace. . . . They imprisoned many women and men here because of what they were saying, putting them to torture, and expelling many from the city.[9]

that will do justice to their ideas ("the flowing, curative waters of Wittenberg, as one pamphlet described them) as well as to social and cultural factors, and to trace the way in which groups and individuals tuned in and tuned out of the messages they heard, developed their own idiosyncratic "take" on issues, and spoke out bravely or prudently kept their peace.

I would argue for an approach that respects but does not absolutize the role of ideas, spiritualities, and theologies—which can be valued as genial articulations and responses to the issues generated by the socioeconomic and cultural matrix—but gives equal emphasis to how communities and individuals wove such credos into the warp of their own particular lives. Most communities, after all, expressed their deepest beliefs not in propositional form but in song and ceremony, whether in Catholic processions and pilgrimages or Protestant celebrations of the Lord's Supper or days of fasting and penitence.

DID ANYTHING REALLY CHANGE?

The jury is still out on the question of the "success" of the religious Reformations. Many would argue that they brought about little significant social or cultural change, pointing quite correctly to the reemergence of clericalism, to the censorship of ideas and books, and to the enforced uniformity of the confessional era. Others note the stubborn resistance of rural communities to reforms that looked all too much like impositions from the city slickers. In my own view, the impact and memory of the Reformations, stumbling and compromised as they often were, remained a motor for highly significant change in the mental outlook and actual lives of so-called ordinary people. The audacious expectation of a comprehensive "Reformation," the symbolic language of a new dawn, a new age of light, freedom, truth, and justice, kept recurring in different forms: Puritanism, Jansenism, Neoprotestantism. Even liberation theology, it has been suggested, owes much to its Reformation heritage.

The era's contributions to the Western world we know today are incalculable. New centers of pilgrimage like Wittenberg and Geneva as well as the countless Catholic sites were established. Histories,

February / Man at Fireplace

March / Ploughman

April / Man Pruning

June / Man Hoeing

July / Man Mowing
with Scythe

September / Couple Making
Wine

October / Sower

November / Man Chopping
Wood

December / Disk of Sundays

Fig. 0.4. Woodcuts depicting daily peasant life from a fourteenth-century calendar. Augsburg Johann Schobsser, "Kalendar" (June 1488) in Adam von Bartsch, *The Illustrated Bartsch: German Book Illustration before 1500*, Vol. 86: Part VII, Walter L. Strauss and Carol Schuler, eds. (New York: Abaris Books, 1984), 310–12. See also p. 41 in this volume.

martyrologies, hymnbooks, and "display cabinets," listing eminent men and women, kept fresh the memories of the new saints, scholars, and confessors for future generations. The Counter-Reformation's massive building programs, educational initiatives, and networks of care for the sick and the poor left a legacy for the future that cannot be gainsaid.

All the Reformations really posed the same question. What is the church, actually? By the variety of their answers, their stern challenge to tradition and authority, and the consequent polarization of opinion, new discursive fields were created. The resources of word, song, and literature opened up endless options for the interior life and for communal experiments of all kinds. The dream of a church in the prophetic mold was not to be forgotten.

THE LIFE OF FAITH

Part 1

THE PIETY OF TOWNSPEOPLE AND CITY FOLK

RAYMOND A. MENTZER

CHAPTER ONE

In the mid-1550s, Antoine Cathelan, a former Franciscan monk, departed his native France and, in the course of travel, spent seven months at the nearby Reformed city of Lausanne. Though ultimately unsympathetic to Protestantism, he noted with particular interest the interior arrangement of the edifices for worship: "It is exactly like the interior of a school. Benches are everywhere and a pulpit for the preacher in the middle. The women and children are seated on low benches in front of the pulpit, while around them the men are on higher ones, without differentiation of status."[1] This Catholic eyewitness had plainly grasped the essential pedagogical nature of the new piety, which focused on Holy Writ and its careful, regular explication through the sermon. The faithful now quietly sat—Geneva, for instance, installed pews by the late 1530s—and carefully listened as the pastor explained God's Word as found in scripture and scripture alone. People no longer stood, wandered about, or engaged in individual prayer, as was the case during the late medieval celebration of the Mass. The pastor in the pulpit commanded undivided attention. In Cathelan's description, however, other attitudes and habits appear to have been resistant to change. Received wisdom judged women and children less capable of learning and therefore they occupied benches near the pulpit for better understanding and closer supervision. Men, thought to be more responsible and capable, took seats along the sides and farther back. Still, according to this outside viewer, people gathered and sat without regard for social distinctions in what the modern observer might interpret as remarkable sensitivity and appreciation for the notion of the equality of all believers.

Had Cathelan visited French Reformed congregations less than a century afterward, he might have been equally impressed by the long-term reverberations of the introduction of pews. In response to demands from the faithful, churches everywhere had developed well-delineated, hierarchical seating plans within their temples, which, in France, were the physical structures in which the faithful assembled; the church was the community of believers. The spatial arrangements in these temples not merely took account age and gender but also deferred to social status. Ecclesiastical and political officials—pastors, elders and deacons, nobles, and political officers—had prominent places next to the pulpit. Beyond these designated benches for dignitaries, others in the congregation enjoyed open seating. At least, this was the early ideal.

The church at Castres in southern France soon found that it continually needed to remind people that all benches were common. The reason for the reminder was simple: many worshipers displayed an immediate and strong desire for private seating. Two women of Montauban nailed cushions to their favorite seats in an attempt to lay claim to sacred territory. At Nîmes, families fastened insignia and armorial bearings to benches. Seating squabbles at Alès nearly paralyzed the church during the late 1630s and early 1640s: men and women engaged in bitter personal disputes, complained to the pastor and elders, appealed to the provincial synod, and even lodged lawsuits in the royal courts over who sat where in the temple. Elsewhere, families asserted proprietary rights over pews and insisted upon their orderly transmission from one generation to the next in an explicit system of inheritance. A few persons even resorted to physical brawls. Thus a mother and daughter, members of one of the leading families at yet another French town, attacked the pastor's wife, whom they held responsible for moving their bench to a less prominent spot within the town's temple. The pair "rudely pushed and injured" the minister's spouse and were accused of having pulled her hair and scratched her throat.[2] What had begun as an effort to affirm people's Christian faith by having them sit dutifully and heed the pastor's thorough explanations of scripture soon deteriorated into constant disruption and distraction. Clearly, the Reformation's reconceptualization of Christian theology and devotion had important consequences, and few authorities appear to have anticipated fully the perceptions of ordinary believers. These seating disputes reveal much about the ways in which common folk, firm in their convictions yet sensitive to a multitude of less godly concerns, molded and interpreted innovations in piety and worship.

In all of this, it is worth recalling that the appeal of the Reformation to city dwellers was strong and enduring. Towns across Western Europe from the imperial German world to the Swiss cantons, France, the Netherlands, and the British Isles adopted Protestantism readily and ardently. To understand these extraordinary developments we must ask how religious reform was construed by the urban residents who formed the backbone of support. Explanations have typically centered on educated elites, the politically influential, and the nature of civic bonds. One common account of the attraction of the Protestant Reformation within cities was that it permitted people to achieve full control over all aspects of communal life, civil as well as ecclesiastical. Civic society, the body politic, and the community of the faithful became a seamless whole. The importance of this and related interpretations is not in question. Yet this perspective necessarily concentrates on the most prominent social and economic groups and the municipal political processes they dominated. Far less attention has been given to the broader spectrum of urban residents and their religious insights, liturgical preferences, and devotional habits. What, in short, were the dynamics of piety across the entire range of people living in the urban milieu?

Changes in people's appreciation and performance of religious devotion occurred everywhere and at every level in Reformation Europe. The revisions and adaptations affected persons of all stations, from the highest members of the princely order and urban magnates to impoverished artisans, day laborers, and even unemployed vagrants. The modifications and innovations reached into Anabaptist, Anglican, Catholic, Lutheran, and Reformed circles. Men, women, and children were all affected, if in differing ways and to differing degrees. The process could be volatile and challenging. Some welcomed and encouraged the changes; others resisted. Clashes over these matters—the value of religious images or the manner of celebrating the eucharist, for example—were hardly unknown. The impetus for change and the elaboration of mechanisms to realize it were nowhere more conspicuous than among the followers of John Calvin. Thus it is to the so-called Reformed tradition that we direct our attention.

REFORMING WORSHIP AND PIETY

Scholars now recognize that the religious transformations initiated in early modern Europe meant more than an altered set of theological tenets. Reformers introduced new modes of prayer and forms of worship. The Calvinist Reformation did not, as is sometimes assumed, do away with ritual. Its leaders unquestionably abandoned elements they considered too "popish" and formulaic, yet they labored arduously to institute a new Reformed liturgy. They also faced the considerable task of molding confessional identity, mainly through a careful process of edification and supervision of each and every member of the community. Put slightly differently: learned ecclesiastical authorities sought to reeducate the often unlettered laity and to translate theological insights into a set of everyday devotional routines and Christian standards of moral behavior. Urban Protestants, especially those who constructed their churches on Calvin's Genevan model, mounted their campaign to reform piety on several levels and in a variety of fashions. They sought to instruct the ordinary and generally illiterate members of the congregation through preaching and catechism. The reformers simultaneously worked to purify sacred rites, revitalize communal worship, and eliminate vestiges of medieval "superstition and idolatry." They instituted poor relief programs, which not only materially assisted the impoverished but delivered a strong measure of spiritual, economic, and social direction. Finally, Protestants in the Reformed tradition attempted to quell disputes, regulate the household, chastise sexual misconduct, outlaw dancing, and suppress "sinful" behavior of every sort.

While emphasis varied across traditions, Protestant leaders generally strove to suppress nonscriptural aspects of medieval piety, which could be dear to ordinary laypeople. In Reformed cities, the cult of saints, prayers to the Virgin Mary, images and statues, processions and pilgrimages, memorial masses, and the calendar of religious feasts disappeared, despite occasional popular reluctance. Liturgical space and language, preaching, and participation in the eucharist were also transformed. The Lord's Supper replaced the Latin Mass, and, in the process, the sacrificial understanding associated with the medieval Mass gave way to a shared eucharistic celebration. The Lord's Supper was not, however, the principal weekly focus of worship. It took place only four times each year on Easter and Pentecost, during Christmas-tide, and in mid-September. Even then, the Supper was always embedded in the sermon service, which became the focus of the liturgy. Not surprisingly, some men and women were initially unwilling or unable to adapt. Early on, the Genevan pastors and elders faulted individuals for mumbling and failing to listen carefully during the sermon. The offenders seem to have been praying privately and not paying close attention, just as had been the custom when attending Mass. A few worshipers in France were reluctant to drink from the cup from which the medieval church had barred them. Others had difficulty learning their prayers in the vernacular and felt more reassured when reciting a familiar Pater Noster or Ave Maria. One Genevan mother was so utterly confused yet fundamentally dedicated to her children's spiritual welfare that she taught them their prayers in both French and Latin.

THE VERNACULAR

Reformed churches instituted a vernacular liturgy, which stressed the Word, prayers, partaking of the Lord's Supper, and almsgiving. The newly authorized rituals lessened the separation of clergy and laity while expanding ordinary people's involvement. As such, urban residents and particularly those belonging to the emerging bourgeoisie found these practices immensely appealing. The pastor addressed his sermons directly to the faithful. There was no physical separation, such as the medieval rood screen, which divided the choir and celebration of the Mass from the nave, where those in attendance stood. Nor was there the linguistic distancing of a priest saying the Mass in Latin, of which his parishioners understood little. The replacement of Latin, the privileged idiom of the intellectual and ecclesiastical elite, with the vernacular as the language of ritual and prayer invited greater congregational participation. Still, inclusion was not as extensive as may appear at first glance. The adoption of a vernacular liturgy by the Reformed churches of France offered easier access and greater engagement to a particular, albeit important, segment of society. Beyond the Île-de-France and its immediate environs, French was the language of the middling urban dwellers, who were among the strongest adherents to Protestantism in France. The vast majority of pastors and elders came from their ranks. On the other hand, thousands of artisans and laborers, above all in the strongly Protestant southern provinces, did not speak or understand French well, if at all. The indigenous language of the southern region was Occitan, which was closer to Catalan than to French. Similar linguistic gulfs separating a lettered elite from ordinary believers existed throughout France and in other parts of Europe.

The late medieval church had sermons, but they tended to be given by Dominican and Franciscan monks during the Advent and Lenten seasons as preparation for Christmas and Easter. The Reformation ushered in a regular schedule and concentrated attention on the Word. Geneva had daily sermons, and while less frequent elsewhere, sermons nonetheless became the crux of people's formal religious experience. Everyone was obliged to attend the sermons on scripture, in particular the Sunday morning service, and was expected to arrive promptly, listen diligently, and remain until the conclusion. Failure to do so often meant a summons from the local religious authorities to explain this breach of Christian conduct. The "preaching" service usually began with scriptural readings by a lay elder, deacon, or schoolmaster. The recitation of prayers and congregational singing of psalms also figured prominently. Wealthy churches even hired a cantor—perhaps the most famous was Louis Bourgeois at Geneva—to lead the singing. Once the pastor ascended the pulpit, he spoke extemporaneously for an hour or more. Other elements of worship and devotion were joined to the preaching. The quarterly celebrations of the Lord's Supper, baptisms, and marriages were embedded in the sermon service, thereby underscoring the central position of the Word in Reformed piety. There could be no sacrament—either baptism or the Supper or even the solemnization of a marriage—without Holy Writ.

Though depicting a combination of events that normally occurred separately or in sequence, the famous painting of the interior of the Temple de Paradis at Lyon during the 1560s (fig. 1.1) provides wonderful insight into the complex of devotional habits that punctuated most people's existence at that time. The pastor delivering his sermon from the pulpit is the central visual element. Flanking him are prominent men from the community, who sit on benches draped with fine blue cloth marked by politically symbolic fleurs-de-lis, the French royal coat of arms. Several small boys, perhaps catechism students, are close to the pulpit as well. A group of women sits a bit further back, while the men are situated along the sides and in the gallery. To the left, godparents enter with a newborn, who will be baptized toward the conclusion of the worship and thereby welcomed as the community's newest member. The godfather carries the infant, who is wrapped in linen, while the godmother with pitcher in hand stands immediately behind. Seated in front of the pulpit is a couple, who are perhaps going to be married at the conclusion of the sermon. Both ceremonies were critical public events whose proper celebration required the totality of the faithful gathered to hear God's Word.

Reformed churches obliged the faithful to attend the Sunday sermon worship, and most readily complied. Inevitably, some members of the congregation lacked diligence, preferring instead to doze, chat with neighbors, or even conduct business affairs. Others appear to have genuinely appreciated these explanations of scripture and often discussed the morning's sermon in both positive and negative tones as they spilled out into the street, returned to their homes, or went about their work in the days that followed. That they could be discriminating listeners is demonstrated in other ways. In larger urban centers

> **An Excerpt from the Ecclesiastical Ordinances of Geneva**
>
> *The duty of pastors:* With regard to the pastors . . . their office is to proclaim the Word of God for the purpose of instructing, admonishing, exhorting, and reproving, both in public and in private, to administer the sacraments, and to exercise fraternal discipline together with the elders. . . .
>
> *The frequency, place, and time of preaching:*
>
> On Sundays there shall be a sermon at daybreak in St. Pierre and St. Gervais, and at the customary hour in St. Pierre, La Madeleine, and St. Gervais.
>
> At noon the catechism, that is to say, instruction of little children, shall be conducted in all three churches.
>
> —From "Ecclesiastical Ordinances," in *The Register of the Company of Pastors of Geneva in the Time of Calvin,* ed. and trans. Philip Edgcumbe Hughes (Grand Rapids: Eerdmans, 1966), 35–49.

Fig. 1.1. A painting of the interior of Temple de Paradis. Anonymous, sixteenth or seventeenth century. Bibliotheque publique et universitaire, Geneva, Switzerland. Photo: Erich Lessing/Art Resource, NY.

where individuals had a choice among various sermon services, people sought to avoid incompetent or tedious preachers. One Genevan pastor of the mid-1540s had a reputation for being an ineffective preacher. When parishioners saw him approach their church, they "turned around" and presumably went to another service elsewhere.[3]

THE CATECHISM

The pedagogical goals inherent in the pastor's sermon and its systematic explanation of the Bible extended to catechism as well. The education of ordinary, unlettered folk in the core Christian beliefs and basic prayers had for centuries taken place through participation in the liturgy or in the home at the hands of mothers and fathers.

Protestants adopted a more rigorous and systematic approach. Both Luther and Calvin composed and published catechisms early in their movements. Addressed to an uneducated, often youthful audience, they taught the critical elements of the faith—the Lord's Prayer, Apostles' Creed, and Ten Commandments—along with the rudiments of the sacraments and a smattering of prayers appropriate for morning, evening, and mealtime. The objective was to inculcate the truths of the faith and to do so with precise and intelligible but elementary language. Luther, for example, lamented that people commonly had "no knowledge whatever of Christian teaching."[4] Most Reformed churches held a sermon service on catechism each week on Sunday; it was at noon in Geneva and later afternoon in French towns. Calvin penned a French catechism as early as 1542; the earliest extant edition dates from 1545. Eventually the Geneva catechism contained fifty-five lessons or "Sundays," which presumably framed a pastor's sermons. The Heidelberg Catechism of 1563, used extensively by Dutch, German, and Hungarian Reformed communities, had fifty-two "Sundays." These and other catechisms concentrated on brief questions and responses—the rote instruction that officials thought appropriate for unlettered persons raised in an oral culture. Catechism teachers frequently employed an "echo" technique, whereby the answer repeated a part of the question: "What is the chief end of human life? The chief end of human life is . . ." The Genevan pastor Charles Perrot tells us about the dialogue between pastor and child. He would "come down from the pulpit, . . . sit down on a bench," and then have each of the children "recite in turn."[5] Altogether, catechesis aimed at fostering piety in a manner accessible to a plain and unsophisticated audience.

Catechism was also a lifelong experience, at least in the French Reformed churches. People attended elementary catechism lessons in

> **An Excerpt from the Registers of the Genevan Consistory**
> **Thursday, April 13, 1542**
> **Françoys Mermiez**
>
> The Consistory advises that . . . he be made to give an explanation of his faith in intelligible language. And whether he knows how to pray to God and whether he frequents the sermons. Answers that he never misses a sermon and cannot say his Pater [Lord's Prayer] except in Latin, which he did. And he said the Ave Maria in Latin, and also the Credo [Apostles' Creed] in an unintelligible manner. And that he present himself here in one month.
>
> —From *Registers of the Consistory of Geneva in the Time of Calvin, Vol. 1: 1542–1544*, ed. Robert M. Kingdon, Thomas A. Lambert, and Isabella M. Watt, trans. M. Wallace McDonald (Grand Rapids: Eerdmans, 2000), 40.

their youth, and as adults they assisted at a general catechism in the two weeks preceding the Lord's Supper. Pastors grilled these men and women on their understanding of the faith and their knowledge of the essential prayers. Attendance was an absolute prerequisite for participation in the Supper. Churches regarded absence as a serious fault and sometimes maintained lists of those who were present and therefore eligible for admission to the table. At Nîmes, the deacons composed rosters of the catechized with annotations regarding people's satisfactory or unsatisfactory comprehension. In the custom there as well as at La Rochelle and Montauban, the faithful were catechized, and afterwards the elders issued each a special communion token, which was subsequently collected either at the temple door or at the table on the day of the service. No one could participate without a token.

The primary goal of catechism was to teach the prayers, which were recited and, on some occasions, sung during the worship service. Praying is, after all, a devotional act, and the goal was not simply to know the proper prayers but to say them on a daily basis. Reformed congregations in urban areas held prayer services on weekdays, families were meant to pray together at home, and people presumably said individual private prayers. Gestures associated with prayer also needed to be reoriented. The sign of the cross, like prayers in Latin offered to the saints, was no longer acceptable. Calvin in the *Institutes of the Christian Religion* favored kneeling, baring the head, and extending the arms toward heaven when praying.[6] Less clear is the extent to which his suggestions were taken to heart. On certain occasions, the entire congregation knelt to recite a psalm "in prose" (that is, not sung). The reorientation of gesture extended to daily life as well. Some French pastors insisted that individuals should no longer swear an oath upon the Bible; instead, they ought to raise their right hand to the heavens.

THE LORD'S SUPPER

Transformations in the celebration of the eucharist had an equally profound effect upon the devotional lives of ordinary Protestants, even though some features of the sacrament proved stubbornly impervious to modification. To begin, the Supper took place but four times a year and, in this sense, differed significantly from the daily celebration of the medieval Mass. On the other hand, the involvement of laypersons in the service increased dramatically. Perhaps the two most noticeable changes, at least in the popular mind, were the increased frequency of receiving the eucharist and the laity's reception of the cup. Medieval Christians tended to take communion once a year, most likely with the entire parish at Easter. The Reformed Supper now occurred quarterly. More spectacular was the layperson's taking of both the bread and the wine. During the centuries preceding the Reformation, the wine had been reserved exclusively for the priestly celebrant. Scattered evidence suggests that a few individuals who had grown up prior to these modifications felt uncomfortable with them; they may have hesitated to receive more often than once a year or shied away from the cup.

The Lord's Supper in French Reformed churches followed the *Form of Prayers and Ecclesiastical Song, with the Manner of Administering the Sacraments*, first published by Calvin in 1542. The rite was very much the usual Sunday morning worship, in the course of which the Supper was celebrated. A special prayer introduced the sacrament. The pastor then delivered a general exhortation to the faithful, followed by preparation of the bread and wine. In France the congregants proceeded two by two toward the communion table, which was typically located directly below the pulpit. The communicants were segregated according to gender; the men received first and were followed by the women. Some churches had separate communion tables for the two sexes—a women's table and a men's table. Procedure at Geneva appears to have been analogous. And while the French and Genevan churches conducted an ambulatory service, communicants in the Low Countries and Scotland sat at tables in an explicit image of the Last Supper.

To avoid profanation of the eucharist, only those persons deemed qualified by virtue of correct belief and proper behavior could share in the celebration. Churches used the several weeks prior to the Lord's Supper to prepare. Everyone had to attend catechism and demonstrate knowledge of Christian prayers. Notorious sinners and excommunicates were invited to seek forgiveness and reconciliation. Again, the elders in many churches distributed entry counters—sometimes paper chits, more often lead tokens—to those eligible for participation in the service. If the lay elders assiduously screened participants for the eucharist, they also shouldered substantial responsibility for the conduct of the service. Churches assigned each elder a specific task. One distributed the communion tokens to the members of the community qualified to receive; another collected them at the service. Several elders supervised the faithful as they moved toward the table. One read during the service. Two or three typically furnished the bread, wine, and linens. Yet another elder collected offerings for the poor.

Each participant received an ordinary morsel of bread—there was a conscious rejection of the wafer-like host—and drank common table wine from the cup. The pastor distributed the bread and often, but not always, the cup. Elders at Geneva appear to have distributed the wine. In France, an elder typically handed the cup to the pastor, who presented it to the faithful. Sometimes, and it is unclear how often, French elders administered the cup directly to the people. In the early seventeenth century, one French church had a system whereby the pastor distributed the bread and the "senior" elder the cup. Not everyone, however, was pleased. A merchant balked at receiving the cup from an elder rather than the pastor. Drawing on his reading of Holy Writ, he maintained that Jesus had presented the cup to his disciples and the pastor should do likewise.

In the end, practice varied among churches. The elders, particularly in large congregations, could administer the cup, lest the service take too long. Altogether, Reformed churches substantially enhanced the participation of laypeople, notably lay elders, in the sacramental celebration. They supplied the elements, directed the congregation, and performed a number of ancillary tasks. Finally, the elders sometimes distributed the cup, which medieval communicants could not even receive. The elders' administration of the wine was a stunning practical reinforcement of the laity's place in the Reformed churches. Not only did ordinary people receive the cup; they might even distribute it.

Nonetheless, the Supper could be the occasion for unpleasant and disruptive melees. For many in the French congregations, the sacrament served to reify social distinctions. The order for reception of the bread and wine could easily be a source of friction. Most Reformed churches observed a standard order of reception for the bread and wine: pastor, elders, local nobles, members of the judiciary, city consuls, and, finally, the remaining members of the faithful. Still, problems arose. At Castres in the mid-seventeenth century, several royal judges complained that they had been slighted in the arrangement for taking the bread and wine. Elsewhere, local judicial magistrates and municipal consuls challenged members of the consistory—pastors, elders, and deacons—who asserted a right to receive before the rest of the congregation. In yet another town, the wife of a leading nobleman became engaged in a fierce shoving match with the mother of the chief judicial officer, as each tried to push her way ahead of the other during the celebration of the Supper. These were battles over the privilege and preference that accompanied social rank, fought here in sacramental circumstances. Similar conduct occurred in England. Evidence from the 1620s suggests that people there also received in order of social precedence, with "the ordinarie sort" receiving last. Some parishes in and around London even used two grades of wine, reserving the better quality for the socially and politically prominent. One Englishman declined altogether to participate, seeing the sacrament in socially exclusive terms and commenting that "it was fit only for Gentlefolks and Schollards not for Poor folks to take it."[7]

At the same time, people understood the Supper as a communal activity that functioned as a conciliatory rite within the community. It was a vital symbol of unity and, to borrow the language of anthropology, served not merely to underscore social differentiation but also to facilitate integration. Thus men and women frequently absented themselves if they were in disagreement with another member of the congregation. More dramatically, excommunication, which barred a person from the eucharist and, accordingly, was antithetically related to the sacrament, accentuated the Supper as the centerpiece of a civic and religious experience. Denying the bread and wine to notorious sinners emphasized the crucial position of the eucharistic meal as a shared experience. Again, the two weeks or so preceding the service were the appropriate moment for persons at odds with the church to make amends, reconcile, and reintegrate.

THE PSALMS

In all of these pious activities, among the most ubiquitous elements was psalmody. The Reformed faithful embraced the Psalms enthusiastically. The incorporation of vernacular translations into Reformed worship transformed ordinary people's participation in the life of worship and defined perhaps more than any other element the collective meaning of being Reformed. The French poet Clément Marot had by the early 1540s rendered fifty psalms into metrical French verse. Théodore Bèze, Calvin's lieutenant at Geneva, completed the series by 1562. Louis Bourgeois, Claude Goudimel, and others created tunes, which aided in the memorization and singing of these French psalms. The Genevan Psalter of 1562 was immensely popular. More than 27,000 copies were printed in the first two years. It contained 152 texts: each of the 150 Psalms, the Ten Commandments, and the Song of Simeon. They were set to 125 different tunes. In France men, women, and children regularly sang the Psalms in their temples. The inclusion of women's voices was a genuine innovation, one that Catholic polemicists regarded as scandalous. Psalm singing could also be heard in people's homes and, according to popular tradition, while they labored in their shops and fields. The Psalms became instruments for stirring demonstrations of constancy when Protestant martyrs perished at the stake. Huguenot soldiers sang them as battle hymns when they deployed in defense of the faith, and common folk invoked the Psalms as they marched defiantly in the streets.

FAMILY WORSHIP

The Psalms were also a prominent feature of household worship. The father became a "lesser pastor" who led morning and evening prayers, readings from scripture, and the singing of psalms. The 1545 edition of Calvin's *Catechism* contained several prayers drawn from Psalms for use before and after meals. In the years following the 1562 publication of Marot and Bèze's French version of the Psalms, the Psalter gathered additional prayers, which were explicitly intended for use by heads of household in the conduct of daily prayer. A dramatic example of these

Fig. 1.2. The singing of Psalter undoubtedly helped to root the Reformation in the hearts of lay people. This Scottish Psalter, for use in households, gave rhymed texts and melodies. *The Psalmes of David in prose and meeter* (Edinburgh: Church of Scotland, Heirs of Andrew Hart, 1635). Photo published with permission of the Rare Book & Manuscript Library of the University of Illinois, Urbana-Champaign.

developments comes from a 1635 Scottish Psalter. In the case of Psalm 147 (fig. 1.2), the worshipers had the psalm in meter for singing. The prose text of the psalm, taken from the Bible, appeared in the margins. Psalms were always sung a cappella, that is, without instruments, and when sung during worship service at the church or temple, they were sung without harmonization. This Scottish version for use by the family at home is a four-part harmonization, allowing all members of the household—father, mother, children, and servants—to sing in the appropriate voice: soprano, alto, tenor, and bass. The tenor, likely in a continuation of musical traditions associated with medieval Gregorian chant, carried the melody. The Psalter and the Bible, which was another standard feature of the learned Protestant household, became the printed vehicles for daily family worship. Though these religious routines presumed literacy, the power of the clergy to mediate people's devotion weakened. The capacity of laypersons and the place of the printed book expanded.

Calvin himself likened the household to a small individual church where the devout father, as the head and master of his family, supervised and instructed the members—wife, children, and servants—in accordance with the talents and capabilities that he received from God. The father, the ancient and sacred paterfamilias, once again assumed a sacerdotal role at the heart of the family. Much as he directed other aspects of family life, the father became its spiritual and moral guide. Again, Protestant emphasis on the priesthood of all believers and the Reformation's affinity for patriarchy indelibly marked these familial rites and the father's role in them. On the other hand, mothers undoubtedly continued to teach children basic prayers and inculcate other elements of devotion, much as their maternal predecessors had done in a medieval religious universe. Later, following the 1685 revocation of the Edict of Nantes and the expulsion of ministers from France, domestic worship and the fundamental role of women for transmission of the prayers, gestures, and attitudes associated with Reformed piety became crucial. Men and women, acting within the family, maintained and transmitted vital religious traditions.

CARE OF THE WEAK

Charitable activity was another extremely important facet of urban piety. There were, after all, scriptural injunctions to feed the hungry, clothe the naked, visit the sick and imprisoned, offer hospitality to strangers, and provide for orphans and widows. Members of the faithful were expected to meet these responsibilities in part through almsgiving. French churches, in preparing the Lord's table, invariably designated one of the elders to gather alms. London parishes similarly collected money for the poor at communion. Devout Protestants also developed permanent institutional structures for assisting the poor.

Genevan municipal officials had early on established a General Hospital, which provided a variety of social services. It maintained a spacious building, which housed orphans and foundlings as well as elderly, sick, and incapacitated adults. The Genevan General Hospital also distributed bread to the impoverished and offered temporary accommodations and an evening meal for indigent visitors. The enterprise predated Calvin, who lent his approbation, and deemed the lay administrators and governors deacons. In France the deacons managed cash funds rather than a specific institution. French churches typically had two separate funds: one for the ministry and another for the poor. The first covered upkeep on buildings, travel expenses, and the salaries for pastors and minor employees such as cantors and bell ringers. The other was used to meet the needs of the multitude of poor who inhabited every early modern town. The French deacons were members of the consistory and worked with the pastors and elders in providing clothing, food, cash, and loans to people who were blind or had other disabilities, widows and orphans, religious refugees, and the temporarily unemployed. In each case, they were persons who had no other means to support themselves.

The churches placed poverty-stricken boys in apprenticeships with cobblers, blacksmiths, printers, and other artisans. They found employment for poor young women as servants and eventually gave them dowries so that they could marry. Constructive employment, stable marriages, and secure families were key elements in the maintenance of public order and social peace. Churches in some larger towns—Nîmes, for example—cooperated with civic authorities in creating elaborate lists of donors and recipients in complicated arrangements for the distribution of bread to the needy. These mechanisms for assisting the indigent appear to have eased the burden of poverty while simultaneously regulating and instructing the poor in the economic and social spheres. This control over the poor also entailed supervision of moral behavior and religious faith. Churches required people to be well behaved and devout to receive support. In the Scottish town of Saint Andrews, for example, recipients of poor relief had to be able to recite their basic prayers.

Income for these relief projects derived, in part, from pious legacies. Every French church made a special point of reminding local notaries that they should encourage testators to provide for the poor

> ## An Excerpt from the Ecclesiastical Ordinances of Geneva
>
> *The fourth order of ecclesiastical government, namely, deacons:*
>
> There were always two kinds of deacons in the early Church. The one kind was deputed to receive, dispense, and keep the goods for the poor, not only daily alms, but also possessions, revenues, and pensions; the other kind was to care for and remember the sick and administer the allowance for the poor, a custom which we still retain at present.
>
> —From "Ecclesiastical Ordinances," in Hughes, *The Register of the Company of Pastors of Geneva.*

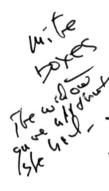

in their wills. And while many devout Protestants left money to the poor, the church sometimes found it difficult to force the heirs to pay these bequests. Money also came from the collection plate. An elder or deacon generally took up a collection at the conclusion of the worship. Sometimes, there was an alms box near the principal door of the temple for those who wished to donate more discreetly; though they produced far less revenue, mite boxes into which people could drop small coins were occasionally scattered in shops throughout the town. Finally, the churches typically levied assessments on persons in the congregation who were deemed financially secure. These more affluent individuals were an important source of funds, and if they failed to pay their monetary "contribution" toward the pastor's salary, poor relief, building maintenance, and the like, the pastors and elders admonished them and even threatened excommunication. These men were dubbed ingrates, who had neglected their moral and religious responsibility to Christian brothers and sisters and to a church that endeavored to assist them in the struggle for eternal salvation.

The various Reformed poor relief programs undertaken by French Protestants clearly served to remind donors of their religious obligations. The lists of donors used for the distribution of bread to the poor, like that of the consistory of Nîmes, for example, were organized in two columns with the names of individual donors on the left and the names of the recipients to the right. In addition, the consistory took great pains to link individual contributors with specific recipients on the distribution rolls. The arrangement of the givers' and receivers' names side by side in a kind of double-entry ledger may have served accounting purposes. Donors and recipients, however, did not engage in direct fashion. The poor received bread, while the affluent contributed money, which the church then used to purchase bread. Yet a style of giving was surely involved. This one-to-one relationship between the individual who was well-off and her or his poverty-stricken neighbor is pointed out on several occasions. A certain Polinaire was to contribute to the support of Perrette Frayssinette. Then the entry was scratched with the remark: "[he] does not wish to provide for Frayssinette." Similarly, a wheelwright balked at contributing to the welfare of Marguerite Blanche's small child, and a wealthy attorney refused to support Claude Chiviol. It suggests a compelling association of donor and recipient. On countless other occasions, the consistory moved recipients about on the relief rolls from one donor to another. Again, there seems to have been some attempt to establish a sense of personal obligation between contributor and beneficiary. In this sense, the structure of social welfare, which the French churches created, offered individual believers a strong and immediate awareness of their Christian responsibility to assist the poor. And people appear to have understood.

Fig. 1.3. Woodcuts (below) for the months of January, May, and August from Augsburg Johann Schobsser's "Kalender," 1488, depict aspects peasant life, including, repast, love, and reaping. From *The Illustrated Bartsch*, vol 86. Part VII: Anonymous Artists 1487–1488.

DISCIPLINE

Most famously, Reformed communities sought to inculcate an acute sense of human frailty and the necessity of discipline to further virtue as well as repress vice. They took to heart Jesus' instruction in Matt. 18:15-17. Every Christian should first admonish his sinning brother in private. If he refuses to listen, then the matter should be taken to the community at large. For the Reformed that meant taking it to the consistory, which was composed of the pastors, the elders, and, in many cases, the deacons. Local Reformed churches throughout Western Europe formed consistories, which met weekly to confer on details of church administration, oversee the distribution of aid to the poor, and discuss the various breaches of Christian conduct that had come to their attention. The consistory was an executive and supervisory body, which functioned as a morals tribunal and a compulsory counseling service. The elders in particular, had a responsibility to watch over the faithful and make certain that people participated in the liturgy and conducted their lives according to fitting religious and ethical standards. Urban churches divided their towns into administrative districts and assigned an elder to each. The elder reported each week to the consistory on the various misdeeds that had taken place within his assigned neighborhood. The elders were even expected to visit each and every family within their districts at least once a year.

At least a few followed to the letter the scriptural injunction in Matthew 18 to show your brother his fault, "just between the two of you." A seventeenth-century Dutch elder at Utrecht reported that when pastors and elders made their obligatory home visits to each

member of the church, they frequently patched up quarrels and allowed drunkards and fornicators to seek pardon for their misdeeds on the spot, thus reconciling them in private ways. Many sinners at Utrecht never appeared before the town's consistory but were nonetheless put on the right path. The extent to which similar, less formal systems operated elsewhere remains a matter of scholarly discussion.

Most consistories worked tirelessly to ensure that people dutifully attended weekly sermon services, the quarterly celebrations of the Lord's Supper, and related catechism lessons. They wished to enforce proper observance of the Sabbath, regulate marriage and strengthen family life, chastise blasphemers, and eradicate all traces of sorcery and magic. Pastors and elders sought to root out other faults. Peacemaking in an admittedly disputatious world was perhaps the largest task to which they applied themselves. They repeatedly mediated verbal and physical quarrels and settled long-standing disputes. Church officials also wished to eradicate scandalous language, sexual misconduct such as fornication and adultery, dancing, games, excesses of food and drink, ostentatious dress, and participation in masquerades and carnival.

> ### An Excerpt from the Registers of the Genevan Consistory
>
> Thursday, August 24, 1542
>
> Jaques Bornant, called Callaz, cobbler
> [Summoned] because of [absence from] the sermons and wasting time in gambling games. Answers that he goes to the sermons on Sundays. Said the [Lord's] prayer and the confession [Creed] and does not know the commandments. The consistory advises that he be admonished to cease to gamble to give an example to others, and to frequent the sermons.
>
> —From *Registers of the Consistory of Geneva*, 113.

In their notions of sin and virtue, Reformed Protestants with their insistence upon the primacy of Holy Writ vigorously underscored breaches of the Decalogue. They certainly made fewer references to faults that had been traditionally associated with the seven deadly sins than they did to sins against the Ten Commandments. Some churches were occasionally quite explicit on this point. The municipal Discipline Ordinance at Basel and analogous legislation in some south German communities went to great lengths in listing particular sins according to the Ten Commandments.

The changes designed to encourage a moral climate consistent with the demands of the Decalogue were manifest in the development of a worship without "graven images," the proscription of all profane activities on the Sabbath, the obligation for the faithful to attend church services each Sunday, and the requirement for regular participation in the eucharist. These reformers stressed, moreover, obedience to parents and other authorities. Adult men and women were scolded for their irreverent treatment of mothers and fathers. They were told to obey and honor their parents, lend financial support when necessary, and cease annoying them. Particularly prominent in the popular mind were Reformed attempts at control of sexuality. Ecclesiastical authorities worked to strengthen the bonds of matrimony and engaged in a determined clarification and enforcement of proper sexual comportment. Couples had to honor betrothal vows, publish marital banns, observe the prohibited degrees of consanguinity, and obtain parental permission to wed. Men and women living together without benefit of holy marriage were told in no uncertain terms to regularize their relationships. Officials invariably summoned and severely punished pregnant but unwed women. The slightest hint of sexual impropriety by women or men led to prompt investigation. The assault on fornication and adultery was vigorous and unrelenting.

Above all, the values promoted by Reformed churches throughout Europe emphasized Christian peace and harmony. Consistorial officials everywhere worked tirelessly to quell strife and settle differences, mediate disagreements, and achieve reconciliation. They wished to reduce conflict, foster concord, and maintain harmony within society. Pastors and elders sought to pacify feuding parties with symbolic handshakes and solemn promises that they would live in peace and friendship. The consistory demanded that bickering persons "extend the hand of friendship" or the "hand of reconciliation." People "touched" one another's hand as a sign of their promise to live in peace and friendship. The consistory of Nîmes sometimes asked persons to "kiss" one another's hands. Altogether, they were to "forget the past," reconcile, and accept one another as "good brothers and friends."

Other rituals of repentance had much the same quality; they aimed at inculcating a sense of the shame of sin and reintegrating the individual into the community. Again, the sense of a shared morality, underscored by the necessity of communal concord, was paramount. Pastors and elders, seated in the consistory, censured and admonished sinners, often demanding that they beg pardon of God and the church in humbling ceremonies of private and public penitence. Blasphemers, for example, typically knelt and confessed their fault in the closed confines of the consistory chambers. Public ceremonies of repentance were a far stronger punishment whose purpose was not merely to correct and chasten a sinner but to serve as an exemplar to others in the community[9] and to facilitate reconciliation between the offender and the congregation. Parents who permitted a daughter or son to marry a "papist" in a Catholic ceremony invariably atoned for this along with the offending child before the entire congregation immediately prior to the Sunday sermon service. Unmarried pregnant women endured similar embarrassing rituals of contrition before the assembled faithful. According to the church, public sin required public reparation.

Falling to one's knees, openly drawing attention to personal failings, and seeking forgiveness in the presence of fellow townsfolk—a person's family and neighbors, close friends, and mortal enemies—must have been an unpleasant experience. In Scotland the sense of humiliation was heightened by having the worst miscreants appear in sackcloth and sit precariously on a tall three-legged stool of repentance. Still, there was a positive element. Public confessions of fault served to square sinners with the congregation and thereby reinforced community bonds. Not surprisingly, these open admissions of egregious wrongdoing and accompanying pleas for collective forgiveness frequently occurred immediately prior to the communion service, the centerpiece of a powerful set of rituals designed to unify and strengthen the moral and spiritual body of believers.

LAY PARTICIPATION

All in all, the prominent roles accorded Reformed elders and deacons underscore the "lay piety" that the Protestant Reformation cultivated. An emerging middle group of lay townspeople from professional and mercantile backgrounds—individuals who could read and write and who owned books—increasingly dominated the Reformed churches, including powerful positions in the celebration of the Lord's Supper, religious education for the faithful in the form of catechism for both young and old, the provision of social assistance to the impoverished, and the oversight of people's religious and behavioral habits. Elders even accompanied pastors as voting delegates to local assemblies known as colloquies as well as to provincial and national synods. They controlled access to the Lord's table through their moral supervision of all members of the community. Indeed, they bore enormous responsibilities for the religious and spiritual well-being of their fellow congregants. At the same time, while this middling urban elite may have enjoyed a privileged position, ordinary persons were profoundly engaged in official and unofficial piety and in ways that were not possible or even conceivable in earlier times.

Some people may have actively resisted or, more often, experienced difficulty adjusting to the new ways, but the vast majority embraced and identified with Reformed piety. Indeed, they found it deeply satisfying and were enormously proud of their scripturally based Christian piety. Although the evidence is anecdotal, people seem to have incorporated the scripturally based piety advocated by Reformed authorities into their everyday existence. The singing of psalms while going about daily tasks is a prime example. In a more negative vein, individuals, when challenging ecclesiastical officials, sometimes located their objections in a reading of Holy Writ. Thus, a notary from Nîmes demanded that the consistory show him where in scripture it was written that he should be obliged to make public reparation for his transgressions. Another man, as noted earlier, refused to accept the cup from an elder based on his understanding of the biblical account of the Last Supper. Ordinary members of the faithful could have notions of piety different from those of the ecclesiastical authorities and were not at a loss to explain why.

The emerging Protestant—particularly Reformed—piety appealed, above all, to socially privileged groups. They had benefit of literacy

---

An Excerpt from the Registers of the Genevan Consistory

Thursday, February 8, 1543

Noble Master Gay the shearer and Jaquemeta, his wife

Answers that he wants to live and die according to the Reformation.... He cannot go to the sermons because of his affairs, and goes to the catechism, and is not a papist, and was at the sermon last Sunday, and cannot say or recite anything of the sermon.... Said the prayer and the confession. The wife does not know how to say it except in Latin as in former times. The consistory gave them admonitions and remonstrances that they be admonished to frequent the sermons more often, and within a month, and go on Sunday to catechism and learn to pray.

From *Registers of the Consistory of Geneva*, 188–89.

and could readily appreciate vernacular Bibles, printed Psalters, catechisms, and prayer books. They understood and valued the learned language of the sermon. Men, especially, assumed prominent roles in the liturgy, led their own families in daily worship, and watched over the religious and moral welfare of the community. These new forms of piety could also retain deeply embedded notions of social differentiation, manifested in preferential seating or precedence in the order for proceeding to the Lord's table. Nonetheless, artisans and laborers participated in this scripturally oriented piety through vernacular recitation of prayers and the singing of psalms. In particular, people knew the words and the tunes from the Psalter and sang the Psalms in both sacred and profane settings. Indeed, the popular associations that permeated the poetic meter and dancelike rhythms prompted Queen Elizabeth to dub them "Genevan jigs." For many adherents as well as opponents, singing psalms came ultimately to define Protestant identity.

The devotional landscape of cities and towns changed enormously with regular sermon services, the introduction of benches for the faithful, more frequent reception and stronger lay participation in the Lord's Supper, communal as well as household singing of psalms, catechism instruction and prayers in the vernacular, active communal charity programs, and resolute endeavors to instill restraint and virtue in everyday deportment. Permeating this approach to piety was a fundamental emphasis on the importance of Christian peace and harmony. In wholly complementary fashion, urban Protestants extolled a shared Christian worship as the foundation for civic accord and unity. For their part, ordinary believers welcomed and embraced the innovations, especially the laity's greater involvement in the liturgy, even as they adapted the practice of piety to their own needs and circumstances.

FOR FURTHER READING

Benedict, Philip. *Christ's Churches Purely Reformed: A Social History of Calvinism*. New Haven: Yale University Press, 2002.

Coster, Will, and Andrew Spicer, editors. *Sacred Space in Early Modern Europe*. Cambridge: Cambridge University Press, 2005.

Gordon, Bruce, and Peter Marshall, editors. *The Place of the Dead: Death and Remembrance in Late Medieval and Early Modern Europe.* Cambridge: Cambridge University Press, 2000.

Green, Ian. *The Christian's ABC: Catechism and Catechizing in England c. 1530–1740.* Oxford: Oxford University Press, 1996.

Karant-Nunn, Susan C. *The Reformation of Ritual: An Interpretation of Early Modern Germany.* London and New York: Routledge, 1997.

Kingdon, Robert M. *Adultery and Divorce in Calvin's Geneva.* Cambridge: Harvard University Press, 1995.

Lualdi, Katherine Jackson, and Anne T. Thayer, editors. *Penitence in the Age of Reformations.* Aldershot, U.K.: Ashgate, 2000.

Mentzer, Raymond A., editor. *Sin and the Calvinists: Morals Control and the Consistory in the Reformed Tradition.* 2nd edition. Kirksville, Mo.: Truman State University Press, 2002.

Parker, Charles H. *The Reformation of Community: Social Welfare and Calvinist Charity in Holland, 1572–1620.* Cambridge: Cambridge University Press, 1998.

Taylor, Larissa, editor. *Preachers and People in the Reformations and Early Modern Period.* Leiden: Brill, 2001.

Wandel, Lee P. *The Eucharist in the Reformation.* Cambridge: Cambridge University Press, 2005.

RURAL AND
VILLAGE PIETY

KEITH P. LURIA

CHAPTER TWO

Not long after taking up his position as bishop of Grenoble in 1671, Étienne Le Camus wrote to a friend that among the people of his diocese, "no one knows anything of religion except confraternities."[1] Though exaggerated, his complaint testified to the importance of these brotherhoods in Catholic religious life and the suspicion with which a Catholic Reformation prelate regarded them. The associations were of great concern both to villagers who sought to manage their own religious lives and to reformers who sought to instill in them a new form of spirituality. Confraternities, therefore, provide a useful way in to examine the development of rural piety during the Protestant and Catholic Reformations.

What were confraternities? They often provided the focus for Catholic religious activities: members gathered to hear the Mass with their confraternal brothers rather than with other parishioners in the parish church, they honored their patron saints with processions and festive meals, they provided charity for each other when necessary, and they buried their deceased brethren with proper rites and memorial masses to speed their souls' release from purgatory. Catholic reformers disapproved of confraternities because laypeople dominated them. The groups engaged priests to say the Mass and lead processions, but priests did not control them. Hence the confraternities provided an alternative to a religious life focused on parish churches under the supervision and control of the parish clergy. Reformers objected to confraternal processions, especially nighttime ones, which they feared dissolved too easily into immoral activities.

They also disliked confraternity banquets, which they believed were too often occasions for excessive eating and drinking.

Cities and towns had numerous confraternities, some associated with specific crafts devoted to their patron saints, others with wider memberships dedicated to divine figures of general interest, such as the Virgin Mary. Villages were not large or economically varied enough to support an array of confraternities, but the groups were not just an urban phenomenon. In the diocese of Grenoble the most numerous of these rural organizations were devoted to the Holy Spirit. They dated to the thirteenth or fourteenth centuries; religious life and charitable activities in many of the diocese's villages were organized around them. When Le Camus complained about confraternities, he had these Holy Spirit groups in mind. Many of them appeared to be in decline, attracting little attention. But he especially disliked the behavior of active groups, such as that in Saint-Ismier, where the confraternal brothers paraded a barrel of wine around the village during their annual procession, or the one in Corenc, the members of which imbibed large quantities of wine during their banquets. Both of these villages were in wine-growing areas, and celebrating with their local product allowed the brothers to link spiritual communion with convivial fellowship as well as to associate their religious aspirations with the fruitfulness of their vineyards. But to a cleric like Le Camus, such festivities were all too typical of a rural piety badly in need of reform.

RELIGIOUS REFORM AND RURAL PIETY

The encounter between the austere bishop and bibulous confraternity brothers of Saint-Ismier and Corenc appears emblematic of a conflict historians have described between religious reform and traditional rural piety. A distinction between the two is easy to draw in stark terms. Rural piety evokes such labels as conservative, timeless, and superstitious. The religion of reformers is associated with progress, innovation, and cultural sophistication. Early modern reformers (both Catholic and Protestant) criticized rural people for being ignorant of true doctrine and immersed in sinful or profane religious activities.

Historians and folklorists have too often adopted a similar point of view, even if they express it in different terms. For them, country folk were preoccupied with seeking divine help for day-to-day problems of illness or threats to crops and livestock. Religion was essentially a form of magic rather than a spiritual endeavor focused on the concern for salvation and proper moral behavior. Rural piety seemed unchanging; people practiced their faith as countless generations of their forebears had done before them. Even historians with more sympathetic views of "popular culture" and "popular religion" have, in their own ways, reinforced this notion of rural religious life, either by insisting on the essential failure of religious reformers to change it or by suggesting that change came to the countryside through a process of "confessionalization" in which the churches' programs only succeeded when state power imposed them on reluctant villagers.[2]

Recent scholarship has shown that the opposing terms used to characterize these two forms of religious life—popular versus elite, unofficial versus official, collective versus individualized, rural versus urban—are far too simplistic to describe the dynamic of religious change in the rural world of early modern Europe. To be sure, we do not search for the origins of new religious movements, such as the Protestant or Catholic Reformations, in the countryside. They take root in urban areas first. But this truism does not mean that the religious life of villages was unchanging until new ideas and practices were imposed upon them from the outside. The rural world had a long history of generating religious unrest, demands for change, and new forms of pious activity. That not all of these changes found official acceptance among Church authorities does not make them any less important as expressions of Catholic piety.

Drawing a stark contrast between official and unofficial or between popular and elite religion does not accurately characterize the differences in Catholic piety. Reformers like Bishop Le Camus did seek to bring rural religion into line with the Catholic Reformation's goals, including greater clerical control of and more propriety in religious practices, a better understanding of Church doctrine, and a heavier emphasis on devotional activities that encouraged the individual examination of conscience rather than communal religious sociability. But the Church did not deny the efficacy of obtaining miraculous divine help by petitioning saints, honoring relics, or visiting shrines. It did not seek to eliminate collective activities important to communities, such as processions on the festivals of patron saints, provided that priests supervised them and they were conducted with greater decorum than in the past. In turn, villagers did not necessarily resist the ideas reformers brought to their villages. Their religious concerns were never limited to the magical manipulation of divine power. They had never ignored the Church's teachings on redemption and proper moral behavior. They wanted priests capable of performing their duties properly and of taking on a central role in parish religious life. They also eagerly adopted new devotional practices.

Thus contrasting the religion of reformers and that of villagers in absolute terms obscures rather than explains the nature of rural piety and the changes within it. A more useful approach starts with the realization that we cannot locate the dynamic of change during the period of the Reformations (Protestant as well as Catholic) exclusively in ecclesiastical institutions on the one hand or villages on the other. Instead, we must realize that it lay in the interaction between churches (along with their political supporters in cities and states) and rural people, in which villagers were neither simply determined resisters nor passive recipients of new ideas and practices. Historians of rural religious life now talk of processes of negotiation and adaptation between countryfolk and reform-minded clerics. Each side had to accommodate the other. But at least for Catholicism if not for Protestantism, these negotiations were made easier by the fact that the two forms of religion—that of the Church and that of the village—were never as completely opposed as we used to think.

> **Parishioners Complain about Their Clergy (Rülzheim, 1700)**
>
> We pray to God that we could get rid of this quarrelsome and troublesome priest. We want to behave as good Catholic Christians should, but [all we get] from him is abuse, ridicule, and insults. What he hears all week long from his spies and other gossipmongers must be preached from the pulpit.
>
> —From Marc R. Forster, *The Counter-Reformation in the Villages: Religion and Reform in the Bishopric of Speyer, 1560–1720* (Ithaca, N.Y.: Cornell University Press, 1992), 209.

Furthermore, it is possible, though as yet research on this question is limited, that in areas where Catholics and Protestants lived side by side, confessional strife helped cement villagers' identification with their ecclesiastical institution and the piety it was promoting. In seventeenth-century Germany, villagers, led by their priests, undertook processions—with "flags flying, crosses held high, singing . . . prayers"—that passed Protestant villages and antagonized their inhabitants. They flocked to shrines that bordered on Protestant territories or that had been founded after anti-Protestant miracles (such as when an image of Mary shed tears in response to Protestant insults or was saved after a Swedish soldier had thrown it into a fire). But elsewhere Catholic and Protestant villagers often appeared willing to coexist, despite their clergy's demands that they not do so. In French biconfessional areas, for instance, Protestants and Catholics intermarried, shared sacred spaces such as cemeteries, and conducted their different religious observances peacefully. And sometimes they told their priests and pastors, to the clerics' great consternation, that people could be saved in either faith, providing they led pious and virtuous lives. Thus villagers proved quite capable of adapting their clergy's religious innovations without adopting their intolerance.[3]

THE SEARCH FOR DIVINE HELP

The processes of negotiation, adaptation, and accommodation become clearer if we examine those seemingly suspect, this-worldly uses to which countryfolk put their religion, those practices that most worried early modern reformers. People petitioned saints for help through prayer, visiting shrines, honoring relics, participating in processions, and so forth. The Church provided the rituals and a long list of recognized and approved (canonized) saints through whom the faithful could seek assistance.

Through their acts of devotion, people promoted new candidates for this list, "local saints," some of whom the Church approved and some of whom it did not did not. Jean-Michel Sallmann estimates that in the kingdom of Naples between 1540 and 1750, people venerated several hundred local holy figures. The Church opened official investigations necessary in the process of beatification for only about a hundred. Few were ever canonized. Thus the Jesuit Bernardino Realino and the Theatine nun Orsola Benincasa gained official recognition, but others, like Alfonsina Rispoli and the friar Ludovico of Monte

Faito, did not. People in this region were devoted to them all. Even some official saints were little known outside specific regions: in the Spanish diocese of Cuenca people sought Saint Quiteria's help in curing rabies; in Savoy villagers petitioned Saint Grat to protect livestock. Others, such as Saints Sebastian and Roch, both of whom combated the plague, were well known across Europe. The most important of the helpers was Mary. Often devotion to her was very localized and associated with a particular village or rural shrine sanctified by the miracles that had occurred there. But the most important of the pilgrimage shrines, such as Altötting in Bavaria, Wagheusel in the Rhineland, or Montserrat in Catalonia, were also devoted to Mary and drew their pilgrims from vast areas.[4]

Protestants criticized the instrumental use of saints' cults as superstition. Catholic reformers also disliked what they considered its vulgar rituals and the widespread belief that vows to saints were contracts in which petitioners' promises of devotion were conditional upon saints providing miraculous help. But Catholic reformers never opposed the cult of saints and never denied the validity of miracles people obtained through it. Following the program of the Council of Trent (1545–1563), they did target certain of the cult's traditional features. They wanted to remove unapproved saints from the local pantheons of sacred figures to whom villagers were devoted and to focus people's attention on the Church's central divine figures, especially Christ, Mary, and the new saints of the Catholic Reformation. They also wanted the clergy to exercise more control over the cult's ritual activities. Yet the reformers' efforts did not undermine the uses to which local people put the cult of saints. Indeed, by importing new saints, relics, and rituals into local religion, reformers often revitalized its traditional purposes.

> ### The Council of Trent on Reforming Popular Devotion (1563)
>
> The images of Christ, of the Virgin Mother of God, and of the other saints are to be placed and retained especially in the churches, and . . . due honor and veneration is to be given to them; not, however, that any divinity or virtue is believed to be in them by reason of which they are to be venerated, or that something is to be asked of them, or that trust is to be placed in images . . . but because the honor which is shown them is referred to the prototypes which they represent, so that by means of the images which we kiss and before which we uncover the head and prostrate ourselves, we adore Christ and venerate the saints whose likeness they bear. . . . Furthermore in the invocation of the saints, the veneration of relics, and the sacred use of images, all superstition shall be removed, all filthy quest for gain eliminated, and all lasciviousness avoided.
>
> From *Canons and Decrees of the Council of Trent,* trans. H. J. Schroeder (Rockford, Ill.: Tan Books, 1978), 215–16.

Country people did not always give up older saints but, instead, added new ones to their lists of devotions. Cults associated with Christ and Mary attracted the most interest. Villagers established chapels in their parish churches devoted to the eucharistic cult of the Blessed Sacrament and to the Marian one of the Rosary. But in many places people substituted new saintly miracle workers for old because they were thought to be more efficacious. Especially important were the saints of the Holy Family (particularly Joseph and Anne) and those of the Catholic Reformation, like the reforming bishop of Milan, Carlo Borromeo, or the Jesuits Ignatius of Loyola and Francis Xavier.

Because of their multiplicity of meanings, the cults of these saints exemplify the process of accommodation and adaptation in rural piety. The Church understood a Borromeo, Ignatius, or Xavier as a

Fig. 2.1. In this dramatic painting Saint Carlo Borromeo intercedes with the Virgin Mary on behalf of the plague-ridden people. Francesco Antonio Meloni; *The Illustrated Bartsch*; vol. 43. Masters of the Seventeenth Century.

figure worthy of devotion because of the example he set of piety, self-sacrifice, and labor on behalf of the Church. But Catholic reformers did not necessarily reject more instrumental understandings of these saints, even if they felt uncomfortable acknowledging them. Jesuit missionaries in rural areas sometimes carried with them Saint-Ignatius or Saint-Xavier water, which could protect villagers from malevolent forces.[5] With these powerful antidotes to evil, the missionaries may have hoped to increase their prestige, attract people to their missions, and eventually wean them away from questionable beliefs. But nothing prevented villagers from adopting the new saints to serve their own needs, even as they listened to the missionaries preach a more "interiorized" and "spiritualized" form of religion.

> **Church Leaders in Speyer on the Training of Priests (1572)**
>
> It is not necessary to place highly educated people in all of the parishes. Instead, if the young [priests] are brought up piously here [in Speyer] and receive a reasonable foundation in the humanities, law, grammar, dialectic, and rhetoric, and learn the rudiments of theology, especially the catechism, they will know how to give fine sermons and will be very useful in the parishes.
>
> —From Forster,
> *The Counter-Reformation*, 65.

Thus villagers near Milan adopted Borromeo's cult because he protected them against the plague, just as Xavier did for his devotees in the kingdom of Naples. In the diocese of Cuenca, people gave up Saint Quiteria and adopted Anne instead. As a member of the Holy Family, they expected her healing powers to be superior to those of the discarded saint. Along the coasts near Naples, Saint Anne cared for sailors and fisherman, and in the mountains near Grenoble, she protected villagers from avalanches. Joseph's popularity stemmed from the variety of saintly roles he took on. Religious orders, such as the Jesuits, saw him as an example of poverty, chastity, and obedience. His chaste relationship with Mary made him a model of virtue, and his guardianship of Jesus made him an exemplary paternal figure. He was also the patron saint of the "good death," teaching his devotees how to die peacefully, accepting God's will. In addition, he was a traditional craft patron saint for carpenters.[6] Villagers who honored him did not necessarily choose only one of these senses of Joseph's cult and reject the others, but neither did the Church of the Catholic Reformation.

One result of clerics promoting reforms and of people shaping their own religious lives was that the liturgical calendars of villages reflected a combination of the universal and the local in Catholic ritual practice. Villagers observed the Church's major annual feasts. They added to them saints' festivals that the Church endorsed and perhaps also those it did not. They understood the significance the Church attributed to the saints but also venerated them in their own ways for their own reasons. For example, in southwest Germany, the villagers of Birndorf in the late seventeenth century celebrated Catholicism's major annual holidays but also festivals of particular importance such as that of Saint Wendelin, Saint Sebastian (who protected them from the plague), and Saint Agatha (who protected them from fire). They had also adopted Saint John of Nepomuk (whom the Jesuits sponsored), but rather than honoring him in the parish church under the watchful eyes of their priest, they went in procession to a statue of him they had placed on a local bridge.[7] (They knew the legend that the saint had been martyred by being thrown off a bridge in Prague.)

The same interweaving of the universal and local, elite and popular, official and unofficial was evident in the veneration of relics. Protestants denounced the belief in relics, and Catholic reformers wanted to purify the practice by getting rid of those that had no proper verification. Villagers were frequently unwilling to give up relics when they still brought results. But sacred remains of which the Church approved could be powerful. In the sixteenth century, large numbers of properly authenticated ones were shipped from Rome and Germany (where they were under Protestant threat). People from all social levels—not just villagers—craved them. Actually, most ended their journeys not in poor villages but in much more luxurious surroundings, such as the Escorial of Philip II, who amassed thousands.[8] The austere, Jansenist-leaning Bishop Le Camus in the late seventeenth century insisted that the relics of his diocese be properly documented, displayed, and treated. Priests (not laymen) should carry them in processions, and they should not be paraded around "in a superstitious manner, or plunged in water to plead for rain" or employed in any way to acquire "temporal favors from God." They were "sacred instruments that God uses. . . . There is no grace necessarily . . . attached to them."[9] But the bishop did not deny their validity; he even collected them avidly. Meanwhile his flock continued to seek "temporal favors" from relics, and the reformer's efforts to ensure their authenticity and holiness strengthened rather than weakened their usefulness as means of obtaining divine aid.

The search for divine aid reached its greatest intensity at pilgrimage shrines, locations where divine power was especially potent and where the possibility of receiving hoped-for miracles was especially strong. They were, therefore, of concern both to laypeople and to clerics bent on reforming religious life. Pilgrimage centers were not a feature of rural piety in particular. People from cities as well as villages, princes as well as peasants, set off from their homes in great numbers on pilgrimages to seek miracles. But many of the shrines were located in the countryside, and thus they can provide a useful example of how the interests and concerns of the Church and the people could coincide in the rural world and serve each other.

For the reforming clergy, pilgrimage shrines presented a problem. They often sprang up after a layperson's experience of a miracle or vision, which the clerical hierarchy had not always substantiated. They attracted great crowds of fervent pilgrims not under the supervision of priests. They were often located on mountaintops, in woods, or in fields far from parish churches or other institutions under Church control. And yet the clergy never denied their value as sources of contact with the divine or their importance in Catholic piety. Religious orders were eager to superintend the shrines. Priests compiled the records of miracles that publicized and drew pilgrims to them. In Germany after the Council of Trent, the clergy encouraged a revival of pilgrimage piety, which the spread of Protestantism had previously undermined, as a way of asserting Catholic identity. Though their efforts bore little immediate fruit, in the wake of the Thirty Years' War crisis, old shrines were revived, new ones established, and Catholic pilgrims took to the roads with great enthusiasm.

As was the case with relics and saints' cults, pilgrimage piety was not simply a matter of popular as opposed to elite piety. In 1571, the Bavarian Duke Albrecht V undertook a pilgrimage to the shrine of Our Lady at Altötting to fulfill a vow he had made the previous summer when he had been caught in a storm on a lake. His subjects would have understood what the duke was doing; many of them had made similar journeys even if they could not present gifts to the shrine as expensive as those the duke brought with him. The visit to Altötting was just the start of a ducal program to revive once-active shrines, which had declined during the years of Protestantism's growth. The plan was in part a calculated political strategy to express the duke's allegiance to the Church, combat Protestantism, and solidify his control over his territory. But Albrecht and his successors also firmly believed that honoring pilgrimage shrines sacralized the territory they ruled and thereby gained divine protection for Bavaria while promoting its spiritual welfare. In this respect, the duke's attitude toward shrines was no different from that of the villagers he governed, who also sought divine aid by undertaking pilgrimages.[10] His activities enriched the piety of villagers by offering them more places where they could seek miraculous help and by conferring over these places the prestige of the ruling house.

As they absorbed new religious ideas and applied them to their lives, the faithful remade rural Catholic piety in tandem with the Church's official policies, not by resisting them or simply by being subjected to their requirements. The same conclusion can be drawn concerning religious change in the Protestant rural areas, though historians have examined them much less than Catholic ones. Protestantism was slow to penetrate the countryside. The gap between rural religion and that of the Protestant Reformation was much wider than that between rural religion and the Catholic Reform. Rural people proved to be strongly attached to Catholic piety and what it offered them. Nonetheless, studies suggest that the process of negotiation and adaptation found in the Catholic rural world was under way in the Protestant one as well.

For example, C. Scott Dixon's work on the rural parishes of Germany's Brandenburg-Ansbach-Kulmbach region during the sixteenth century demonstrates how villagers adopted Lutheran ideas but accommodated them to the needs of their traditional village religion.[11] The Lutheran religious reform proceeded here essentially as an act of state that the local margrave legislated.

> ### Church Leaders in Speyer Instruct Otterstadt's Parish Priest (1580)
>
> "Pastor" Bettenhöfer should, every Sunday and holiday after the sermon in Otterstadt, explain, teach, and inspire . . . the children and adults about the Our Father, the Hail Mary, the Apostles' Creed, the Ten Commandments, and the general confession . . . in distinct and understandable German. In this way the adults will learn from him, their minister, what their elders had neglected, and their children will be brought up in respect and fear of God's power.
>
> —From Forster,
> *The Counter-Reformation,* 114.

His regulations called for an even more complete abolition of customs deemed irreligious or immoral than that any Catholic bishop attempted. Nocturnal festival celebrations, dances, spinning bees, and church fairs all were outlawed. The new clergy was to exercise greater supervision over marriages and sexual activity in villages than their Catholic predecessors had ever managed. They were also supposed to inculcate in their flocks a Lutheran understanding of the sacraments to replace an older, instrumental one. No longer were villagers to think of the consecrated host as a miracle-working object or baptism as an exorcistic rite that protected an infant by expelling demons.

As Dixon shows, the Lutheran clergy fell far short of all these goals. Villagers did not give up village customs that offered them divine protection as well as a means of encouraging village sociability. They continued to think of the host as possessing powers that they could manipulate for their immediate purposes. They did not stop trusting in the protective value of a wide range of sacred objects and practices, such as images, charms, bell ringing, and the saying of certain prayers. But it is not correct to think that these German villagers merely resisted the Lutheran Reformation and their ruler. They eagerly adopted the Reformation's call for the preaching of the gospel. They insisted that their clergy preach the Word clearly in a manner they could easily comprehend. But hearing the gospel still served an immediate purpose: it taught them how to live in accordance with God's directives and avoid divine anger. It thereby provided them with an alternative to Catholic ritual as a path to salvation. Besides, clear preaching of the gospel was their right, granted to them in the margrave's legislation.

Villagers also adopted and adapted other parts of the Lutheran message. Protestant reformers criticized the recourse to rituals as a means of magically manipulating divine power. They targeted charms, popular medical remedies, wise women, and cunning men, and they diabolized these practices by teaching that magic was a temptation of the devil. According to Dixon, the reformers' message took hold in villagers' minds, not, however, because they changed their beliefs about the efficacy of such practices. Instead, they recognized that to continue them was to invite the unwelcome attention of state and church investigators. Country people learned the lesson of demonism their preachers had taught but deflected it onto others by scapegoating women they accused of witchcraft. They had adopted at least this one aspect of the reformers' message, but the results were sometimes tragic.

THE CREATION OF THE "SOCIAL MIRACLE"

While the search for divine aid was central to villagers' religious lives, it was not the sum of rural piety. Traditional ceremonies and beliefs had multiple purposes. In the official teachings of the Catholic Church, they provided a means to salvation. And they did so for villagers just as much as for better-educated or higher-ranking Catholics. Country people were no less concerned than their social superiors with the proper administration of the sacraments, and they complained to bishops visiting their villages when their parish priests failed to provide this. They prayed, made their confessions, worried about fulfilling the requirements of charity, and buried their dead with proper ceremonies just as the Catholic elite did, though with much more limited means at their disposal.

But in addition to fulfilling doctrinal requirements, the practices of rural piety also performed another vitally important function. They helped produce what John Bossy has referred to as Catholicism's "social miracle."[12] The rituals of village religion worked to create social bonds and unity where rivalries and enmity might otherwise have prevailed. Processions, for instance, brought villagers together in collective endeavors that defined their communities and demonstrated to the individual participants the importance of working together in the search for divine aid and salvation. The sacraments of penance and communion reconciled quarreling neighbors and family members. They helped establish peace in what were often conflict-ridden communities. The consecrated host was an extraordinarily powerful representation of social concord and a means to achieve it. Religious practices thus had the power to create a more harmonious community. But as the example of confraternities shows, these practices were also profoundly shaped by the tensions and conflicts of rural society.

As we have seen, village confraternities left religious reformers like Bishop Le Camus exasperated. Yet neither he nor his colleagues sought to eliminate them from religious life. Instead, they wanted to promote new organizations to replace the old. The new groups were dedicated to devotions the Catholic Reformation emphasized, particularly those venerating Christ or Mary. These cults tied local worshipers to the central spiritual concerns of the church; they promoted uniformity in worship rather than local diversity. Reformers wanted the new associations firmly under control of the clergy. Confraternity brothers would not gather together for raucous banquets or set off on nighttime processions. They would assemble for the Mass; undertake charitable endeavors; and engage in individualized, meditative prayer. To judge from the diocese of Grenoble, the Catholic Reformation's program appears to have been a success. Holy Spirit organizations largely disappeared from the region's villages, replaced by new associations dedicated to the eucharistic cult of the Blessed Sacrament or to the Marian devotion of the Rosary. In the villages of this region the Rosary was especially successful. Membership in Blessed Sacrament groups was often limited to the local elite; Rosary confraternities incorporated villagers from different social levels, and they included women and men. Elsewhere throughout southern France, as well as in Spain, southern Italy, and southwestern Germany, parishioners flocked to join Rosary confraternities.[13]

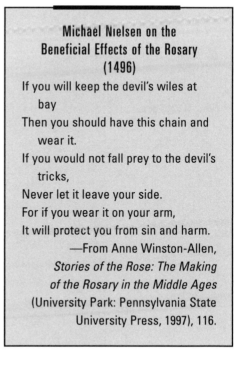

Michael Nielsen on the
Beneficial Effects of the Rosary
(1496)

If you will keep the devil's wiles at
bay
Then you should have this chain and
wear it.
If you would not fall prey to the devil's
tricks,
Never let it leave your side.
For if you wear it on your arm,
It will protect you from sin and harm.
—From Anne Winston-Allen,
*Stories of the Rose: The Making
of the Rosary in the Middle Ages*
(University Park: Pennsylvania State
University Press, 1997), 116.

Rosary groups promoted a form of piety in accord with the Catholic Reformation's goals. The devotion honored Mary and thereby offered participants a way of demonstrating their attachment to the Virgin, one of the Church's central cultic figures. Members of Rosary confraternities practiced a disciplined, meditative recitation of prayers, including "Hail Marys" and the Lord's Prayer, counted out on chaplets or strings of beads. Praying the Rosary fostered an interiorized and individualized spirituality. Confraternal brothers and sisters observed the five annual Marian festivals: the Purification, the Annunciation, the Assumption, the Nativity, and the day of Our Lady of the Rosary. They also confessed and took communion regularly, and they submitted themselves to the clergy's direction. In southwest Germany, Rosary confraternities organized Sunday afternoon prayer recitations, along with monthly prayer meetings and weekly ones during Lent. Rosary prayers were integrated into the regular parish liturgy, thereby engaging worshipers in a more active form of worship than that to which they had been accustomed. The prayers were also incorporated into the traditional cult of saints. In the village of Birndorf, for instance, parishioners prayed the Rosary during the celebration of Saint Sebastian's and Saint George's festivals.[14]

Fig. 2.2. Caravaggio's famous depiction of the Madonna of the Rosary reminds us of the centrality of the Rosary for the piety of this period. Kunsthistorisches Museum, Vienna. Photo: Erich Lessing / Art Resource, NY.

In other respects, however, the new organizations continued to fulfill the time-honored requirements of local religious life. Members undertook the meditative and individualized prayer recitations, but they also shared in the merit earned by members in the Rosary groups. They gained indulgences by joining the associations and by participating in festivals. They also organized processions, sometimes monthly but certainly on Marian festivals. They prayed for the souls of the dead in purgatory. And the Rosary devotion provided them with a new means to seek divine help. For example, in southern Italy during the seventeenth century, Rosary beads worked miracles after people touched relics or holy men (such as Jesuit missionaries) with them. The beads helped cure people from fevers and warded off evil. The practice was not simply the consequence of "ill-informed" or "superstitious" villagers manipulating the Rosary cult. Dominican friars, noted along with the Jesuits for promoting the devotion, encouraged the beads' use as miracle-working objects.[15] Thus the Rosary devotion propagated a new form of piety but also fitted into the traditional ritual system of village religion.

In a manner reminiscent of older confraternities, Rosary associations reflected villagers' determination to exercise control over their religious lives. Clerics promoted the new groups and arranged for their bishops' approval of them. But they worked with parishioners and, indeed, frequently responded to lay initiative in creating the

confraternities. Once they were established, lay leaders often supervised the groups' funds. The organizations also fulfilled village
religion's traditional function of building bonds of social affinity.
Confraternity membership often included virtually the entire village
population. Initiation rituals and common religious observances
bound the brothers and sisters to each other. So too did the processions members undertook on Marian festivals. The confraternities
also worked to establish the bonds of brotherhood and charity among
their confederates. They mediated conflicts among
their members, and the wealthier confraternity
brothers provided aid for their poorer associates.
The groups also took over the funerary duties of
the older confraternities they were supplanting by
burying confraternal brothers and sisters and saying masses for their souls. Hence Rosary confraternities maintained the role of traditional groups
in providing an associational life for villagers that
defined their sense of community and provided
an important vehicle for their sociability.

However, we cannot assume that religious
activities and confraternal organizations were
always successful in creating unity in villages. The
critical role of lay initiative in directing communal religious life allowed for the possibility that
religious endeavors could foster social competition. A constant tension existed between religion's
powerful harmonizing and communitarian effect
and the problems of the social world of which it
was a part. Religion could not entirely overcome
these problems; indeed, it could contribute to
them, when pious activities became another arena
in which villagers played out the competition evident in their political and economic lives.

As an example we can return to Le Camus's
diocese of Grenoble and the small village of
Entraigues. Although each community's spiritual
history is, in many respects, unique, the means by

> **The Benefits of Confraternity Membership (from a 1483 Ulm Handbook)**
>
> This confraternity frees from hateful-
> ness and enlightens blind spirits. It
> fortifies the person in good thoughts,
> protects from distractions and from
> hindrances to devotion in prayer and
> meditation. This brotherhood pro-
> duces fruitfulness of virtue and curbs
> cursing tongues. It fills the soul with
> good works and increases purity of
> spirit. Indeed, through this associa-
> tion quarreling and disunity, envy,
> hate and offensiveness are banished.
> Help comes to the poor, prisoners are
> released. Worldly and carnal individu-
> als become godly people and children
> of God like unto angels. To be sure,
> this brotherhood generates good and
> averts evil, and Christians are drawn
> to the praise and love of Christ and
> his dear mother.... For this is not a
> brotherhood of earthly riches but of
> the spirit and of the achievements of
> virtues and of all spirituality.
>
> —From Winston-Allen,
> *Stories of the Rose*, 118–19.

which Entraigue's religious life developed may well have been typical of what happened in many villages.[16] Entraigues is located in what was in the seventeenth century a remote alpine mountain valley. But it was not isolated from the outside world. Members of the village's better-off families undertook regular commercial voyages throughout France as well as in Italy, Spain, and Portugal. They returned bringing with them not only foreign products but new religious ideas as well.

In 1642, the villagers sent a request to Grenoble's bishop, Pierre Scarron, for permission to establish a Rosary confraternity in the village. We do not know how they came to learn of the devotion. No evidence exists of Dominicans, Jesuits, or Capuchins having visited Entraigues to preach and sponsor the Rosary devotion, nor does the parish priest appear to have played a very active role. Apparently, villagers—not the clergy—brought the Rosary to the community. The fate of another confraternity that clerics did encourage reinforces the conclusion. Two years after the establishment of the Rosary a representative of the arch-confraternity of Saints Sebastian and Roch came to the village carrying Scarron's authorization to promote the organization in the diocese. The people of Entraigues signed his membership roll, but no other record of the confraternity exists. Plague continued to be a threat in the 1640s, and Sebastian and Roch were still popular devotions in many areas. But their organization gained no hold in Entraigues, likely because it had not grown out of the community itself but had been brought in from the outside.

The Rosary confraternity, however, did develop out of the community's desire for a powerful new devotion and the associational life it fostered. At the same time, it gained entry into the village because of competition among the community's elite families. The history of the confraternity's establishment and pious activities demonstrates both sides of this tension. In their request for permission, the founders promised to build a chapel in the parish church dedicated to the Rosary with a painting over the altar of Mary giving the Rosary chaplet to Saint Dominic. They endowed a Mass to be said on the festival of Our Lady of the Rosary, and they promised to follow the Mass with an orderly procession in which the members would march two by two behind a confraternal banner they would purchase. And, of course, they would say the Rosary prayers by holding regular prayer vigils. As was the case with Rosary confraternities throughout Europe, the piety of Entraigues's group would therefore combine the individualized prayer-oriented activity the Catholic Reformation encouraged with the collective endeavors, such as the procession, common to traditional village religion.

The confraternity was an enormous success. In this village of approximately 430 people, 244 joined in the first year and 90 the next. Interestingly, the majority of names inscribed on the organization's roles belonged to women—171 the first year and 70 the second. Scholars have suggested that women found the Rosary devotion attractive because the private prayer recitations could be easily accommodated to their domestic lives. Men presumably had less free time to say the prayers.[17] But such an interpretation cannot explain why Entraigues's women flocked to join the confraternity. They were not confined to a domestic realm separate from the community's public life, an idea of little relevance to village life. Instead, village women actively engaged in their community's economic affairs, owning land and managing crops and livestock. The Rosary prayers did provide them with a new pious endeavor, but the confraternity also offered them a means to participate with other women in associational life. The organization had offices for women that were counterparts to the men's positions of prior, subprior, and chorister. In seeking these positions, women could help pursue one of the goals that brought their families into the confraternity: the acquisition of prestige and prominence vis-à-vis other families in the community.

The chief rivals in Entraigues were the Bernards and the Buissons, the community's richest families. They competed for political leadership in the village, and their economic endeavors brought them frequently into dispute. Their contest carried over into the village's religious life. The heads of all the village's prominent families, including Guillaume Buisson and Jean and Pierre Bernard, signed the 1642 appeal to the bishop for permission to establish the confraternity. They all donated money for the organization and its chapel. But for years following the group's establishment, the Bernards controlled its leadership positions. Jean Bernard was prior in the confraternity's first two years, and his sons and grandsons held the office many times over the rest of the century. Guillaume Buisson never held a position in the group, and it was not until 1686 that a Buisson, Guillaume's son Guigues, achieved the rank of chorister. Only in 1701 did a Buisson gain the priorship. Guillaume's exclusion from a leading role in the confraternity did not diminish his pious attachment to the devotion. He asked his son and heir to endow masses to be said in the Rosary chapel on behalf of his soul. But the confraternity was a Bernard-dominated organization.

Guillaume Buisson responded to the Bernard gambit in 1657. In that year, ten of the village's leading men drew up a contract for establishing a chapel in the parish church. They dedicated it to the Holy Savior and the Transfiguration of the Lord. The devotion did not involve a confraternity and thus did not offer a new associational outlet for communal piety, as had the Rosary. But like the Rosary confraternity, the chapel was a community enterprise, and the village assembly agreed to use parish funds to maintain it. Neither the Holy Savior nor the Transfiguration was a new cult, but they fit into the Church's program of encouraging Christocentric devotions. They thereby offered local devotees a prestigious connection with the spirituality of the Catholic Reformation.

We do not know how the cults came to the village, but Entraigues's chapel was part of a very localized upsurge in devotion to the Transfiguration. Perhaps it was a particularly significant cult for villagers in this mountainous region, since Christ was transfigured on Mount Tabor. A number of nearby villages established Transfiguration chapels in these years, suggesting the presence of religious as well as commercial exchange among these communities. The devotion's spread also suggests the importance as cultural intermediaries of local merchants who traveled between these communities. One of them was Guillaume Buisson. He gave far more money to endow the chapel than any of the other contributors. In return, he insisted on building a bench there and a family tomb beneath it. Benches and tombs in churches were very visible signs of family prestige. Buisson's large donation and the demand for the tomb suggest that the chapel was his idea, just as the Bernards had been the motivating force behind the Rosary. Indeed, the contract establishing the devotion provides another insight into Buisson's motives. It ordered the chapel to be constructed directly across from and exactly the same size as the Bernards' Rosary chapel.

The Bernards did not want to lose ground to their rivals. They, in turn, demanded space for a tomb elsewhere in the church.

The importation of the Catholic Reformation's new modes of piety thus allowed important village families, like the Bernards and Buissons, to act as cultural brokers between their communities and the religious activities of the world outside the village. And religion gave them another arena where they could pursue their contest for prestige and social advancement. But their ventures also enriched the spiritual opportunities for the entire community. The village assembly supported the establishment of both devotions. Villagers endowed masses at the Transfiguration chapel, and they flocked to the Rosary confraternity in droves—even the Buisson family joined. It is important to note that, since Bishop Pierre Scarron was an indifferent reformer at best, this flowering of communal piety in the remote village occurred a full decade and a half before the arrival in the diocese of the official Catholic Reformation with Scarron's successor Le Camus.

The Catholic Reformation program was not, therefore, simply imposed on the faithful as a means of instilling within them an interiorized and spiritualized form of piety. New religious ideas entered communities as much, if not more than, from lay as from clerical initiative. The people who joined Rosary confraternities did undertake the meditative prayer recitations; they did, in other words, associate themselves with what Catholic reformers hoped to achieve. But they also adapted new ideas to their own, sometimes quite traditional ends of seeking divine protection and help, promoting communal sociability, and engaging in social competition. New religious undertakings fed a desire for collective activities: the Rosary in Entraigues helped build a sense of community as it drew support from the village assembly, incorporated large numbers of the villagers, sponsored communal processions, and encouraged charity. Individual prayer coexisted with collective engagement. But the devotion also provided a means for families to further social rivalries. The practice of rural piety did not exclude one or the other of these objectives; it allowed for both.

The Catholic villagers of the diocese of Grenoble and the Protestant ones of Brandenburg-Ansbach-Kulmbach have essentially the same lesson to teach us about rural piety. We cannot continue to think of village religion as a repository of timeless customs, as conservative and resistant to change. From the villagers' point of view, their religion was a vital and ever-changing system of beliefs and practices that responded both to the requirements and teachings of their churches and to the conditions of communal life. They were open to the new ideas and pious activities reformers brought them; indeed, they sought out such ideas and activities to reshape their own religious lives. But what they imported from the outside had to be accommodated to their purposes. Hence they welcomed an innovation such as the Rosary devotion and its new form of interiorized and individualized spirituality, but they also adapted it to fulfill their desire for collective religious sociability and to meet the ever-present yearning for divine help and protection. Within their communities religious endeavors helped create the possibility for people to live together in concord. But the impulse toward communal harmony, strong as it was, could not simply overcome the impulse toward disunity in villages; the two forces existed in tension. As a result, pious activities could themselves become objects of contestation, as villagers used them in competition with each other. The result of these tensions, negotiations, and accommodations was a people's religion alive and creative, always adaptable to changes while still serving the religious needs of its faithful.

FOR FURTHER READING

Bossy, John. *Christianity in the West, 1400–1700*. Oxford: Oxford University Press, 1985.

Châtellier, Louis. *The Religion of the Poor: Rural Missions and the Formation of Modern Catholicism, c. 1500–c. 1800*. Translated by Brian Pearce. Cambridge: Cambridge University Press, 1997.

Christian, William A., Jr. *Local Religion in Sixteenth-Century Spain*. Princeton: Princeton University Press, 1981.

Dixon, C. Scott. *The Reformation and Rural Society: The Parishes of Brandenburg-Ansbach-Kulmbach, 1528–1603*. Cambridge: Cambridge University Press, 1996.

Forster, Marc R. *The Counter-Reformation in the Villages: Religion and Reform in the Bishopric of Speyer, 1560–1720*. Ithaca, N.Y.: Cornell University Press, 1992.

Gentilcore, David. *From Bishop to Witch: The System of the Sacred in Early Modern Terra d'Otranto*. Manchester: Manchester University Press, 1992.

Hsia, R. Po-Chia. *The World of Catholic Renewal, 1540–1770*. Cambridge: Cambridge University Press, 1998.

Luria, Keith P. *Territories of Grace: Cultural Change in the Seventeenth-Century Diocese of Grenoble.* Berkeley: University of California Press, 1991.

Nalle, Sara T. *God in La Mancha: Religious Reform and the People of Cuenca, 1500–1650.* Baltimore: Johns Hopkins University Press, 1992.

Soergel, Philip M. *Wondrous in His Saints: Counter-Reformation Propaganda in Bavaria.* Berkeley: University of California Press, 1993.

A PEOPLE'S REFORMATION?

MARGO TODD

CHAPTER THREE

It was once the case that students learned that the impetus for the Reformation was a combination of new theological ideas appealing to virulent popular anticlericalism and the aggressive sponsorship of self-interested magistrates. Historians charted its progress mainly in terms of easily accessible printed documents: royal proclamations and statutes, published sermons, mandated liturgical change, and—the sole data on the popular side—reports of iconoclasm and of martyrdoms. Historians still incline to the passive voice when asserting that Protestantism "was accepted" or "came to be established," rather than tackle head-on the difficult questions of popular agency, reception, and (on the other side) resistance.

In the last generation, however, scholars' interest in Christianity in the pew, and their increasing commitment to archival research and to the use of material as well as textual sources, have enabled us to examine how the new faith was received, promoted, opposed, and negotiated at the parochial level. The question of whether Protestantism was imposed from above on an unwilling or indifferent population, or spurred from below by popular religious fervor and dissatisfaction with the traditional church, is not a new one. But we can now begin to answer it not just in terms of elite mandate but with new evidence of the beliefs, or at least the actions, of ordinary and mostly illiterate folk. The answer to the perennial question is no simpler than it ever was; indeed, it seems to have become more complicated, more nuanced, as historians have looked more critically at older presumptions and more deeply at manuscript and material data. It will be, however, all the more persuasive for its admission of complexity.

Recent histories of the Reformation in the British Isles provide the best case study of the new approaches taken and new conclusions drawn by students of Protestantism's "popularity." This is in part because of prolific publication by recent historians of the British Reformation, in part because of its very contentious nature, and in part because the Isles played host to three very different Reformations. One (in England) took a relatively conservative, Erastian form, with monarchs dictating religious policy. Another (in Scotland) comprised Europe's most radical national Reformation and commenced as a lay and clerical movement *against* the queen's wishes. And the third (in Ireland) failed miserably. The three Reformations were united by the Calvinism of their adherents, by the relative popularity of earlier Catholic tradition and weakness of anticlericalism in Britain compared to continental Europe, and by the interplay of politics and religion that complicated the process at all levels. Here we shall examine each of these three Reformations in turn and then stand back and assess the question of popularity for Protestantism in the multiple realms of the British Isles.

ENGLAND

The received version of the English Reformation has long been that popularity had nothing to do with it, that it was a purely political act. Henry VIII needed a male heir to secure his dynasty and required a divorce from the aging Catherine of Aragon in order to marry a younger wife. The pope, under military threat from Catherine's nephew, the emperor Charles V, was in no position to comply, so Henry had himself made the supreme head of the Church of England by an act of parliament in 1534.

Did this constitute Reformation? Henry separated his church from Rome, but he hardly made it Protestant. The service remained in Latin, the clergy remained more or less celibate, and even the most Lutheran-looking of the new Articles of Religion, the Ten Articles of 1536, left room for transubstantiation and purgatory. The English Bible authorized in 1539 gave the nod to Protestantism, but a vernacular translation was in any case on the agenda of Catholic humanist reformers. But Henry got to marry Anne Boleyn (and four more after her), and perhaps just as important to him, he was able to abolish monasticism and seize the enormously valuable properties of the religious houses.

It was at Henry's death in 1547, with the accession of his nine-year-old son, Edward, and the rise to power of his Protestant Protectors, that the statutory Reformation began to look truly Protestant. Edward's parliaments dissolved the chantries (chapels where masses were said for the souls of the dead), authorized a vernacular service with the *Book of Common Prayer*, permitted clergy to marry, and published Articles of Religion that were not merely Protestant but unabashedly Calvinistic.

Fig. 3.1. The title page of the English Bible, featuring Henry VIII (top center) distributing copies to clergy, courtesans, and laity. Edward Whytchurche, printer, 1540.

What evidence do we have that this Reformation from above was popular—or not? Historians have asserted both. The older view that Reformation was imposed from above, in rather short order, on a largely indifferent population, was challenged in the 1960s by A. G. Dickens. He argued instead that the instigation came from beneath, that people distressed with the corruption of the Catholic Church welcomed Protestant ideas with open arms, so that Henry's agenda meshed conveniently with a movement already in progress. By the 1980s, a revisionist view emerged, Christopher Haigh and others producing evidence that not only was Reformation imposed from above, but it was enforced on an unwilling and resistant populace and took generations to take hold. Eamon Duffy's work on the popularity of late medieval English Catholicism seemed to clinch the argument. More recently, historians like Diarmaid MacCulloch have formulated a counter-revisionist interpretation, granting that Reformation was a slow process, but insisting that the ideas of Protestantism, not the pressure of politics, were the impetus for what must be defined as a change of hearts and minds and that the English people really did embrace the new religion.

The evidence itself, unsurprisingly, is mixed. Certainly the Protestant preachers who had been active as itinerant evangelists since the 1520s claimed to have made numerous converts, particularly in the heavily populated southeast. Some paid for their success with their lives, though Henry VIII burned about as many Catholics as Protestants in his campaign for uniformity with his own shifting definition of orthodoxy. The vernacular Bible had an undeniable appeal, as Henry must have anticipated. Why else would so conservative a monarch have issued an English Bible? Henry was in many ways an astute politician, well aware that he would need broad-based support for so drastic an act as separation from Rome. Perhaps in the English Bible we are getting his own "read" of the degree to which Protestant preachers had succeeded. The masses of common people pictured at the bottom of the Bible's title page, welcoming the scriptures with thanks to the king who had provided them, may be our best contemporary assessment of how the initial, tentative Reformation of the 1530s was received. The title page is a study in visual propaganda for the royal supremacy, but for propaganda to work, it must incorporate a grain of truth. Indeed, by 1545, Henry himself seems to have been taken aback by the Bible's success among the people. It had become *too* popular, unleashing individual lay interpretation in an age that valued conformity and hierarchy.

But there is counter evidence as well. The dissolution of the monasteries was easily pushed through a parliament attended by men who would buy up those properties at bargain prices from a cash-hungry king, but it was not so well received by ordinary folk. In 1538, a massive riot

---

Henry VIII to Parliament, 1545, on the Danger of Giving the Bible to the Laity

You of the temporalty be not clean and unspotted of malice and envy, for you rail on bishops, speak slanderously of priests, and rebuke and taunt preachers, both contrary to good order and Christian fraternity.... Be not judges yourselves, of your own phantastical opinions and vain expositions, for in such high causes ye may lightly err. And although you be permitted to read holy Scripture and to have the word of God in your mother tongue, you must understand that it is licensed you so to do, only to inform your own conscience, and to instruct your children and family, and not to dispute and make Scripture a railing and a taunting stock against priests and preachers (as many light persons do). I am very sorry to know and hear, how unreverently that most precious jewel the word of God is disputed, rhymed, sung and jangled in every alehouse and tavern, contrary to the true meaning and doctrine of the same.

—From Edward Hall, *Henry VIII*, ed. C. Whibley (London: T. E. and E. C. Jack, 1904 [1548]), 2:356–57.

in defense of the monasteries broke out in the north of England. This "Pilgrimage of Grace" denounced the Protestant reforms in no uncertain terms, its thousands of participants marching into battle beneath the Catholic banner of the five wounds of Christ. Nor would this be the last of the religious riots. We might presume that a service in English would have an immediate appeal to worshipers with no Latin; however, in 1549, thousands of opponents of the vernacular service and other reforms launched the Prayer Book Rising in the southwest. The Cornish folk among them pointed out in their manifesto that the "vernacular" of the new English service was not their own, Celtic tongue: they preferred familiar Latin to foreign English.

Part of the problem the English reformers faced was that people seem generally to have been happy with the Catholic Church. On the eve of the Reformation, there were no problems with clerical recruitment, tithe disputes were few, and people readily resorted to ecclesiastical courts for quick and relatively cheap justice. Bequests to chantries continued right up until their dissolution. And when Edward VI's government ordered that altars and images of saints be removed from parish churches, many people quietly hid the images away in their cupboards and barn lofts, ready to bring them out again when the religious winds shifted. We know this because when the wind did change, at the accession in 1553 of Edward's Catholic half sister, Mary, out came the altar stones and icons. Reception of the early Reformation, then, was mixed at best.

If Protestantism had succeeded in winning hearts and minds in its first generation, why did Mary Tudor's parliaments so readily pass legislation returning the English church to Rome? The fact that monastic lands would remain in the hands of their lay purchasers was clearly more important to members of parliament than Protestant worship or an English Bible. But what of their social inferiors? Much has been made by historians arguing for Reformation from below of the numbers of people—women as well as men, poor as well as rich—willing to die at the stake for their faith. But there were, on final count, fewer than three hundred Protestant martyrs in Mary's five-year reign, among England's four and a half million people. About eight hundred more went into exile to continental Lutheran and Calvinist cities. The remainder of the people either had never been truly converted, were indifferent, or prudently kept mum about their faith. Knowing well the very real power of a strong Tudor state, and gauging carefully the better part of valor, most English people were compliant in their outward behavior.

The argument for popular Protestantism begins to convince only for the second half of the sixteenth century. At Mary's death in 1558, her half sister Elizabeth succeeded and restored Edward's Protestant Articles of Religion and service book. More important, she opened the way for the two universities to recommence the training of Protestant preachers that had begun during her brother's short reign. As the reformers had insisted all along, the religion of the Word must be instilled by preaching of the Word. Now, at last, enough preachers could be provided to make change at the parish level possible. It would take time, of course. But by the 1580s, English people began to define themselves as Protestants.

The process of popularizing Protestantism was aided by two forces apart from preaching itself—propaganda and the Spanish threat. The most notable propaganda effort came from the pen of the Marian exile John Foxe. His *Acts and Monuments*, abridged for cheap publication as the *Book of Martyrs*, took the raw material of Henry's and Mary's martyrs, together with a few early Christians and medieval heretics and martyrs like Wycliffe and Hus, and built them into a new Protestant history of England whose popular impact is hard to overestimate. As its title page attests, the *Book of Martyrs* gave the English people that all-important foundation for a new identity—an evil Other against which they could define themselves. In both text and abundant illustration, Foxe depicted the English along with continental Protestants as defenders of the true faith against the forces of Antichrist and Satan himself. There is a "plotline" in the images on the title page, read from bottom to top, "good guys" on the left, "bad guys" on the right. The true worship of God as Word pictured on the left side of the page might lead to martyrdom, but martyrdom in turn led to heavenly reward. The idolatrous and superstitious worship of Catholics on the right side, however, ended with advocates of the old religion escorted out of heaven by the demons who in fact hold up the frames of the right-side pictures. This "us versus them" mentality in a format that appealed to illiterate folk and readers alike would do as much to recruit people to Protestantism as any number of sermons. As numerous reprintings demonstrate, Foxe sold well. We know that illiterate people purchased the *Book of Martyrs*, hoping for visitors who could read it to them. Heads of households read stories from Foxe to their children and servants. And the pictures of martyrs inside reinforced the message of the title page: Catholicism was idolatry or worse; Protestantism was the true, biblical faith. Some of these pictures were large foldouts that people removed from the book, colored, and hung on the walls of their cottages. The stories told in image and word provided new Protestant saints of both sexes and all social standings for popular emulation. What Englishwoman would not admire outspoken heroines like Anne Askew, courageously talking back to her vicious and ignorant clerical inquisitors from her obviously superior knowledge of the vernacular scriptures?

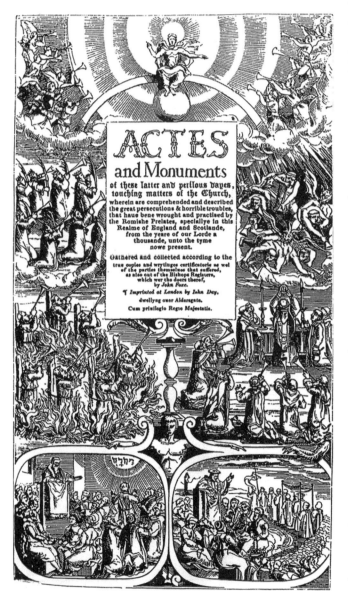

Fig. 3.2. Title page of John Foxe's *Actes and Monuments*, abridged for a popular readership as the *Book of Martyrs*. John Dey, printer, 1570.

The political events that cemented English popular identity with Protestantism began with a Catholic rising in 1569 and the papal bull of 1570 excommunicating Elizabeth and calling for her deposition as a heretic queen. It culminated with the abortive naval invasion by the Spanish Armada in 1588. The northern earls who rose in rebellion in 1569 sought to replace Elizabeth with her ill-fated Catholic cousin, Mary Stuart, Queen of Scots. Easily put down by royal forces, it was followed by a series of assassination attempts against the queen, in many of which Mary Stuart had a hand. In 1580, the Jesuits appeared in England and worked to feed such plots with their insistence that a heretic had no right to rule. Elizabeth, disinclined to make religious martyrs, may have had as many as two hundred Catholics executed, but in each case for treason, not heresy, and by beheading, not burning. Rather than making martyrs to inspire English Catholic recusants, she emphasized the danger that Catholics now posed to the security of the realm in myriad popular pamphlets illustrated with images of papists as diabolical traitors. Finally, Philip II's naval attack in 1588 under a papal banner made it quite clear to English people of all sorts that Catholicism, castigated as "popery," was now to be equated with treason. And the Armada's destruction by a combination of English privateers and providential storms allowed the queen and her pamphleteers to claim that God was on her and the Protestants' side. Popular annual celebrations of the Armada's defeat, with bonfires, bell ringing, and feasting in the streets, reinforced the message

---

Anne Askew on Using the Scriptures, 1546

First, Christopher Dare [the inquisitor] . . . asked if I did not believe that the sacrament hanging over the altar was the very body of Christ really? Then I demanded this question of him: wherefore St Stephen was stoned to death? And he said he could not tell. Then I answered that no more would I assoil his vain question. Secondly, he said that there was a woman which did testify, that I should read how God was not in temples made with hands. Then I showed him the 7th and 17th chapters of the Acts of the Apostles, what Stephen and Paul had said therein. Whereupon he asked me how I took those sentences. I answered I would not throw pearls among swine, for acorns were good enough. Thirdly, he asked wherefore I said I had rather to read five lines in the Bible than to hear five masses in the temple? I confessed that I said no less: not for the dispraise of either the epistle or the gospel, but because the one did greatly edify me, and the other nothing at all. As St Paul doth witness in the 14th chapter of his first epistle to the Corinthians where as he sayeth: if the trumpet giveth an uncertain sound, who will prepare himself to the battle? . . . He asked me what I said concerning confession? I answered him by meaning, which was as St James sayeth, that every man ought to knowledge his faults to another, and the one to pray for the other. . . . He asked me if I did not think that private masses did help souls departed. I said it was great idolatry to believe more in them than in the death which Christ died for us. . . . Then the bishop's chancellor rebuked me, and said I was much to blame for uttering the Scriptures. For St Paul (he said) forbode women to speak or talk of the word of God. I answered him that I knew Paul's meaning as well as he, which is in I Corinthians 14, that a woman ought not to speak in the congregation by way of teaching. And then I asked him how many women he had seen go into the pulpit and preach? He said he never saw none. Then I said he ought to find no fault in poor women.

—From John Foxe, *Acts and Monuments* (London, John Daye, 1576), 1205.

with public festivity. What Englishman, after the 1580s, would wish to call himself a Catholic?

There were still Catholics, of course, but not many. The queen's government prosecuted only their clergy and some of their noble protectors. But the number of Catholics was kept small by the need to worship in secret, hiding itinerant priests and hoping that their neighbors did not report suspicious activity. Many avoided the charge of recusancy by attending Church of England worship at least on Christmas and Easter. And most rejected the Jesuits' radicalism and insisted on their loyalty to the queen. These were not the sort of Catholics likely to implement Tridentine reform in England; they were survivors, and no more.

Does the fact that by the 1580s most people would claim to be Protestants mean that the new faith can be called "popular"? Were most people now Protestant believers? Here the answer depends very much on who is asking. By the later sixteenth century, the Church of England was already internally divided, between zealots (dubbed "Puritans" by their foes) and outward conformists (or, to Puritans, "worldlings"). Given illiteracy rates, most of the "mere conformists" give us scant insight into their beliefs or the nature of their piety. We must take care not to accept too easily their enemies' judgment that they were indifferent, like the "lukewarm" of Laodicea. Judith Maltby's work on the popularity of the *Book of Common Prayer* suggests very real conformist devotion. Puritans, more inclined to keep spiritual journals, to worry about their election to salvation, and to complain about their less godly neighbors, give us a bit more to work with. In their view, the biblical principle that the elect are but a remnant of humankind, the true Israel surrounded by a mass of Philistines, applied to their own situation. Their presumption was that the godly were always a small minority within the visible church, explaining why there remained within that church so many "dregs of popery"—clerical vestments, the liturgy itself, the sign of the cross in baptism.

Puritans sought further to Protestantize the church from within (never to separate themselves from it) and to impose on all parishioners a "reformation of manners" on the principle that a true church will effect a change in behavior. They criticized the established church for not exercising effective discipline—enforcing Sabbath observance; punishing sexual dalliance, drunkenness, and blasphemy; barring from communion those whose behavior was not above reproach. A few went so far as to criticize episcopacy (rule of the church by bishops) as a polity ill suited to good discipline. Their own "us versus them" view of the world thus went beyond the anti-Catholicism of Foxe. It is visible in the title page of Thomas Young's treatise on Sabbath observance. Here, the godly (again on the left) perform the *opera lucis* (the works of light), while their neighbors labor, dance, feast, and gamble when they ought to be attending sermons and reading their Bibles. Puritans represent a style of piety not likely to qualify as "popular," but they would insist (with some hubris) that this was the indicator of election to "God's little flock," surrounded by reprobate wolves. Was the Reformation popular? Puritans were sure that, properly understood, it could not be. Was it claimed by most English people? By Elizabeth's reign, yes.

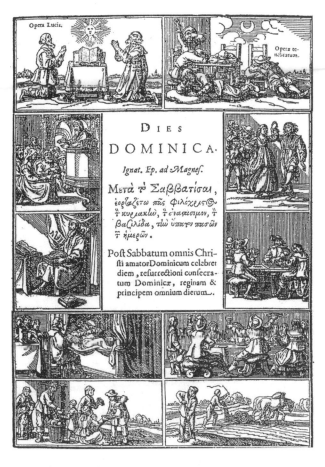

Fig. 3.3. Title page of Puritan Thomas Young's (1587–1655) book on observing the Sabbath, 1639.

SCOTLAND

North of England's border, the Reformation took a course also shaped by politics, but veering in a much more radical direction and negotiated and shaped to a very great degree by the laity at the parish level. The new religious order would have a profound impact on the daily lives of ordinary folk, demanding a rigorous moral and doctrinal discipline legendary even in its own time. But while that discipline

The Martyrs of Perth (1544)

There were many accused of the crime of heresy, yet these persons were only apprehended: Robert Lamb, William Anderson, James Hunter, James Ronaldson, and his wife, Helen Stirk, and James Finlayson [all craftspeople]. . . . Robert Lamb was accused in special for interrupting the friar in the pulpit, which he not only confessed, but also affirmed constantly, that it was the duty of no man which understood and knew the truth, to hear the same impugned without contradiction. . . . The said Robert also, with William Anderson and James Ronaldson, were accused for hanging up the image of St Francis on a cord, nailing of a ram's horns to his head, and a cow's rump to his tail, and for eating of a goose on Allhallow's even [a fast day]. James Hunter being a simple man and without learning, and a flesher by occupation, could be charged with no great knowledge in doctrine; yet because he often used the suspect company of the rest, he was accused. The woman, Helen Stirk, was accused for that in her childbed she was not accustomed to call upon the name of the Virgin Mary, being exhorted thereto by her neighbours, but only upon God, for Jesus Christ's sake, and because she said in like manner that if she herself had been in the time of the Virgin Mary, God might have looked to her humility and base estate as he did to the Virgin's in making her the mother of Christ—thereby meaning that there were no merits in the Virgin Mary which procured that honour to be made the mother of Christ . . . but God's only free mercy exalted her to that estate. . . . These forenamed persons upon the morrow after St Paul's day were condemned and adjudged to death. . . . There was great intercession made by the town to the governour for their lives, . . . but they altogether refused. . . . Thereafter they were carried by a great band of armed men (for they feared rebellion in the town, except they had their men of war) to the place of execution. . . . The woman was taken to a place to be drowned, and albeit she had a child sucking on her breast, yet this moved nothing the unmerciful hearts of the enemies. So after she had commended her children to the neighbours of the town for God's sake, and the sucking bairn was given to the nurse, she sealed up the truth by her death.

From David Calderwood, *Historie of the Kirk of Scotland*
(Edinburgh, 1625), 1:171–73.

has been seen by earlier historians as an imposition by the clergy on the people, recent research has shown laypeople actively participating in its design and implementation, and voluntarily submitting themselves to its demands.

The official Reformation came only when the Scots parliament in 1560 enacted it as part of the nobility's campaign to eliminate the French influence that had long dominated Scottish politics. The 1542 death of James V had left an infant daughter as heir, with a shifting regency that eventually settled on the child's mother, Mary of Guise. The young queen of Scots grew up a Catholic in France, only returning to Scotland in 1561, after her mother's death. By 1557, the nobility had endured quite enough erosion of their own power at the hands of French courtiers; they decided that an appeal to England's Elizabeth was not too steep a price to pay for military aid against the regent's forces, even if Elizabeth's Protestantism came into the bargain.

Protestant ideas were already present in Scotland. Towns like Edinburgh and Dundee, closely tied to North Sea trading partners, had been importing the new ideas and books right along with other merchandise since the 1520s. Lutheranism had caught on among university students and some of their teachers in Saint Andrews and among friars in many towns. Their active, vernacular, reformist preaching in the 1540s and 1550s would help to lay a popular urban groundwork for Reformed beliefs. The burgh of Perth is a case in point: there the converted friar John Row would become the first Protestant minister of the town. The new faith had won over significant groups of craftspeople by the 1540s, when popular resentment of the wealth of the town's four religious houses boiled over in a protest that ended in five dramatic martyrdoms. The facts that the town pleaded for the martyrs' lives and that the five required a military escort to their executions lest the people intervene certainly suggest broad popular support for Reformation in this burgh.

It is impossible to say just how popular Protestant ideas were in those early years, though. Scotland's martyrs were very few indeed—only twenty or so to England's nearly three hundred. And in the same towns where the martyrs died, bequests to chantries and altars, donations for reliquaries and icons, abounded through the 1550s. Complaints about clergy were relatively few, even in Perth, and as in English towns, guildsmen and burgh councils hired and controlled their own priests, rather undermining the strength of anticlericalism. James VI certainly exaggerated when he claimed that the Reformation was instigated in Scotland "by a popular tumult and rebellion."[1] Still, vernacular preachers had set the stage for what happened in 1558–1559.

At that time the noble "Lords of the Congregation" took up arms in the cause of Protestantism (and their own political opportunism) and found as they marched to towns like Perth that the citizenry came out in their support. Doubtless it helped that the Lords at the gates of Perth had put ropes around their own necks in imitation of the Perth martyrs. They knew as well as Foxe the polemical advantage of the image. The Lords defeated and would in 1567 depose Mary Stuart in favor of her infant son, whom they raised with strictly Calvinist principles.

It was what happened after the Reformation parliament that would most drastically transform the religious experience and culture of the Scottish people. Scotland's Protestantism was not England's. Inspired by its clerical leaders' experience in Geneva, it was Calvinist not only in doctrine but also in government. First in Lowlands towns, then in more rural areas, each parish set up its own consistory court, or "kirk [church] session," to oversee the religious and moral life of the parish. The session was comprised of the minister and a dozen or so lay elders, chosen from among the merchants and craftsmen of towns, middling landowners in rural areas. These were men of substance but not great nobles and not clergymen. They were initially elected by the congregation, though they later became self-selecting; even then, the congregation had veto power and periodically subjected both elders and minister to a rigorous vetting to expose any faults in their doctrine or behavior. By the 1580s, parish sessions would form a network in the new organization of presbyteries, whose representatives would in turn meet occasionally in provincial synods and in a national General Assembly to discuss matters of doctrine and discipline. The system was by no means democratic, but at the parish level it was certainly dominated by laymen and commoners rather than nobility. For the first time, laypeople not of high birth had a real say in how their church was to be run.

It was run with great fervor and intensity. From their founding, sessions ran a campaign of Sabbath observance, catechism and examination, and close moral oversight that would put even the English Puritan agenda to shame. Absentees from Sunday sermons were fined, and while elders in the kirk took attendance, others were designated "searchers" to prowl the parish during the service and detect absentees. Boys found playing golf were whipped; drinkers in alehouses paid heavy fines. Town sessions enforced attendance at weekday sermons as well, ensuring that the Protestant message became firmly embedded in the minds of the people. Parents were told to instruct their children in religion, supplementing the regular Sunday afternoon catechism in the kirk. A translation of Calvin's *Catechism* was provided, along with John Knox's Scots *Confession*, in the *Book of Common Order* published regularly after 1562; a Gaelic translation of this volume was published in 1567 for use in the Highlands and Isles. And to ensure that the catechism took hold, the entire population of the parish underwent individual examination by elders before each communion. If they passed, they received a token that would admit them to the sacrament. If they failed, they would be "dealt with" by the session and fined for failure to communicate. Clinging to Catholic ideas was in Scotland an expensive proposition.

Misbehavior cost even more—not just in money, but in public humiliation. Those "searchers" also made unannounced weekday visits to their assigned households to seek out fornicators, adulterers, drunkards, blasphemers, and quarrelers, as well as anyone who might be celebrating a forbidden holiday (including Christmas and Easter). These unfortunates were then prosecuted and subjected to a distinctively Scottish form of public humiliation. In each parish church, a new piece of furniture appeared after 1560—the "stool of repentance," where moral offenders were ordered to sit in penitential garb through the Sunday service. They stood on the stool after the sermon to confess their sins aloud, often holding some symbol of their offense. An abusive wife in Leith, for instance, had to appear in sackcloth holding both the staff with which she had injured her husband and the napkin used to staunch his wound; an Inveravon man had to hold a stalk of grain for "breach of the sabbath in shearing of corn."[2] People who had slandered their neighbors followed their public confessions with a procession to the place where they had misspoken and apologized on their knees to their victims, who then shook hands or kissed them in token of reconciliation. Few would escape the elders' rigor; those not found by the searchers were very often reported by their neighbors.

Too often modern students conclude from the invasiveness of the sessions that they must have been unpopular. The challenge for us is to set aside modern notions of privacy and individual rights and to explain why communities in fact accepted indeed, sponsored and actively collaborated with—the new discipline. This is a system that could not have worked at all without a great deal of popular cooperation. And surviving minute books of sessions attest to the fact that it *did* work. We find in those books that some people *voluntarily* confessed to the elders sins that would otherwise go undetected—a married couple admitting sexual intercourse during a fasting season, for instance. Clearly, many perceived a value in public confession as a way of relieving guilt. The kirk's discipline presumably also garnered popular support for its relatively even handed policies. There was, for

example, no sexual double standard: male as well as female fornicators underwent punishment. Social status impinged rather more; still,
lairds, lords, elders, and ministers can be found right along with their
social inferiors and parishioners repenting from the stool. And what
better way to reconcile quarrels and reduce the violence level of a still-
feuding society than public chastisement of the troublemaker?

The sessions were run by the common people, at the most local
level; they were therefore quickly responsive to the needs of the community. They provided a range of useful social services designed to
build a more orderly society. They administered poor relief, schools
(for girls as well as boys), and fostering of orphaned or abandoned
children. They intervened in domestic violence, requiring abusive
spouses and parents to mend their ways, and they forced absent
fathers to support their children and adult children to sustain their
aged parents. They rescued the reputations of the slandered, and they
mitigated violence by offering binding arbitration of quarrels. However distasteful modern people might find their prying and punishing,
they served early modern communities much as the police and welfare
agencies of the modern state do.

The lay governors of the Reformed kirk also broadened its
appeal by exercising some flexibility in discipline. The clergy might
rail against dancing and festivity, for instance, but the elders in
fact punished it lightly, reserving their sterner penalties for high-
priority offenses like Sabbath breach. They were no fools. They knew
that if their priorities were set on sermon attendance and catechism,
the transformation of hearts and minds would be accomplished more
efficiently, and "superstitious" festivals would die off in due course.
As to popular magic, sessions did sometimes initiate the charges of
witchcraft that give early modern Scotland such a bad name. But
the witch craze was most vehement when the circumstances of the
community were most dire—in times of local disasters like dearth
or pestilence. Popular healers carried on for years without being
troubled by the authorities; only when their potions ended in otherwise unexplained deaths, or the community fell prey to diseases of
cattle or crops, did their neighbors begin to associate them with new,
clerical theories of diabolic witchcraft. Until then, we find elders and
even ministers acknowledging a parallel cosmology of amoral sprites

and fairies, the Gaelic tradition of "second sight," natural magic and healing charms, running alongside their rigorously Calvinist system. John Aubrey called the same phenomenon in England "the remains of gentilism," and David Hall has shown us that New England's Puritans believed in similar "worlds of wonder."[3] We ought to bear in mind that early modern belief was multifaceted and more syncretistic than we generally suppose. The Reformation succeeded best where its converts were allowed a bit of room to accommodate the competing cosmologies of their experience. It was a tacit negotiation between evangelical clerics and ordinary folk that helped to ensure the ultimate success of the cultural change demanded by Protestantism.

The negotiation took a different form in the Gàidhealtachd, the Gaelic-speaking, clan-based society of the Highlands and Isles. In those sparsely populated regions it was more difficult to organize kirk sessions than in the towns and villages of the Lowlands and eastern coast; there were probably very few until after the turn of the century. But the reformers had met the challenge of evangelizing across language and cultural barriers with characteristic flexibility. They adapted to Gaelic culture, rather than trying to change it, by first recruiting the support of powerful chieftains and of the "learned orders"—the poets, bards, and *sennachies* (historians) who maintained the oral tradition of Gaelic learning (and were equally conversant in Scots and Latin). The fifth earl of Argyll, chief of Clan Campbell, was particularly influential in the process. With this base, Protestant bishops in Galloway, Orkney, and Argyll distributed Bishop Carswell's translation of the *Book of Common Order* and recruited Gaelic-speaking preachers and readers. The latter translated the scriptures into the language of the people as they read weekly in parish kirks to a nearly universally illiterate population best attuned to oral transmission of ideas. By the time Franciscan missionaries finally showed up to reconvert the Highlands in the 1620s, they found a population won over by decades of fervent Protestant preaching and catechizing. Modern estimates of Catholic survival at the turn of the century for all of Scotland are around 2 percent—no mean achievement.[4]

Finally, in Scotland as in England, the perceived political threat of popery cemented popular affiliation with Protestantism, so much so that any hint of a return to "popish superstition" inspired violent

Description of the Saint Giles Riot of 1637

When the next sabbath, July 23 came, the bishop of Edinburgh (after that the ordinary prayers had been read in the morning) about ten o'clock brought in the Service Book to the pulpit, and his dean sat in the reader's seat with his Service Book before him, in the Great Kirk of Edinburgh. . . . Now so soon as the bishop did open his Service Book, and began to read thereon, and the people perceiving the dean opening his book also, all the common people, especially the women, rose up with such a loud clamor and uproar, so that nothing could be heard. Some cried, "Woe, woe!" Some cried, "Sorrow, sorrow! For this doleful day, that they are bringing in popery among us!" Others did cast their stools against the dean's face, others ran out of the kirk with a pitiful lamentation, so that their reading upon the service book was then interrupted; . . . therefore, the bishop left his reading, and taught a sermon, but a very short one. After sermon, when the bishop came out of the pulpit and went out of the kirk, he found the street full of people who ran about him crying that he was bringing in a new religion among them, and bringing in popery upon them. The bishop put in a great fear ran up the nearest stair to have gotten into my lord Wemys' lodging, crying to the people that he had no wit of the matter. . . . The [afternoon] sermon being ended, and the bishop going home in a coach with my lord Roxburgh, to save himself from the violence of the people, was all the way pursued with stones casten, until he came to his own house in the abbey. . . . The next sabbath, July 30, very few women came to sermon to the Great Kirk of Edinburgh.

—From John Row, *The Historie of the Kirk of Scotland* (Edinburgh: Maitland Club, 1842 [1637]), 408–9.

popular protest. This was particularly true after the 1605 Gunpowder Plot— a conspiracy of Catholic radicals to blow up both houses of the Westminster parliament on its opening day on November 5, when King James would be present, and replace him with a Catholic monarch. Catholicism was by the seventeenth century perceived as treason in both realms. In Scotland, where the set liturgy had been abolished at the Reformation, popular antipopery was most strikingly displayed when James's successor, Charles I, tried in 1637 to impose an English-style liturgical service on the kirk. Like the English prayer book, the structure of the service was based on the Mass; unlike the English, the Scots would have none of it. All sorts of people—not just clergy or Puritans—protested the book. The bishop of Brechin reportedly had to read it holding a pair of loaded pistols aimed at his angry congregation, and in Edinburgh's Saint Giles parish both women and men, humble and well-off alike, protested by throwing their stools at the dean reading the despised service. There is surely no clearer evidence of the popularity of this most radical Reformation. A bloody civil war wracked both realms in the 1640s, as Scots "Covenanters" defended their austere service, and English Puritans called for stricter Calvinism, more rigorous discipline, and an end to "superstitious ceremonies" in their own church. However different the two Reformations, in both kingdoms popular belief served as an impetus for religious war.

IRELAND

In 1641, the Irish too entered the civil wars. But they did so on the other side, for the Protestant Reformation there had proved a decisive failure. Some attribute this fact to a generalized Irish distaste for things English. But how can we then understand Reformation in Scotland, a realm that had spent centuries at war with England, right up to the 1540s? Others explain it as a linguistic problem. Few Irish people spoke the language of the English Bible and *Book of Common Prayer*; they spoke Irish Gaelic. But again, the folk of Scotland's Highlands were not Anglophone. There were, moreover, efforts to surmount the language barrier in Ireland. A Gaelic catechism appeared in 1571, printed with a specially made set of Irish type paid for by the notoriously frugal queen Elizabeth. There was no Gaelic Bible until 1685, but the Scots Gaelic Bible was also slow to appear, and we have seen that a resort to the tradition of "oral literacy" sufficed there for Protestant purposes. The language barrier had also been overcome in Wales, another Celtic-language region. There, too, native preachers bridged the gap, though with the advantage of a Welsh Bible in 1588. A native Protestant preaching ministry never appeared in Ireland, however.

Fig. 3.4. Pictorial representation of the Saint Giles Riot of 1637. Anonymous woodcut, seventeenth century.

University provision for the training of ministers is a partial explanation of the difference. Welshmen attended both Cambridge and Oxford (where places were specially designated for them in Jesus College). Scotland had three universities at the time of the Reformation and added a fourth in Edinburgh in the 1580s. But in Ireland, would-be ministers had to study abroad until the belated foundation in 1594 of Trinity College, Dublin—an institution not particularly friendly to Gaelic students in any case. Without preachers, the people could hardly be expected to embrace Protestantism. Still, this is a very partial explanation.

We must again turn to politics fully to understand the people's response to Reformation. The great difference between Ireland and the other British realms was that Ireland's English rulers did not treat its people as they treated the Welsh or Highlands Gaels. Wales had been incorporated into a United Kingdom with England in the 1530s, with parliamentary representation and mostly native administration of church and shires. The Scots Highlands, of course, were never subject to English administration: the union of crowns, when James VI succeeded Elizabeth in 1603, did not subjugate the independent realm of Scotland. But Ireland had been a "lordship" of the English crown since the Anglo-Norman conquest of the twelfth century. In 1541, in the wake of a major Irish rebellion, it became in effect a colony when Henry VIII claimed the title of king, not just overlord, of Ireland.

The Irish population in the sixteenth century was divided into three very unequal parts: the most numerous and least powerful Gaelic Irish; the "Old English," or semi-Gaelicized descendants of the Anglo-Norman conquest living in or near the Pale around Dublin; and the "New English," or post-Reformation arrivals often given land confiscated from Irish rebels. The New English also got the most powerful and lucrative administrative positions. The Gaelic Irish and Old English, unlike the Scots, certainly never invited English alliance. Henry, Edward, and especially Elizabeth were their oppressors. Real parliamentary power lay in Westminster; the Irish parliament could only do as it was told. English planters had fiscal and tax advantages over natives and occupied lands seized violently from Gaels. And to hold land at all after the Reformation, one had to swear the oath of supremacy, acknowledging the English monarch as supreme head of the church in his or her realms. The Irish people came to recognize Protestantism as part of the machinery of oppression.

Despite the negative associations of Protestantism with English domination, there were a few early successes for Protestants in Ireland.

The Elizabethan government sensibly permitted a Latin translation of the *Book of Common Prayer* in 1559, so that some people were lured in by the similarity of the service to the familiar Mass. A particularly zealous Protestant preacher, Bishop John Bale, won a few converts in Ossory and Kilkenny. And the first Jesuit mission of 1542 reported "the few faithful [Catholics] are too poor to support us" and others had been "subdued by fear."[5] They gave up the mission after just a few weeks and fled to Scotland, where they were arrested. But at this early stage, the Irish seem rather more confused than persuaded by Protestantism.

The situation changed dramatically when Elizabeth determined to impose the new faith by force, along with a systematic repression of Irish culture—language, music, dress, law, and religion. Catholics' estates were forfeit to the Crown, and one whose property was valued under £20 could be imprisoned for a year. Now the traditional and very popular faith long maintained by the preaching friars in close alliance with the *aes dána*, the Gaelic learned orders of Ireland, provided the banner of resistance to English domination at all social levels. Counter-Reformation missions strengthened the resolve of the Irish people to wield that banner in the face of real persecution. Irish students returned from Spanish and French seminaries to build on the popularity of the mendicant orders working from centers in the west of the island, beyond effective English rule. Chantries beyond the Pale had never been dissolved and now supported Catholic clergy. Observant Franciscans led successful missions, joined by Jesuits in 1542, 1560, and especially 1598. Ordinary people flocked to hear them say masses and preach, whatever the danger. As one scribbled notebook entry indicates, the people had come to

A Gael's Lament for Irish Religion

And the ruler of England and Ireland at this time is Queen Elizabeth.... And the English are saying that she is the supreme head of religion, and that is a lie, because we are certain that the pope is head of the holy Catholic church and what the English say is true in the sense that she is indeed supreme head of their own evil religion in her own dominions, for there is no fast or Lent or . . . holy day under their law, though God ordained their observance, nor is there honour or love of sacred buildings. And further, they are the greatest murderers and the proudest people in all Europe, and I am surprised that God tolerates them so long in power—except that he is long-suffering and that his avenging hand is slow but sure, and besides, that the Irish themselves are bad, and that this misfortune is to chastise and correct them. I shall say no more, because I should use up all my ink and paper on this subject!

—From a late sixteenth-century manuscript, "The Irish Church in the Sixteenth Century," trans. Canice Mooney, *Irish Ecclesiastical Record* 99 (1963): 111, quoted in Samantha Meigs, *The Reformations in Ireland* (London: Macmillan, 1997), 60.

understand English Protestantism not as a path to spiritual freedom but as divine punishment for their sins.

Periodically over the course of the century, Gaelic chieftains raised rebellions against English tyranny. These were always brutally repressed, the families of the defeated often systematically starved out in the aftermath when the Crown seized vast tracts of Irish land and turned it over to English and Scots "planters." The Ulster plantation of 1609 was the culmination, settling radically Calvinist Scots in the Gaelic heart of the north, where Hugh O'Neill's rebellion had recruited so many and failed so miserably in the 1590s. For the Irish people, all things English—including Protestantism—were thus impossibly tainted. Reformed religion was part of a foreign attack on Irish identity. The *aes dána,* so effectively enrolled for Protestantism in Scotland, became the voice of Ireland's vigorous, irretrievably Catholic identity. In their writings we find a startling image of the Reformation's failure in Ireland: by 1600 the usual Gaelic word for "Protestant" became *albanać* or *sasanać*—"Scot" or "Englishman."[6]

SUCCESS AND FAILURE

Where the Reformation succeeded as a genuinely popular movement, it was because Protestant leaders adapted themselves to the culture of the people. The Scots laity made it their own when their mostly local authorities took the reins of its disciplinary system, modifying it to address their own agendas and turning over the transmission of its message in the Highlands to the bardic orders. The English grafted it onto their parochial and episcopal system and embraced it as part of their communal identity as the threat of popish Spain grew. In both realms concessions were made to persistent folk beliefs. In neither were the common people passive recipients of orders from on high; they negotiated, compromised, and actively reshaped the new order. In Ireland, however, the authorities seeking to spread Protestant belief lost their opportunity by making the Reformation a culture war. It is one that continues to this day.

FOR FURTHER READING

Dickens, A. G. *The English Reformation.* 2nd edition. University Park: Pennsylvania State University Press, 1991.

Duffy, Eamon. *The Stripping of the Altars: Traditional Religion in England, c. 1400–c. 1580.* New Haven: Yale University Press, 1992.

Haigh, Christopher. *English Reformations: Religion, Politics, and Society under the Tudors.* Oxford: Clarendon, 1993.

MacCulloch, Diarmaid. *The Later Reformation in England, 1547–1603.* British History in Perspective. New York: St. Martin's, 1990.

———. *The Reformation.* New York: Viking, 2004.

Maltby, Judith. *Prayer Book and People in Elizabethan and Early Stuart England.* Cambridge Studies in Early Modern British History. Cambridge: Cambridge University Press, 1998.

Todd, Margo. *The Culture of Protestantism in Early Modern Scotland.* New Haven: Yale University Press, 2002.

FROM CRADLE
TO GRAVE

Part 2

ENTERING THE WORLD

DAVID CRESSY

CHAPTER FOUR

In Tudor and Stuart England, childbirth was a private event with public significance, a domestic occurrence of which the commonwealth took note.[1] In the household, as in the kingdom, the birth of a child established new relationships and new prospects as men, women, and children negotiated their roles as parents, offspring, successors, and heirs. Without childbirth there could be no patriarchy, without human procreation no social reproduction. The woman's work of childbearing made mouths to feed and hands to work, as well as new subjects, citizens, and Christians.

The primary work of childbearing, however, was not the production of a child but the deliverance of a woman. Attention focused on the female body and its punishing trials and tribulations. As all around her knew, the childbearing woman underwent a series of transformations affecting her physical, hormonal, emotional, social, domestic, and cultural condition. From conception to quickening, through all the anxieties of carrying and gestation, to the climax of labor, parturition, recovery, and the rewards of suckling and motherhood, each woman participated in a series of commonly shared experiences, performances, and ceremonies. Nature governed the biological parameters of her progress, but culture gave childbirth its social meaning. Each stage of the transformation was nuanced by social scripting and social construction. Every phase of the process was invested with emotional, cultural, and religious significance. Though not formally ritualized or liturgically performed like the life-cycle services in the *Book of Common Prayer*, the ceremonies of childbirth were deeply embedded in the popular culture of Tudor and Stuart England. Women of every social background understood the protocols of pregnancy, midwifery, and female fellowship around the childbed. Indeed, many of the social and economic differences between elite and humble women were dissolved in the primal activity of birth.

Childbirth was women's work, in which men played distant supporting roles. Very few men gained intimate entry to the birthroom or knew what happened behind the screen. The transformations belonged to a powerfully gendered domain in which women relied on each other. Women were the central figures in childbearing, sharing the pain and the peril. Women were the guardians of its mysteries, the custodians of its lore. This poses particular problems for historians, since the bulk of the documentation of early modern society was generated by men. Women, for the most part, were illiterate, and they rarely set forth their experiences in writing. With a few remarkable exceptions, our sources are confined to the viewpoints of husbands, fathers, ministers, doctors, and scribes. Gynecological handbooks and medical manuals, domestic conduct books and herbals, religious exhortations and diaries, and court records and correspondence are all heavily weighted to the male point of view. Exploiting this evidence and seeing beyond its limits require an unusual effort of empathy and imagination. Most of what we know about the childbed mysteries comes from the other side of the veil.

The ceremony of childbirth began with the recognition of pregnancy, gained pace with the sensation of quickening, progressed to preparations for labor, developed urgency with the ministrations of the midwife and her attendant women, and climaxed with the deliverance of the woman and the birth of the child. Its ritual aftermath included lying in, gossips' feasts, the child's christening, upsitting, the woman's "month," and the ecclesiastical ceremony of churching or thanksgiving. Each stage involved a host of procedures and traditions that varied in detail between social groups and regions and were subject to subtle modulations over time. Every aspect of the ceremony was subject to complications and controversies.[2]

GOD'S BABIES:
THE SPIRITUAL CONSTRUCTION OF CHILDBIRTH

The Christian culture of early modern England provided the master narrative for understanding the mystery of childbirth. Other systems of explanation—especially the learned traditions of ancient science, medieval medicine, and renaissance anatomy—addressed the physiology of childbearing but fell short in describing its deeper spiritual significance. Indeed, Elizabethan churchmen thought that to construe childbirth as merely "a natural and ordinary work of nature" was to deny honor due to God and to reprieve Christian parents of limitless spiritual comfort.[3] In the sixteenth and seventeenth centuries the miracle of reproduction was swathed in religious meaning. The Christian church, predominantly a male institution, provided the language and told the stories that governed thinking about human reproduction. But the extent to which the public Christian discourse on childbirth was echoed within the private womanly domain of the birthroom is something we may never know.

From the point of view of the church, a woman in childbirth experienced both the curse of Eve and the grace of Christ. Motherhood, from the perspective of the pulpit, recapitulated the entire spiritual history of humankind. The woman bore children and suffered because she was stained by original sin. Yet miraculously, through Christ's redemption she could be saved. Childbirth involved sorrow, shame, and chastisement, yet under Christ the woman's labor was part of a covenant of sanctification, mercy, and eternal comfort. Sermons, prayers, and pious meditations reiterated this theme in countless disquisitions on childbearing in Elizabethan and Stuart England.

The Old Testament set forth the story of God's punishment of Eve's transgression and the consequent curse that descended to all womankind through the ages. "Unto the woman he said, I will greatly multiply thy sorrow and thy conception; in sorrow thou shalt bring forth children; and thy desire shall be to thy husband, and he shall rule over thee" (Gen. 3:16, King James Version). The pain and the peril of childbearing, the exercise of patriarchal authority, and the politics of reproduction all descended from this awful judgment.

Characteristically, the New Testament offered fresh hope, though no diminution of female subordination. "The woman being deceived was in the transgression. Notwithstanding she shall be saved in childbearing, if they continue in faith and charity and holiness with sobriety," explained Paul to Timothy (1 Tim. 2:13). This epistle, according to one seventeenth-century clergyman, offered "heart-reviving words to every drooping woman."[4]

Religious writers usually insisted that sexual activity, conception, and childbearing were joyful and lawful activities, so long as they took place within marriage. They were part of God's plan (at least the revised postlapsarian plan) for his creation. "We are plainly taught of God that the seed of faithful parentage is holy from the very birth," opined Richard Hooker. "The fruit of marriage is birth, and the companion of birth, travail." The newborn child was the "pledge of love" between husband and wife, "a joyful benediction" to be welcomed as a future Christian, repeated many a seventeenth-century sermon. It became a commonplace of English Protestant instruction that "children are a blessing, an inheritance, a crown, a reward unto us of the Lord." William Hinde in his eulogy of the Puritan squire John Bruen repeated that "children are the inheritance of the Lord, and the fruit of the womb his exceeding rich reward."[5]

Nor was this exclusively a male or clerical perspective. Guided by faith, the devout Elizabeth Joceline wrote in 1622 that she "earnestly desired of God that I might be a mother to one of his children." Elizabeth Clinton, the Countess of Lincoln, wrote after eighteen pregnancies that "children are God's blessings," though she also saw childbearing as the consequence of Eve's transgression. "It pleased God to give me the blessing of conception," wrote Alice Thornton of her first pregnancy in 1652, and God was her constant companion whenever she was big with child or came to term. "God gave her conception," wrote John Angier of his wife in 1642, though he himself surely had something to do with it. "Blessed be to God for his mercy to her," exclaimed John Evelyn when his wife was "bearing" again in 1664.[6] Pious laymen and women shared with the clergy this popular theology of reproduction.

Using biblical imagery more resonant of the Mediterranean than the temperate environment of northern Europe, early modern preachers likened a man's productive wife to "the fruitful vine, and the number of his children like olive branches round about his table." Adopting this imagery, the childless Sarah Savage in the 1680s longed to be "a fruitful vine." It was a common conceit in religious writing, as well as in literature and folklore, that the woman was like a tree or a vegetable, her offspring the fruit of her womb. God was a gardener and, with God's husbandmen on earth (husbands indeed), set out to shape the branches and tend the vine. "A man's yard [i.e., penis] is, as it were, the plough wherewith the ground is tilled, and made fit for production of fruit," observed the seventeenth-century midwife Jane Sharp, adding, "man . . . is the agent and tiller and sower of the ground, woman is the patient or ground to be tilled." Under God's guidance, in popular medical writing, the seed became flesh in a ferment of water, blood, and milk. It was through the woman's body, through its ingoings, outcomings, and cultivation, that humankind could go forth and multiply.[7]

Everyone agreed that childbearing was an obligation for married women. Matrimony existed, so the wedding service reminded everyone, "for . . . the procreation of children." Giving birth was a Christian duty that was fully consonant with God's law. Avoiding pregnancy was a sin. But a tension existed between interpreters who emphasized the spiritual rewards of procreation and those who stressed the inherent sinfulness of the carnal act. Religious ambivalence about the godliness or sinfulness of childbirth reflected similar strains between Christian readings of the New Testament and of the Old, between joy and despair. The familiar words of the baptism service, repeated in countless sermons, reminded listeners

Fig. 4.1. This is a particularly vivid depiction of the birth room scene, with the mother and child surrounded by other women. It is taken from an Augsburg handbook about pregnancy and midwives: Eucharius Roesslin, *Der Schwanngeren Frawen und Hebammen Rosegartten* (1529).

that "all men be born and conceived in sin." The ninth of the Thirty-Nine Articles, the official statement of the beliefs of the Church of England promulgated in 1563, on the subject "Of Original or Birth Sin," explained "that the flesh lusteth always contrary to the spirit, and therefore in every person born into this world it deserveth God's wrath and damnation."[8]

Few preachers went so far as to suggest that lawful sexual intercourse was unclean or that childbirth inherently involved pollution. But some of the sterner sort drew attention to the fundamental corruption in which all human beings were conceived and born. This sinful state, of course, was a consequence of humankind's postlapsarian condition and had nothing directly to do with the processes of reproduction. But some godly writers were so overwhelmed by the discourse of sin and salvation that they could not mention childbirth without reference to defilement and the "spot of child-bed taint." The Jacobean preacher Daniel Featley reminded a christening congregation in 1619 of "that filth and corruption which we draw from the loins of our parents." Similarly, Sampson Price, in a sermon of 1624, associated birth with nakedness, sin, and shame: "Man . . . enters into the world bathed in blood, an image of his sin. . . . Our nativity is miserable because vile and unclean." The remedy was to be born again. In the same vein, though with a different religious sensibility, the Puritan artisan Nehemiah Wallington grieved that he was "born in sin and came forth polluted into this wicked world."[9]

John Donne's preaching on the subject of childbearing emphasized the sinfulness, uncleanness, and filthiness of human origins. "Our mothers conceived us in sin; and being wrapped up in uncleanness there, can any man bring a clean thing out of filthiness?" Donne asked at the churching of Lady Doncaster in 1618. And he continued, "We come into this world as the Egyptians went out of it, swallowed and smothered in a red sea, *pueri sanguinum, et infirmi,* weak and bloody infants at our birth." The newborn babe was contaminated by spiritual and material stains, its physical loathsomeness, *a maternis visceribus* (from the innards of the mother), a symbol of the vileness of the human condition. One can imagine the charmed discomfort of his auditors as Donne piled on extravagant references to dung, excrement, blood, and rottenness, as well as falsehood, treachery, and deceit. This may seem strange for a sermon of thanksgiving after childbirth, especially one preached before members of the Jacobean aristocracy, but the point of Donne's rant was to emphasize the horror of sin that was common to all and to indicate its partial remedy in baptism.[10]

Some of the ministers who associated childbirth with defilement, Donne included, did so in the course of polemical, historical, and liturgical discussions about purification, thanksgiving, and the churching of women. This was a controversial subject, reaching to the heart of religious ceremony and ecclesiastical discipline. References to childbirth in this context might then be understood to have more to do with theology, liturgy, and church politics than with close observation of natural processes. The language of religious polemic shaped this part of the spiritual construction of childbirth. Unfortunately, we seldom hear this debate from a lay point of view, even more rarely from that of a woman.

In unreformed popular culture as well as in fastidious high-church circles, the opinion still circulated that childbirth involved some kind of pollution and that an unchurched mother was in some sense "green" or unclean. Reacting against the view that there was something loathsome or corrupt in natural reproductive processes, Puritans often argued that it was absurd to treat a recently delivered woman, in the month before her churching, as if she had committed "some grievous offence." But the mainstream Church of England never regarded the thanksgiving ceremony of churching as purification. No "purification" was necessary if nothing impure had taken place, though each newly delivered mother was obliged to give thanks.

Like their early Stuart predecessors, high Anglican clergy of the later seventeenth century sometimes made reference to "the stains of childbirth," especially when preaching their Candlemas sermons. But Candlemas (February 2), commemorating the Purification of the Blessed Virgin, invoked unreasonable comparisons between the purity of Mary under ancient Judaism and the condition of ordinary childbearing women in early modern England. Once again, the rhetoric of preaching supplied language about childbirth that was not necessarily applicable to the birthroom. When the church discussed childbirth, it talked about godliness, not gynecology.

Sermons were not the best place to discuss the physical details of procreation, and at least one preacher admitted that treating the topic at all required exceptional delicacy. Public discussion of childbirth by men would be considered an indelicate intrusion into the female domain. The Jacobean preacher John Day, in a Christmas sermon commemorating that most remarkable of all childbirths, cut short his classical, historical, and biblical disquisition by saying, "but I spare your ears in this place, and so much the rather for that sin hath made our bringing forth so full of shame, that we can hardly speak thereof, though never so warily, but we may be thought by women kind to pass our bounds." Day's discomfort may also have been shared by some of the parishioners of Much Totham, Essex, whose vicar, Ambrose Westrop, was said to "profane the ordinance of preaching, by venting in the pulpit matters concerning the secrets of women." Westrop was acutely misogynistic, well beyond the ministerial mainstream of his time, and he was said to have regarded both marital sexual intercourse and normal menstruation as sources of pollution. Not surprisingly, radical Puritans took the opportunity to remove him from his parish in the sequestrations of 1643.[11]

Eve's sin explained women's pain, but not everyone received the story of the fall with due awe and reverence. The Stuart minister John Ward tells the story of "a woman in Warwickshire, being in travail and sorely afflicted with pain, they could not rule her, but sent for my Lady Puckering to try what she could do; when she came she exhorted her to patience, and told her that this misery was brought upon her sex by her grandmother Eve, by eating an apple. 'Was it?' says she, 'I wish the apple had choked her,' whereupon my lady was constrained to turn herself about, and go out of the room and laugh."

In May 1662, Samuel Pepys "heard a good sermon of Mr. Woodcock's at our church. Only, in his later prayer for a woman in childbed, he prayed that God would deliver her from the hereditary curse of childbearing, which seemed a pretty strange expression."[12] Popular Pelagians, among whom Pepys might be numbered, were disinclined to worry about original sin and more prepared to treat childbirth in sexual rather than spiritual terms. This may have been the most widespread view among the laity, but it is slenderly represented in the surviving records.

COMFORTS FOR CHILDBEARING WOMEN

Whether the pain of childbirth was natural or spiritual in origin, a consequence of female physiology or the ancestral curse of Eve, women took measures to lessen its intensity and reduce its accompanying peril. Midwives, wise women, and many of the sorority of matrons who gathered in the birthroom knew special phrases as well as concoctions and applications of sympathetic magic that would help a woman through pregnancy and labor. The female subculture of childbirth included intimate practices and beliefs that were barely suspected by husbands or priests, were long resistant to reform, and remain virtually inaccessible to historians. Late medieval midwives are said to have used the following Latin charm: "*O fans, sive vivus, sive mortuus, exi foras, quia Christus te vocat ad lucem*" (O infant, whether dead or alive, come forth, because Christ calls out you to the light), which sounds more learned than popular. A Leicestershire midwife was reportedly heard intoning, "In the name of the Father and of the Son and of the Holy Ghost, come safe and go safe, what have we here," during the course of a difficult delivery in 1569. Others may have used less recognizably Christian prayers.[13]

Herbal medicine, primarily in the female domain, offered a variety of remedies for hastening or easing delivery. "Kitchen physic" yielded salves and candles that could be administered with or without accompanying prayers. A diligent midwife's physic garden would include lilies and roses, cyclamen or sowbread, columbine or aquilegia, all of which were believed to ease the pains of birth or to hasten delivery. Traditional herbals included remedies "to help conception," "to nourish the child in the womb," "to stay the longing of woman with child," "to procure an easy and speedy delivery to women in travail," "to bring down the afterbirth," and "to increase milk in women's breasts." Printed herbals, which were frequently refined and republished in the sixteenth and seventeenth centuries, served as botanical histories and pharmacological reference works for apothecaries and physicians, but they also gave scholarly botanical precision to the folkloric general knowledge of wise women and midwives. In addition to traditional herbal concoctions for women in labor, laudanum became available in late Elizabethan London, to be joined in the seventeenth century by such questionable remedies as the exotic Maldiva nut.[14]

Traditional Roman Catholicism offered an armory of comforts to the childbearing woman, many of which were discredited with the Reformation. Under the old dispensation, a woman in labor could call on Saint Margaret or the Virgin or one of a host of local supernatural helpers, and she could supplement this saintly intercession by clutching religious relics, girdles, amulets, and fragments of the consecrated host. Only through inquiries at the dissolution of the monasteries in 1536 do we learn that the convent of Bruton, Somerset, treasured "our lady's girdle of Bruton, red silk, which is a solemn relic sent to women travailing which shall not miscarry *in partu.*" Other monastic houses loaned out holy girdles or belts, necklaces, and relics as aids to women who were pregnant or lying in. Bishop Nicholas Shaxton of Salisbury thought it necessary in 1538 to prohibit the use of "any girdles, purses, measures of our Lady, or such other superstitious things, to be occupied about the woman while she laboureth, to make her believe to have the better speed by it." In some places, it was believed, a woman's own girdle would serve to ease labor if it had been wrapped around sanctified bells. Village wisdom and folk religion provided additional assistance in the form of special stones, charms, and potions that promised a safe deliverance or relief from childbed pains.[15]

In traditional popular Catholicism, the holy sacrament was the most powerful medicine of all. The Sarum Missal, one of the most popular formularies of pre-Reformation worship, included masses "on behalf of women labouring with child" and supplications to Saint Mary, "the benign assister of women in travail." The Catholic Bishop Bonner admonished childbearing women in mid-Tudor England "to come to confession and to receive the sacrament especially when their time draweth nigh." Some people believed that attendance at Mass in this condition helped the unborn child as well as the expectant mother, and that its spiritual benefits extended to a child who might die before baptism. If the woman could not come to Mass, then the Mass, or some part of it, might be taken to the woman. Alice Thornton, a staunchly Protestant Yorkshire woman, took the sacrament in 1665 in readiness for lying in. "After this great mercy in the renewing of our vows and covenants with God," she declared, "I was fully satisfied in that condition, whether for life or death." In later seventeenth-century variants on this tradition, Margaret Godolphin "received the heavenly Viaticum" (her name for the eucharist) at the onset of labor in 1678, and John Evelyn's daughter took the sacrament a week after giving birth in September 1694. Like the Mass a century or more earlier, the eucharist served to settle the soul in preparation for an unpredictable outcome.[16]

The Elizabethan Jesuit John Gerard told the story of Lady Grisell Wodehouse, who seemed to be dying after childbirth. "An old priest, one of those ordained before the beginning of Elizabeth's reign [came] to give the lady all the last rites of the church. After making her confession she was anointed and received Viaticum and (this is the wonderful thing) within half an hour she was recovered and was out of danger." Gerard marveled that her husband, Sir Philip Wodehouse, a Protestant, "wondered how it had happened. We explained to him that one of the effects of the holy sacrament of Extreme Unction was to restore bodily health when God judged it to be for the soul's good. This completed the husband's conversion." Protestants would have been shocked by this recommendation of unction and by other signs of resurgent Catholicism. Reforming churchmen sought to suppress traditional practices they deemed superstitious, including women's semisecret rituals surrounding childbirth. The Protestant attack was most ardent during Elizabeth's reign, when 'superstitious' customs were still deeply entrenched. But unauthorized practices continued in the perilous intimacy of the birthroom long after the establishment of the Reformation, and not only in the much maligned "dark corners of the land." Protestant hostility to potions and charms formed part of the larger campaign for the reformation of manners and the expunging of superstition. It was not explicitly misogynist, although it stripped away some female comforts. The Church of England no longer countenanced a woman's promise to go on pilgrimages if God gave her an easy labor. Bishop Barnes of Durham instructed his clergy in 1577 to discipline "all such woman as shall . . . at the child's birth use superstitious ceremonies, prisons, charms or devilish rites or sorceries." Midwives were put on oath not to "use any kind of sorcery or incantation" and to inform against any who so offended.[17]

Many traditional practices survived the Reformation, and not all were corrected by Protestant instruction. Richard Greenham, ministering to his parishioners in Elizabethan Cambridgeshire, observed many things to be corrupted by superstition which were good in their first original, as, when women drawing near the time of their deliverance do require the prayers of the church, as in a farewell commit themselves to the intercessions of the saints, partly for that they are about to enter into a dangerous travail, partly for that they shall be long without the public means of the assembly, and therefore stand in need of the grace of God watching over them.[18]

Though it was perfectly understandable that women should clutch at whatever helped sustain them through the travails of childbirth, it was offensive to advanced Protestant sensibilities if those props were tinged with Catholicism and superstition.

Catholic families were especially instrumental in keeping traditional practices alive, including recourse to holy girdles and invocations of the saints. But one did not have to be a follower of the old religion to turn to eagle stones or other childbirth talismans. One such wonder was offered to Margaret Cavendish, the Countess of Newcastle, to ease her labor in 1633. Anne, Viscountess Conway, secured another, which she wore while pregnant in 1658 for its "great virtue in hard labour." So-called eagle stones (aetites, a stone within a stone) reputedly came from Cyprus or Africa, but they were readily "to be had in London" and were strongly recommended. The seventeenth-century midwife Jane Sharp advised expectant mothers to wear one, "for I have proved it to be true, that this stone hanged about a woman's neck and so as to touch her skin, when she is with child, will preserve her safe from abortion, and will cause her to be safe delivered when the time comes." Other medical manuals repeated this advice. The nested stones apparently worked through the principles of sympathies and signatures, the stone within the stone signifying the security of the child within the womb. Alternatives to the eagle stone included therapeutic lodestones and "the skin of a wild ox" tied to the woman's thighs.[19] Rather than deriding such practices as superstitious, the more thoughtful commentators commended the goodwill shown by friends who provided these items and the solicitude of husbands who sought to protect their wives and future offspring by every means their culture afforded.

English Protestantism continued to provide a powerful range of spiritual comfort and assistance to women in need. Although the Church of England no longer countenanced special masses for child-bearing women or prayers to the saints on their behalf during labor, it strenuously encouraged the use of prayer. In the crisis of child-birth, when life and death walked hand in hand, a pious family had but one place to turn. Domestic prayers and religious exercises were designed to attract God's attention; they petitioned, they assuaged, they explained; and they provided a pathway to reconciliation if any-thing went seriously wrong. Thomas Bentley's massive *Monument of Matrons*, published in 1582, includes model prayers for "women with child, and in childbed, and after their delivery," as well as prayers for midwives and prayers of thanksgiving.

Devotional exercises for use during pregnancy and labor formed part of the revived religiosity of early Stuart England. They were written by mainstream Calvinists as well as by advanced Arminians. Though framed by reference to Eve's transgression, their prayers did not dwell on pain and punishment but stressed instead the blessings of fruitfulness, the honor to women, divine deliverance, and the prospect of salvation. Popular devotional manuals such as Robert Hill's *Pathway to Prayer and Pietie*, which went through eight editions between 1606 and 1628, included model prayers and meditations for women in travail. So too did Samuel Hieron's *A Helpe Unto Devotion*, which reached its twenti-eth edition in 1636. Daniel Featley's *Ancilla Pietatis: or, The Hand-Maid to Private Devotion*, which went through six editions between 1626 and 1639, similarly offered prayers and admonitions to the childbear-ing woman. Addressed to the middling and better sort, the message of these handbooks was invariably one of stern comfort. For the woman commencing labor, Hill observed, "her sin is great, her danger is not small, her pains will be grievous, and the hour of life is now at hand." "Religious women," Featley advised, "ought patiently and comfortably to endure the pains of childbirth," not least because "child-bearing hath a promise annexed unto it of a blessing temporal/spiritual if the mother be faithful and so continue."[20] Neither Featley nor Hill would wish these trials and rewards for themselves, but their mainstream Christian per-spective gave high value to the reproductive fulfillment of women and reemphasized the spiritual construction of childbirth.

Competing directly with Featley, John Cosin's *Collection of Private Devotions,* which went through five editions between 1627 and 1638, also featured prayers "to be used by women that travail with child" and for "thanksgiving after childbirth." The expectant mother would pray for protection "against all the dangers and pains of my labour and travail" and ask God that "I may be safely delivered of this happy fruit which thou hast created in my womb." The newborn child, "a joyful benediction, even the fruit of mine own womb," would "forthwith" be readied to be "born again by baptism." In a similar vein Samuel Rowlands printed "a prayer for a woman in time of her travail," and George Wither composed hymns for "when a woman hath conceived" and "when a woman is safe delivered." A later work, John Oliver's *A Present for Teeming Women,* included "a prayer before childbirth" and "scripture directions for a woman with child" written for Mrs. Bridget Seymour of Hanford House, Dorset. This was printed by a woman, Sarah Griffin, and published by another, Mary Rothwell, as a further commendation to the ladies.[21]

Surviving diaries and letters sometimes show laymen and women adapting these prayers or making their own in stressful domestic circumstances. "Childbirth is God's work," Lady Massingberd counseled her daughter, "pray spare yourself as much time as you can for meditation and prayer to acquaint yourself with God." The pious Elizabeth Egerton, Countess of Bridgewater, typically turned to prayers and meditations to ease her through childbearing: "Oh God, to thee I give all praise and glory, that thou hast been pleased to bless me, that I have conceived again with child. . . . I beg of thee to have compassion on me in the great pain I am to feel in the bringing forth of this my child." Even when praising God, her mind did not stray far from reflection on "the great torture of childbirth." She died in childbed in 1663, at age thirty-seven, after bringing forth several children.[22]

Other godly families engaged in prayer, together with more mundane preparations, at the critical moments of a pregnancy. Devotional handbooks were unnecessary if the prayers came freely from the heart. In 1638, the Northamptonshire Puritan diarist Robert Woodford raised his own heartfelt prayers for "my dear wife who is now in travail." During each of Hannah Woodford's pregnancies her husband self-consciously looked to the Lord; her own spiritual preparations are unknown. In July 1640, amid the burgeoning crisis of the kingdom, Woodford prayed for those closest to him: "Lord look upon my dear wife in her present condition now great with child, Lord give her a gracious delivery, give her strength to bring forth, preserve her life, give the child right shape and form, continue her life of it and of the rest, make them instruments of thy glory and vessels of mercy." And the following year, awaiting the outcome of his wife's fifth pregnancy, Woodford prayed, "Lord order every conveniency, give her a gracious delivery in thy due time, the sentence on her is to bring forth in pain and on me to get my bread by the sweat of my brows, Lord stand by her thy servant and support her graciously. Lord, many have lately died in childbed. . . . Lord build up and continue our family still."[23]

The Essex clergyman Ralph Josselin likewise "sought to God" on the eve of his wife's labor in 1645, praying that "God would order all providences so as we might rejoice in his salvation." In 1654, after another satisfactory outcome, the diarist recorded, "I am persuaded my particular earnest prayers were moving for her in the very moment of her delivery." In 1657, at the time of Jane Josselin's quickening, "the women met with her in prayer," but since her husband was not with them, there is no indication of what they said.[24] Typically the male diarist was concerned to prevent loss, while his wife prayed to endure pain. It was his burden to beget and multiply, hers to suffer the curse of Eve.

Seventeenth-century dissenters, like their conforming brethren, argued that the pain and the peril of childbearing could be alleviated by religious exercises and attention to prayer. Richard Adams, a nonconformist under Charles II, advised that a godly life laid "a sure ground of a comfortable exemption from the curse in childbearing, and of the removal of that original guilt which otherwise greatens the sorrows of women in such a case." It was Adams who glossed the words of Paul to Timothy as "heart-reviving words to every dropping woman."

Later Stuart nonconformists conducted days of prayer and fasting on behalf of women in childbed. In December 1661, the Manchester minister Henry Newcome recalled, "I was sent for out to the poor woman that was in labour and prayed with her, but she died this evening." In November 1672 Newcome went "to Benjamin Booker's to a private day, on the account of his wife who is with child." Oliver Heywood "sought God" while his wife lay in and "praised God" when she brought forth a son. And in his public ministry Heywood "kept a private fast at Mr. Dawson's house for his wife to beg mercy for her in childbearing" in May 1673. In May 1678 Heywood and his wife visited Isaac Balmes at Boulin, Lancashire, and "kept a fast there for his wife near her time," adding, "God helped." In September he "kept a private fast for young John Kershaw's wife in Wyke, great with child," and the following August again "kept a fast with many women for Esther Kershaw's safe deliverance in childbearing."[25] These nonconformist gatherings provided spiritual fellowship and material support at critical moments, and they needed neither handbook nor prayer book to guide their religious rituals.

Just as devout households prayed for the safety of the mother and the happy deliverance of her womb, so the kingdom—the family writ large—was similarly called to prayers during the pregnancy of a queen. In 1605, for example, the government of James I printed prayers "for the queen's majesty's safe deliverance in her childbirth" and appointed them "to be used in the church at morning and evening prayer by every minister." Those who complied found seven variant prayers asking God to preserve Queen Anne from "the great pains and peril of childbirth." They prayed God that "through thy heavenly protection she may be safely delivered of the blessed fruit of her body, and become a joyful mother of a happy issue." So might any husband pray for his wife, or any minister for his parishioner. God had appointed "to all the sons of Eve one and the same entrance into life through the sorrows and pangs of childbirth," and the royal family was not exempt. A short while later came another little prayer book containing prayers of thanksgiving "for the queen's majesty's safe deliverance" on April 9, which proved to be just one of the deliverances of 1605. The nation was likewise asked to join in prayer during the reign of Charles I to seek God's protection of Queen Henrietta Maria as she produced her "long desired" and "happy issue."[26]

The vocabulary of deliverance linked public and private blessings. Christopher Hooke's lecture on the occasion of Elizabeth Savile's deliverance in childbirth in 1590 made explicit reference to the nation's "miraculous deliverance from the Spanish invasion" two years previously. England's deliverance from the Gunpowder Plot could be likened to the deliverance of the Stuart queens. The official prayers of thanksgiving printed after November 5, 1605, exactly matched the design of those for the safe deliverance of the queen six months before.[27]

SUFFERING AND DEATH

Conventional Christian counsel considered the two most likely outcomes for the woman in childbed, "a comfortable sanctified deliverance here, or a blessed translation to heaven," the former "to reap in joy what was sown in tears," the latter joy everlasting.[28] Two lives were at stake, that of the mother and her newborn baby, and death was a prospect for them both. But childbirth meant more than a calculus of souls.

Every stage of the childbirth experience exposed the woman's vulnerability and summoned intimations of mortality. Even uncomplicated childbearing involved laborious travail, sharp discomfort, and the prospect of lingering distress. Women otherwise blessed with robust good health often feared that childbirth might kill them. The pain and the peril—Eve's legacy and nature's course—was a rite of violence through which all mothers passed and which a minority would not survive. This was no time for subtle discussion of predestination or the possible torments of hell (although strict Calvinists spoke of both), but rather for soothing words about deliverance and salvation.

Hearing the screams from the birthroom, some men were astonished that their women came through alive. Others accepted the continuance of life as a matter of routine. Pain was to be expected, death to be feared. The Elizabethan separatist Henry Barrow thought "the safe deliverance of these women . . . though a singular benefit of God, yet a thing natural, ordinary, and common." The Jacobean Puritan William Gouge was more impressed by the mystery of survival and more inclined to give praise, considering the safe deliverance of women from childbed "near a miracle . . . wherein the Almighty doth so evidently manifest his great power and providence."[29] Most of the popular devotional manuals included prayers of thanksgiving after childbirth as well as prayers for its successful outcome.

Male diarists report their wives' fears and their own anxieties at these critical junctures. Richard Rogers, the Puritan minister of Whethersfield, Essex, learned of a neighbor's death in childbed in 1588 and worried that his own wife, Barbara, might die likewise: "I, seeing by much pain in wife and near childbirth many likelihoods of our separation, considered how many uncomfortablenesses the Lord had kept from me hitherto by those which I then saw must needs come if he should part us." Among his concerns was the complication of having to marry again. Fortunately, Rogers could follow this diary entry with another a few weeks later, "*Natus est Exechiel meus* [my Exechiel (Ezekiel) is born] and my wife hardly escaped."[30]

Ralph Josselin recorded that his wife Jane was "oppressed with fears" at the onset of labor in 1645. She "was wonderfully afraid and amazed" and experienced "great fears" and "sad pains and sadder fears" during subsequent deliveries. Yet Mrs. Josselin brought forth ten children from at least fifteen recorded pregnancies, and she outlived her husband. In June 1654, as Jane Josselin struggled to deliver her seventh child, her husband struggled with the Lord. "My heart was sensible in some measure how great a loss it would be if God took her from me, and yet my spirit was borne up in expectation of the mercy."[31] Fear was a recurrent companion, though obviously different for women and men.

The Cambridgeshire minister Isaac Archer likewise noted in his diary in 1670, "my wife growing nearer her time was troubled with fears she should die, and I feared it too. She was much taken up, I saw, with such thoughts, and I was glad, because it was an occasion of seeking God." After giving birth again in 1672, Mrs. Archer experienced "the very agonies of death, as she thought, and was seized all over with intolerable pain, and possessed with a persuasion she should die that night. Her father and mother were with her, and we all had grief enough." Once again she recovered. Archer's diary, to be examined in detail below, shows Mrs. Archer surviving nine completed pregnancies and several miscarriages, yet her fear, and the fear of those around her, was real enough.[32]

Several diarists saw some of their worst fears fulfilled. Nicholas Assheton recorded in February 1618, "my wife in labour of childbirth. Her delivery was with such violence, as the child died within half an hour and, but for God's wonderful mercy, more than human reason could expect, she had died; but he spared her a while longer to me, and took the child to his mercy." John Angier's wife, Ellen, had premonitions of dying in childbed and indeed died soon after giving birth in 1642. According to the diarist, "after her conception her weakness and weariness increased, and was not mitigated, as usually, after she quickened, so that she feared she should not come to her time, and often said it would be her death." She was delivered on November 21, 1642, "in the evening after hard labour." The child survived, but Mrs. Angier never recovered and died three weeks later.[33]

John Evelyn's friend, Margaret Godolphin, was similarly unfortunate. She appeared "exceeding well laid" in 1678, but "so careful and provident she was to prepare for all possible accidents that, as if she foresaw her end, she received the heavenly Viaticum but the Sunday before, after a most solemn recollection; and putting all her domestic concerns in the exactest order, left a letter directed to her husband, to be opened in case she died in childbed." Mrs. Godolphin gave birth on September 3 and died six days later, most likely of puerperal fever.[34]

The classic story of Christian fortitude, forbearance, and spiritual preparation concerned Elizabeth Joceline, a godly Jacobean gentlewoman who looked on her first pregnancy in 1622 as a likely sentence of doom. "When she first felt herself quick with child, as then travelling with death itself, she secretly took order for the buying a new winding sheet," and called for this winding sheet to her childbed. She survived parturition, giving birth to a daughter, but died nine days later of "a violent fever" at the age of twenty-six. Mrs. Joceline's pious meditations, published posthumously as *The Mothers Legacie to her Unborn Child*, were frequently reprinted with a eulogy of her life, and the account of her morbid preparation was often retold. The tale provided a model of faith and fortitude for all expectant mothers.[35]

Fearful expectations abound in the records, and examples of women dying in childbed are not hard to find. But it would be misleading to deduce from this evidence that childbed mortality was common. In fact the opposite is true. Most women survived childbirth without complications, and most mothers quickly recovered. Childbirth was a natural occurrence, notwithstanding the pain and the peril, and emphatically had more to do with life than with death. A leading Jacobean medical manual, repeating ancient wisdom, asserted optimistically that of a thousand births, there is scarce one found that is amiss.[36] Modern demographic calculations also suggest that early modern childbirth was not so dangerous as was feared, though the chance of death was more like one in a hundred.

In an important essay titled "Did the Mothers Really Die? Three Centuries of Maternal Mortality in 'The World We Have Lost,'" Roger Schofield calculates that 9.3 per one thousand or just under 1 percent of mothers died in childbed in Elizabethan England. The rate deteriorated in the seventeenth century, as demographic conditions generally worsened, to a peak of 15.7 per one thousand in the reign of Charles II. Conditions were always worse in London—sometimes twice the national rate—with maternal mortality as high as 23.5 per one thousand in Aldgate parish in the 1590s. But London is a special case, in this as in so many other things. Contrary to popular myth, women were not in "a state of virtually perpetual pregnancy" in the early modern period. On average they could expect six or seven pregnancies (not all successful), and therefore, according to Schofield, "A woman . . . would have run a six to seven percent risk of dying in childbed at some time in her procreative career." But mothers, like other people, also died of other causes. Schofield has calculated the risk to women of dying during their nonchildbearing intervals, and he concludes, "the risk she ran of dying in childbed was no greater than the risk she ran every year of dying from infectious disease and a whole variety of other causes."[37] If we accept this evidence, we have a broad demographic framework in which to set particular experiences. Most pregnancies turned out successfully for both mother and child. But one does not need actuarial precision to be frightened.

THE ARCHERS: A FAMILY HISTORY

Isaac Archer's account of his wife's childbearing experience is worth reporting in detail. Not yet widely known, though as lively and informative in some areas as the celebrated diary of Ralph Josselin, Archer's diary provides a candid and conscientious account of successive childbirths as well as spiritual and professional difficulties.[38] Inevitably,

Mrs. Archer's childbearing is reported entirely from her husband's point of view. Isaac Archer was the vicar of Chippenham, Cambridgeshire, and Freckenham, Suffolk, during the reign of Charles II. Born in 1641 and educated at Trinity College, Cambridge, during the Protectorate, he became a godly Anglican minister with pronounced sympathy for nonconformists. Married in November 1667, Archer expressed delight in his change of estate. "I found my wife perfectly devoted to please me, and I bless God for giving me one with a meek and quiet spirit, and well disposed," he wrote the following February. Like many other seventeenth-century diarists Archer never writes his partner's name, referring to her throughout as "my wife."

Anne Archer became pregnant in 1668, and on April 3, 1669, "she was delivered of a lusty girl . . . after six hours pains." After greeting his firstborn daughter, Archer confided to his diary, "I prayed for a boy." A frightening incident occurred three days after the birth, when the house caught fire as Mrs. Archer lay helpless in her enclosed chamber. After the blaze was quenched, her husband declared it a deliverance, comparable to Mrs. Archer's deliverance from the pains and perils of childbearing. This child died one year later.

Anne's second pregnancy in 1670 prompted her husband's morbid reflections. "My wife growing nearer her time was troubled with fears she should die, and I feared it too. She was much taken up, I saw, with such thoughts, and I was glad, because it was an occasion of seeking God, as I know she did." These fears were almost realized, for shortly after giving birth to another daughter on November 27, 1670, Mrs. Archer came close to death. "About one o'clock my wife began to faint, through an overflow of blood, and was without sensible pulse or colour; we gave her over and she took leave of me (which much concerned me); the women told me she would lose all her blood." Fortunately, the hemorrhage ceased, and she recovered, though not without general distress. Her own thoughts and fears on this occasion are unrecorded.

A third pregnancy quickened in 1672. On June 1, 1672, Archer wrote, "my wife was newly with child when we came from Chippenham, and had many pains for a week; and we had the midwife with us because we live in a solitary place. This night, at 10 of the clock, she was delivered of a boy, lusty and large, but lean; this was the eve of

Trinity Sunday, and as we had counted, the time was just come about." Once again Mrs. Archer came close to death. Two weeks after giving birth, on June 13, "my wife fell grievously sick and faint by reason of some noxious and venomous impurities that nature should have cleaned her of; she had the very agony of death, as she thought, and was seized all over with intolerable pain, and possessed with a persuasion she should die that night. Her father and mother were with her, and we all had grief enough." Fortunately, once again, Mrs. Archer recovered. The long-wished-for son lived less than three years.

Mrs. Archer gave birth to another daughter in December 1673 after four hours of labor. The diarist had little else to say on the matter except that the child was "fat and lustier than usual." Next came

Fig. 4.2. Midwives attending a woman in childbirth. Jacob Rueff, *Ein schön lustig Trostbüchle von den Empfengknussen und Geburten der Menschen* (Zurich, 1554).

another short-lived son who was born prematurely in August 1675. Archer wrote on August 25, 1675, "I had taken a nurse into the house to suckle it because my wife was not able, as having suckled the last too long. The woman knew of its illness, and yet told us not of it, so it died while she slept, and unbaptised." The minister agonized over the spiritual consequences of this neglect but managed to convince himself that the child would still be taken to God's bosom.

By the spring of 1676, Anne Archer was pregnant for the sixth time. On April 25, the diarist noted, "my wife was with child, it seems, and had gone about three months." Sadly, she miscarried on August 22, "through a sudden fright, upon an unhappy occasion." Within a few months, however, she was pregnant again, and by June 10, 1677, the signs of impending delivery appeared secure. "My wife is now with child, and we hope past the danger of miscarrying, having been let blood twice," wrote Isaac Archer, adding, "I have in an earnest manner begged a son." Then on October 6, "about four of the clock in the afternoon my wife was delivered, two months before her reckoning, and of a girl, which came wrong, and stuck so long with the head in the birth, that it was dead when fully born, though alive in the time of travail, and so next day 'twas buried in Freckenham chancel on the north side of the little boy, under a stone."

Chastened by this loss, Archer prayed for his wife. "I thank God she is hearty, and I hope may be healthful in time, after so much cleansing." And he reflected on himself, the father of so many dead babies, "perhaps I am not worthy of a son. . . . The loss is the less because 'twas a girl, though we could have wished the life of it. God's will be done." Archer continued to brood on his losses, lamenting children as "chastenings sent by God for the good of parents." "Since God took away my two boys I ceased not privately to pray for another to make up my loss. My wife miscarried twice, and then had a girl dead, and now after all God's time is come."

The longed-for second son was born on February 14, 1678, after another painful delivery. Archer relates, "my joy however was somewhat dampened when the women thought the child would not live because it changed colour and frothed at the mouth," but the boy lived to be baptized Isaac like his father, a son of prayer. This baby died on July 29, 1678, at the age of five months, and his six-year-old sister Frances died two weeks later.

Mrs. Archer miscarried once more in October 1680, "when she reckoned she had gone about eighteen weeks." Predictably, within a few months she was pregnant again. Isaac Archer spent an anxious summer, fearful of a further miscarriage, "for she was quick," and no doubt hoping for a boy. Then on August 21, after three hours' labor, his wife was "delivered of a girl." Again the birth was premature, "eight weeks before her reckoning," and again it went badly. "She came wrong and was wasted; it lived half an hour, and died." In his prayers Isaac Archer begged good health for his wife and reproached himself, "I have too eagerly desired children."

Finally, in September 1682, Mrs. Archer came to term once again, and was "delivered of a lusty girl, fatter and larger than any yet." Archer wrote in his diary, "I bless God that we have a living child; I never so much as asked of God a son, though we thought it would have been one by all signs." But this daughter, named Frances in memory of her lost sister, was also dead within three months.

After fifteen years of marriage and at least ten pregnancies, the Archers had one surviving daughter. Mrs. Archer had been racked with pain and had known dire peril. Several times she came close to death. Twisted with hopes and disappointments, the family accommodated itself to grief. The Reverend Isaac Archer had buried most of his offspring, some of them before they could be baptized. Mrs. Archer would have two more miscarriages, in January and July 1604, but no more live children. Her procreative career was at an end, despite Archer's egotistical patriarchal prayers. "I begged a child if God saw good. . . . The loss to me is very unkind; but God's will be done." Clearly the husband cared for his wife, the carrier of his children, but his happiness was incomplete without a son, a male child to serve the Lord and carry the Archer name. Anne Archer lived until 1698.

Isaac Archer's diary captures the urgency and anxiety in this minister's attempts at family formation. It provides valuable glimpses of the management of pregnancy in the seventeenth century, together with insights into the emotional religiosity, humility, and vanity of the man as husband and father. This particular family's history should not be regarded as typical, but several features of its childbearing regime were common: the shared recognition of pregnancy and the husband's gendered preference for a son, fear of miscarriage and preparations for labor, supervision by the midwife in company with other women, the wife's experience of pain and fear of dying, the hours of labor and danger of complications, the loss of blood and risk of infection, lying in, occasional wet nurses, and the premature death of young children. Archer himself would not normally have entered the room where his wife was giving birth, instead relying on "the women" to give him reports. While the diarist wrestled with his self-consciousness, the mystery of childbirth remained veiled.

FOR FURTHER READING

Fides, Valerie, editor. *Women as Mothers in Pre-Industrial England*. London: Routledge, 1990.

Gélis, Jacques. *History of Childbirth: Fertility, Pregnancy, and Birth in Early Modern Europe*. Translated by Rosemary Morris. Boston: Northeastern University Press, 1991.

Porter, Roy, editor. *Patients and Practitioners: Lay Perceptions of Medicine in Pre-Industrial Society*. Cambridge: Cambridge University Press, 1986.

Scribner, R. W., and R. Po-Chia Hsia, editors. *Problems in the Historical Anthropology of Early Modern Europe*. Wiesbaden: Harrassowitz, 1997.

Thomas, Keith. *Religion and the Decline of Magic: Studies in Popular Beliefs in Sixteenth and Seventeenth-Century England*. New York: Oxford University Press, 1997 [1971].

von Gennep, Arnold. *The Rites of Passage*. Chicago: University of Chicago Press, 2001.

BAPTISM AND CHILDHOOD

KAREN E. SPIERLING

CHAPTER FIVE

In May 1547, eleven years after the city of Geneva had adopted the Protestant Reformation, a Genevan named Claude Rousser and his wife appeared before the consistory, the morals court run by ministers and elders of the Reformed church of Geneva. The court had summoned the couple to respond to the accusation that they "have their children in a Catholic place." Rousser explained that his wife had sent their children to him when he was staying with his brother. Although he had returned to Geneva, the children had remained "at the home of their uncle, who is taking good care of them." Rousser stated further that the uncle was willing to send the younger child back to his parents in Geneva because he had fallen sick. But "the other, who is older, his said brother wants to keep." When the consistory suggested that *both* of Rousser's children should be raised in Reformed Geneva, Rousser responded that his brother had threatened to break off all relations with the couple if they insisted that he return their son to Geneva. Rousser asserted that he did not want to "lose the love of his brother" by demanding the return of his son. Nevertheless, the consistory rebuked Rousser for his decision, telling him that "he should prefer above all things the salvation of his child." For the members of the consistory, this meant raising children in a Calvinist community where they could learn the tenets of the Protestant faith.[1]

Despite their disapproval of Rousser's decision, the court did not force him to retrieve his son from the boy's new home. Twelve years later, however, the consistory heard the case of another Genevan,

Françoys Vuichard, who also had sent his son to live with an uncle in a Catholic town. Vuichard reported that the uncle was "a rich merchant, who does not have any children," and he refused to retrieve his son from his new life. The consistory had grown more assertive during the intervening decade, and they now demanded that Vuichard bring his son home within fifteen days and then reappear before the court, "on pain of being punished and chastised as a rebel." Vuichard complied with their demand.[2]

During the Reformation, in Geneva and across Europe, parents like Claude Rousser and Françoys Vuichard struggled with church and civic authorities regarding the raising of children. Arguments about who should raise children and where they should be raised, such as we see in the two cases above, affected how those children would be educated and which Christian faith they would learn as they grew up. Protestant reformers and their followers believed that the survival of their newly Reformed churches and communities depended upon the successful raising of their children to be faithful church members and responsible citizens of the community. Similarly, Catholic reformers held that the nurture and education of children was vital to the defense of Catholicism. These convictions directly affected the ways in which children of the sixteenth and seventeenth centuries grew up and experienced the world.

It would be an overstatement to say that the Protestant reformers "discovered" children and childhood; there is plentiful evidence that medieval children held their own special place in family and society. But it is fair to say that Reformation leaders took a new step in placing children and their relationship to their parents not only at the center of society but at the center of a faithful religious life as well. Protestant reformers saw fulfilling one's responsibilities to one's parents or children as an inextricable part of living a godly life, and they emphasized the mutual obligations that children and parents held toward one another. Many reformers seemed to reinforce traditional patriarchal ideas in their insistence that fathers held final responsibility for the religious care of their families and that sons held more responsibility—financially, at least—toward their parents than did daughters. Often, however, the reformers challenged traditional gender roles by insisting on stricter enforcement of paternal responsibilities and by upholding maternal authority when the mother in question was considered to be a faithful Christian.

Generally speaking, Protestant reformers' visions of a faithful society required that both boys and girls be educated and raised to be pious and diligent Christians, parents, and members of the community. Combined with traditional social and familial concerns, Protestant and Catholic teachings regarding the nurture and education of children shaped the ways that children experienced and participated in the society around them, including their involvement with the church, their education, and their interactions with their parents.

CHILDREN IN EARLY MODERN EUROPE

The histories of children and of childhood are elusive subjects, especially before the nineteenth century. Archival records from early modern Europe most often focus on adults involved in legal, financial, or religious interactions with religious and governmental authorities; few sources provide details about the activities, thoughts, or feelings of children. Scholars must comb historical records with exceeding care in order to gather information regarding children and their experience of life

Fig. 5.1. Children had their own pastimes, even in the sixteenth century. Here children are playing a variety of games, including a sixteenth-century version of "leapfrog." Pieter Bruegel the Elder, *Children's Games*, 1560. Kunsthistorisches Museum, Vienna. Photo: Erich Lessing / Art Resource, NY.

during the Reformation. Nonetheless, an increasing number of historians are taking on this challenge, and our understanding of the Reformation's impact on children is growing as a result of their work.

Scholarly interest in and debate about the history of children and childhood in Europe was first sparked with the 1960 publication of Philippe Ariès's *L'Enfant et la vie familiale sous l'ancien régime*, published as *Centuries of Childhood* in English in 1962. Ariès argued that until about the seventeenth century, no concept of childhood that we would recognize today existed. Rather, Ariès suggested, parental affection and attachment to one's children was a more modern development. He argued that medieval parents were emotionally detached from their children, partly because of high child mortality rates. He also asserted that medieval children were incorporated into the adult world almost from birth—in other words, medieval Europeans did not think of childhood as a distinctive phase of life. Scholars including Lawrence Stone and Edward Shorter built upon Ariès's suggestions, stating the argument even more strongly. Beginning in the 1970s, in reaction to the work of Ariès, Stone, and others, medieval and early modern historians began refuting Ariès's claims based on evidence from regions across Europe.[3]

Among scholars of family history, the accepted view now is that long before the seventeenth century, parents developed strong attachments to their children, loved their offspring, went to great lengths to try to secure their well-being, and grieved when a child died. Nonetheless, the ideas of Ariès and Stone are deeply embedded in popular images of historical childhood. Commonly accepted notions about the history of childhood tend to oversimplify Ariès's argument into a straightforward idea of progress: parents of the past treated their children

---

Luther's Letter to Justus Jonas on the Death of His Daughter (1542)

I believe the report has reached you that Magdalena, my dearest daughter, has been reborn into the everlasting kingdom of Christ, and although I and my wife ought to do nothing but joyfully give thanks for such a felicitous passage and blessed end, by which she has escaped the power of the flesh, the world, the Turk and the devil, nevertheless, so great is the force of our love that we are unable to go on without sobs and groanings of the heart, indeed without bearing in ourselves a mortal wound. The countenance, the words, the gestures of our daughter, so very obedient and respectful both while she lived and as she died, remain firmly fixed in the old heart so that the death of Christ (in comparison to which what are all other deaths?) is unable to drive out sorrow from our inmost depths as it ought to do. You therefore give thanks to God in our stead!

—From *Luthers Werke: Kritische Gesamtausgabe: Briefwechsel* (Weimar: H. Böhlau, 1930–1985), 10/3794.20–29, cited in translation in Jane E. Strohl, "The Child in Luther's Theology: 'For What Purpose Do We Older Folks Exist, Other Than to Care for . . . the Young?'" in *The Child in Christian Thought*, ed. Marcia Bunge (Grand Rapids: Eerdmans, 2001), 157.

as little adults and did not express emotion or truly love their off-spring; modern parents love their children. Modern life is better.

True, life in sixteenth-century Europe was difficult in very basic ways, and the survival of children was not to be taken for granted. Infant mortality rates varied widely over time and across geographical regions in early modern Europe. England and northern Germany had significantly lower infant mortality than, for example, France and southern Germany. Still, scholars estimate that on average, the mortality rate for infants younger than a year old was 20 percent; about half of all children died before the age of ten. These rates were higher or lower depending on breast-feeding practices and environmental factors. Across Europe, children who were breast-fed by their own mothers survived at much higher rates than did children who were sent to wet nurses or children who were fed cow's milk. Within the same country and in areas with similar cultural practices, children raised in mountainous and more sparsely populated areas tended to survive longer than children who lived in marshy regions with stagnant water and more polluted air.[4] Neither the Protestant nor the Catholic Reformation directly affected infant mortality rates, but the ideas of both Reformations spread among populations faced with the reality of significant—and, at the time, seemingly uncontrollable—infant mortality. This did not mean that parents remained detached from their children or that society did not care about children until they had survived to adulthood, as Ariès and others have argued. Protestant reformers—and some Catholic reformers, as well—paid considerable attention to children and to the question of how to provide for their material and spiritual needs by incorporating them into church and society and raising them as faithful Christians.

INFANT BAPTISM

The most obvious ways in which the Reformation affected children concerned the alteration of church ceremonies and educational practices. During the sixteenth century, many churches tried to extend, or reestablish, the influence of religious principles and beliefs in people's daily lives. These efforts had an impact on the ways that children were disciplined, educated, and taught to conceive of themselves and their roles in society. Most churches' influence over these aspects of a child's life began with the ceremony of infant baptism, when the child was recognized as a member of the church community.

Traditionally, baptism was the first of seven official sacraments that marked the stages of a person's life and of his or her participation in the Christian community. Sixteenth-century Protestant reformers reduced the number of sacraments from seven to only two: communion and baptism. As one of the two remaining sacraments, baptism was vitally important as a church ritual. And while church members were expected to receive communion at least once a year, baptism occurred only once in a lifetime. This singular importance meant that the significance and proper execution of baptism became a matter of debate not only among reformers but between reformers and laypeople as well.

Since the early Middle Ages, a child's first official encounter with the Christian church had been at his or her baptism. During the first millennium of the church's existence, the sacrament of baptism had evolved from a ceremony initiating adult believers into the church to a ritual that incorporated an infant into the church community, cleansed him or her of sin, and ensured that, in the event of sudden death, he or she would still be welcomed into heaven. In the 1520s, "radical" Anabaptist reformers began to teach that infants should not be baptized. For these reformers, a valid baptism required that a child be old enough to make a statement of faith and to *choose* to be baptized. When some Anabaptists came to be associated with political and civil unrest, religious and civic authorities began to regard adult baptism itself as threat of social disorder.

Partly as a result of this negative association, "mainline" reformers including Martin Luther, Huldrych Zwingli, and John Calvin maintained the practice of infant baptism in their churches. In addition, for these reformers, baptism was an example of the limitless nature of God's grace and of the importance of faith rather than of any particular human action. The sacrament of baptism was effective not simply because the minister said the correct words or performed the required steps; rather, baptism had an effect because of the faith of the participants and the working of God's grace. But the precise nature of this effect was disputed among the reformers and their followers.

While they continued to baptize infants, just as the Catholic Church did, each Protestant reformer had a particular understanding of what exactly was happening during the sacrament. Luther, for example, kept the Catholic idea that baptism was a moment of cleansing, when a baby was purified of original sin. At the opposite extreme, Zwingli defined baptism as a symbol of the Old Testament covenant between God and God's people and a ritual that bound the community together as all of the participants and witnesses remembered the significance of their own baptisms. Neither physical nor spiritual purification was part of baptism for Zwingli. Calvin's view of baptism lay somewhere between Luther and Zwingli—he asserted that baptism was a symbol of spiritual purification *and* a seal of the Old Testament covenant. Calvin did not think that the physical act of baptism cleansed a child of original sin, but it was an important reminder for the church community of God's love for faithful Christians. All of these reformers distanced themselves from the long-held belief that baptism was absolutely necessary for salvation and tried to emphasize the importance of the baptismal ceremony for *all* of the participants. Consequently, baptism became increasingly important as a mark of incorporation into the earthly Christian community.[5]

These theoretical and theological differences resulted in concrete changes from Catholic to Protestant practices. During the Middle Ages, baptism had become an opportunity for a grand celebration, sometimes involving as many as a dozen godparents in addition to neighbors and relatives. Godparents would present a child at church for baptism while the mother and father remained at home, the mother still recovering from childbirth and the father preparing for the festivities after the church ceremony. The baptismal rite and the party that followed provided the chance to establish or reinforce social ties and networks. During the Reformation, baptism came to serve as an even more official marker of a child's entrance into society; at the same time, church and civic leaders often tried to limit the money and time spent on baptismal celebrations. In Geneva, the Reformed church required that all baptisms take place in a church and be performed by a minister, after the sermon and in front of the congregation. The father was required to be there to participate in the ceremony; the mother was welcome but most often remained at home to recuperate from the birth. Godparents were permitted, but the number was limited to one godfather and one godmother. The names of both parents were recorded in the baptismal registry, thereby officially recognizing parents and child as a family. If the child had been born out of wedlock, this record was used by church and city to hold the father responsible for the financial support of the mother, at least temporarily, and for the upbringing of the child.[6]

In terms of understanding children's experience of life during the Protestant Reformation, several aspects of infant baptism are important. The ceremonies of infant baptism designed and promulgated by the mainline reformers were intended to serve as a public welcome of the child into the church body and the wider community. As a result of that ceremony, a child was officially recognized either as a legitimate offspring of his or her parents or as the result of a liaison between two people not married to one another and, thus, not legally entitled to inheritance from his or her father but still deserving of financial support and spiritual nurture. Even though the child was not aware of what was happening at the moment of baptism, he or she would be bound for the rest of his or her life by the family ties officially recognized at the ceremony.

In addition, while the tradition of godparents eventually weakened in many Protestant churches, in the sixteenth century godparents continued to participate in a wide variety of Reformed rites of infant baptism. For the child, this ceremony marked the establishment of a special relationship with his or her godparents that would last long past the moment of the sacrament. Both Lutheran and Calvinist church leaders tried to place restrictions on the choice of godparents, insisting that any godparent must be a faithful member of the church in question, able to recite the Lord's Prayer, the Apostles' Creed, and sometimes the main points of the catechism as well. The concern of reformers was that the godparent who presented a child to be baptized was promising to make sure that the child was raised and educated in the Christian faith. Still, some parents continued to choose godparents based on family and social ties rather than on piety and knowledge of the doctrines of a particular church. For example, in 1551, Vincent Retier chose his brother, a Catholic, to be the godfather at his child's baptism in Geneva. In reaction, the consistory admonished

Retier for his poor choice and sent him to the city council to receive further punishment. They did not, however, nullify his brother's status as godfather or delete his name from the baptismal registry.[7] While the actual responsibilities entailed in being a godparent may have varied widely across Europe, the relationship between godparent and godchild could never be unmade once established at the baptismal ceremony.

Finally, the ritual of baptism publicly acknowledged the belief of parents, ministers, and congregation that the infant in question was a child of faithful Christians, was loved by God, and was included in the covenant that God had established with God's followers extending all the way back to Abraham in the Old Testament. This belief would be incorporated into the child's upbringing and religious education and would provide a foundation for his or her own understanding of his or her religious faith and responsibilities and role in society.

CATECHISM

The ceremony of infant baptism was only the first step in a child's involvement in the church community. Whether a child was born into an Anabaptist, mainline Protestant, or Catholic community, religious education was an important part of his or her childhood. For Anabaptists, educating children in the Christian faith was vital in preparing them to choose whether to be baptized. For reformers such as Luther and Calvin, the ceremony of baptism marked the commitment of parents, godparents, and church members to ensure that the child would be raised and educated in the Christian faith, so that he or she would grow to fully comprehend God's promise as represented in his or her own baptism. Since infants could not understand what was happening at their own baptisms, these reformers believed that it was vital that, as they grew up, children learned what their baptism meant and how they should participate as faithful church members. Protestant and Catholic clergy and devout parents were concerned that their children should learn the "correct" Christian faith and should not be misled by the wide variety of Christian ideas proliferating in the sixteenth century.

To address this need, church leaders composed catechisms for their followers. In some parts of late medieval Europe, church synods encouraged priests to give classes specifically for children, and some literate laity owned prayer books that they may have used to instruct their children. Traditional catechism lessons did not, however, require literacy; they were designed to be spoken aloud and memorized. The sixteenth-century reformers placed a new emphasis on instructing children and designing catechism books specifically for them. These lessons were presented in question-and-answer format to aide in memorization. Both Lutheran and Calvinist reformers expected parents to teach their children the catechism at home. Church officials held fathers ultimately responsible for overseeing this instruction, but they expected that mothers would teach their children as well. In addition, many Protestant churches held weekly catechism services on Sunday afternoons for children, uneducated servants, and anyone else who had not yet learned the main tenets of the Reformed faith. In Scotland, the Calvinist church expected that by the age of six, children would have learned from their parents the Lord's Prayer, the Ten Commandments, and the Apostles' Creed so that they would be prepared to learn more advanced Christian teachings at church catechism lessons.[8]

Printed catechisms provide evidence of what church leaders thought was

---

John Calvin's Catechetical Explanation of the Fifth Commandment (1545)

S[tudent]: It begins, "Honor thy father and mother."

M[inister]: What meaning do you give to the word "honor"?

S: That children be, with modesty and humility, respectful and obedient to parents, serving them reverentially, helping them in necessity, and exerting their labor for them. For in these three branches is included the honor which is due to parents.

M: What is the meaning?

S: That, by the blessing of God, long life will be given to those who pay due honor to parents. . . .

M: What of those who are contumacious to parents?

S: They shall not only be punished at the last judgment, but here also God will take vengeance on their bodies, either by taking them hence in the middle of their days, or bringing them to an ignominious end, or in other manners. . . .

M: Is there nothing more of the commandment remaining?

S: Though father and mother only are expressed, we must understand all who are over us, as the reason is the same.

M: What is the reason?

S: That the Lord has raised them to a high degree of honor; for there is no authority whether of parents, or princes, or rulers of any description, no power, no honor, but by the decree of God, because it so pleases him to order the world.

—From John Calvin, *Catechism of the Church at Geneva,* 1545, translation from Christian Classics Ethereal Library, http://www.ccel .org/pipeline/1-html/4-calvin-treatises /catechis.htm.

important in teaching children about Christianity. They also suggest to us what many children probably learned about their family's chosen faith and church. Across Europe there were hundreds, possibly thousands, of variations, particularly of Lutheran and Puritan catechisms. The questions and answers in most of these catechisms were designed to teach children and others about the fundamental Christian beliefs and about how they should behave as faithful Christians. One Lutheran catechism emphasized a child's duty to honor his father and mother in this way:

> *Question:* What does it mean to honor your parents?
> *Answer:* The law, being a spiritual law, demands not merely external conformity and observance, but asks also for fulfillment in the depth of the heart. . . . This means that you owe your father not only outward respect and honor, but also a fundamentally good will . . . of which your deeds must give proof.

Even in homes where parents remained illiterate or were not diligent with catechism lessons, most children learned lessons about their conduct and responsibility that were reiterated in church catechism lessons. Over the course of the seventeenth century, as Catholic reforms emphasizing the importance of religious education and prayer life within the family spread, catechism lessons and religious inculcation became central moments in family life across Europe. In the most divisive situations of religious persecution, this religious education tied children more firmly to their family's beliefs and traditions.[9]

But just as we should not imagine that no child was loved before the modern period, we also should not assume that all early modern children obediently learned their catechisms or that all of the reformers' ideas came to pass precisely as they envisioned them. Memorization of a catechism did not guarantee an understanding of the theology that underpinned it. And holding a catechism lesson at a church did not guarantee pupils. In Geneva, for example, the reformers' efforts to promote attendance at Sunday catechism services met with mixed success. In 1549, the city council mandated that parents would be fined if they did not send their children to catechism services. Church and city authorities became increasingly frustrated as young people not only failed to attend catechism but gathered outside of the church at service time, playing and fighting loudly enough to disrupt the services. In both Geneva and Nîmes, France, among other places, church and city authorities enacted systems to patrol the streets during catechism services to make sure that children and others were attending. In some cases, consistories dealt leniently with children who skipped a catechism service but generally were considered to be well-intentioned and responsible young people. The Genevan cases suggest that the young people most likely to skip catechism were adolescent boys, not small children. But even children who were present at the church service sometimes disrupted things by laughing, wandering around the church, or not being prepared for the lesson. Thus catechism books tell us the intentions of reforming ministers, but the historical records also show that some children resisted those intentions, reminding us of one very human aspect of the Reformation.[10]

SCHOOLS

Ultimately, many church and civic leaders became convinced that the inculcation of "correct" religious beliefs was too important a matter to be left simply to parents or only to catechism services. Another important way in which the Reformation affected children's daily lives was in the development of elementary education. During the course of the sixteenth and seventeenth centuries, across Europe, both Protestant and Catholic reformers encouraged and even oversaw the establishment of schools for children. One of the most obvious differences between boys' and girls' experience of the Reformation was in the impact of these educational developments. As we will see, while reformers' plans for developing schools often included education for girls, in practice educational opportunities for girls beyond basic literacy remained limited.

While grammar schools already existed during the Middle Ages, they served only a small portion of the population, generally sons of the wealthy elite. A transformation in education began during the Italian Renaissance and spread northward through Europe during the fifteenth and sixteenth centuries. The humanist curriculum that developed during the Renaissance focused on five areas of study: grammar, rhetoric, moral philosophy, literature, and history. Initially, this type of education was meant to prepare young men for careers in civic service. As humanist ideas spread northward through the European community of scholars, they began to influence not only politicians and diplomats but also religious scholars. A fundamental theme of humanist education was the necessity of mastering the linguistic tools to read and edit original texts; this was considered vital to the study of both literature and history.

As northern scholars such as Erasmus absorbed humanist ideas, they put those tools to use on Christian texts, including the Bible. Here, humanist ideas had a great influence on the Protestant Reformation. As reformers including Luther and Calvin began to preach their ideas in the 1520s and 1530s, they emphasized the importance of reading scripture in order to understand God's will for humanity. If children were to be raised to read and discuss scriptural teachings themselves, rather than relying entirely on the clergy to provide interpretations for them, then it was imperative that children be literate. Since the majority of adults remained illiterate at the start of the Reformation, the education of children could not be entrusted entirely to parents. As a result, establishing schools for both boys and girls was a significant part of Protestant and Catholic reform efforts.

In Germany, Lutheran church officials went to great lengths to promote the spread of Lutheran teachings through both catechisms and the establishment of local, vernacular schools. The success of these schools was limited by a variety of factors, from the value placed on education to practical issues of transportation and weather. In Saxony, people were "unwilling to send their barefoot children to the school in Grossenbuch during the winter months" because "the cold, snow and storms are so severe that no one would chase a dog over the raging brooks and narrow planks."[11] Nevertheless, by the mid-sixteenth century, local schools were established across most of the German cities and principalities, in part at the urging of reformers and in part because local inhabitants increasingly wanted to be literate. But it would still be centuries before universal education existed in most of Europe.

It should not come as a surprise that the reformers' vision of widespread education was difficult to put into practice. In Geneva, the city's main school, the *collège*, suffered during the first half of the sixteenth century, both before the Reformation and during its first decades. Once the Reformation had begun, the city magistrates and the ministers had great interest in restoring the quality of the school, but financial straits and disagreements over teachers presented difficulties until the 1550s. In the first decades of the Reformation, some Genevan boys continued to attend better schools in nearby Catholic towns. When church and city officials learned about a child attending school outside of Geneva, they would summon the child's parents and insist that the child return to Geneva. Parents sometimes defended their decisions to send their children away by pointing to the poor state of education in Geneva. In 1537, Jehan Corajoz, a shoemaker, sent his child to a nearby Catholic school not, he said, to learn about Catholicism but "because the school here is not good." The city magistrates dismissed any such resistance and insisted that children should be educated in Geneva. In these cases, clearly, the Reformation directly affected children's educational opportunities. The Genevan educational system eventually recovered, but in the meantime children and their parents were forced either to make do with the education available within the city or to risk a confrontation with city and church authorities by sending their children to school in neighboring towns.[12]

The most important educational development in the Catholic Reformation was the establishment of the Jesuits and their dedication to educating Catholic boys. A new female order, the Ursulines, founded schools for girls, too, but there were fewer of them, and they did not spread as quickly and as far as the Jesuits did. Between the traditional urban Latin schools, sometimes enhanced by Protestant efforts, and the new Jesuit schools, well-off boys had plentiful access to education by the end of the sixteenth century. Rural education lagged behind, but it also increased significantly during the sixteenth and seventeenth centuries in Protestant areas. Gaps remained between the education of the elite and others, and, as mentioned above, between boys and girls. In some places, including Germany, schools were established for both boys and girls, but generally girls were instructed in separate buildings, their instruction was only for part of the day, and they were not expected to continue their education beyond basic reading and writing (enough to read the catechism and scriptures at home) and perhaps "feminine" skills such as needlework. In practice, significantly more boys than girls attended school. Most girls who pursued their education beyond this were members of wealthy families whose parents were particularly dedicated to education.[13]

Despite the uneven nature of the spread of literacy and education during the Reformation, there is no question that the sixteenth and seventeenth centuries were an important period of transition. For both Protestants and Catholics, one important incentive in educating their children was the necessity of reading—whether a catechism, the Bible, or prayer handbooks like those of Saint Teresa and Saint Ignatius—in order to live a pious life. Thus the Reformation contributed to the start of an increase in literacy rates which would progress sporadically across Europe until the Industrial Revolution.

CHILDREN AND THEIR PARENTS

Throughout the Middle Ages and into the sixteenth century, most Europeans believed that God had intentionally organized society in a particular way, imposing certain obligations on people in every societal role, at every level. Protestant reformers built upon this idea in focusing on the nuclear family, convinced that the family was the God-given, fundamental unit in spreading the reform of both church and society. Within the family, there were those responsible for leading and instructing—father first, but also mother—and those in need of teaching and nurture—the children. Both good parenting and responsible behavior on the part of children came to be seen as obligations not only to God and to one's family, but also to the surrounding community.

Even the most idealistic of reformers did not believe that the effective use of catechism books and sermons alone would result in appropriately faithful and responsible children. Physical discipline was required as well. Corporal punishment was common in medieval and early modern Europe—a fact that Ariès and Stone used as evidence that parents in those time periods did not love their children in the

Fig. 5.2. Children were fully integrated into the daily lives of their families, as shown in this depiction of a Flemish household. Maerten van Cleve, *Flemish Interior*, c. 1555–1560. Kunsthistorisches Museum, Vienna. Photo: Erich Lessing / Art Resource, NY.

same way that (ideal) modern parents do. Yet most sixteenth- and seventeenth-century writers who addressed the topic advised restraint in corporal punishment. Most Protestant reformers believed that children needed some moderate physical discipline—including beating—to help them resist the overwhelming temptation to sin. The Anabaptist reformer Menno Simons wrote: "Constrain and punish [your children] with discretion and moderation, without anger or bitterness, lest they be discouraged." This caution against extreme violence was a common sentiment; at the same time, one of the greatest complaints of reformers who wrote about disciplining children was that parents *overindulged* their children. Protestant leaders believed that either extreme—physical abuse or overindulgence—could both harm a child and dishonor God.[14]

Of course, the words of reformers did not translate directly into stricter or more lenient behavior on the part of parents. Nevertheless, their views did have a direct impact on the lives of children in the Reformation. One of the most significant developments during the Reformation, in terms of children's lives, was a heightened emphasis on parental responsibility and an increased oversight of family life by church and civic authorities. It is helpful to view the reformers' increasing attention to enforcing parental responsibility in connection with the Protestant rejection of the cult of saints, which marked a major religious and social change beginning in the sixteenth century. Praying to saints was a fundamental resource for medieval Christians, including parents who sought help caring for their children. Shulamith Shahar tells the story of a woman who, forced to leave her daughter at home in order to fulfill a work obligation to her landlord, prayed to a saint to watch over her child while she was gone. Medieval Europeans, both church officials and laypeople, accepted such dependence on the mercy of saints in people's daily lives. Protestant reformers rejected this role of saints as mediators between human beings and God; they rejected even more forcefully the idea that saints could act to intervene in people's daily lives. This meant that the responsibility of caring for children fell entirely on living human beings: parents, neighbors, and church and civic authorities.[15]

> **Gabriel Harvey on Resolving a Disagreement with His Father (Late Sixteenth Century)**
>
> My father began to chide and square with me at the table. I presently, and doing my duty, rise [sic] from the board, saying only "I pray you, good father, pray for me and I will pray for you."
> —From Nicholas Orme, *Medieval Children* (New Haven: Yale University Press, 2001), 84.

The community, then, was of key importance to the reformers. Particularly in Calvinist areas, church members were strongly encouraged to pay close attention to the behavior of their neighbors and to report any "un-Christian" actions to the consistory. Medieval Europeans also had intervened in the affairs of their neighbors, but with the establishment of consistories in the sixteenth century, people could now report their concerns directly to an immediately responsive authority. Some children benefited from the reports of concerned neighbors. When the Genevan consistory learned that Claude Gardet had beaten her daughter until her face bled, and that she had a pattern of such excessive discipline, they banned her from communion and sent her to the city council for punishment. But consistories did not provide absolute protection for children. Most contented themselves with admonishing parents and then sending them back home, unless they believed a child's life was in immediate danger.[16]

Lest we are left thinking that all early modern parents were abusive, it is also important to note that in other cases church and secular authorities insisted on *more* discipline than parents thought appropriate. In such cases children might find themselves in situations where their parents seemed to be protecting them from the church authorities, rather than vice versa. This could lead to confrontations between consistories and parents, as when the Genevan consistory summoned two men for "not having wanted to do their duty in chastising their children as they had been ordered to by the consistory." Overall it appears that the actual physical treatment and experiences of children did not change drastically as a direct result of the Reformation. Religiously and legally, children had the right to expect that they would be clothed and fed by their parents, but they themselves had little power to enforce this right. Most children remained at the mercy of their parents well into their teenage years (and of their masters, if they were working as apprentices or servants). And most parents sought to provide for their children and to find some method of moderate but effective discipline.[17]

While parents had the responsibility to train and support their children and the right to discipline them, children also had obligations to their parents. These duties sometimes developed into points of conflict as the children became adolescents and young adults who might spend their parents' money carelessly, not support parents in need, or even physically abuse their parents. For young children, however, resistance to family obligations rarely rose to the level of public attention. While it is difficult to be certain about how young children reacted to those expectations, we do know that obligations to their parents were reinforced in many phases of their upbringing, including daily family life, catechism lessons, and even school.

Viewed in one way, the changes provoked by the Protestant Reformation imposed new restrictions on the lives of children—stricter expectations, somewhat more organized attempts to teach the catechism, enforcement of very particular understandings of Christianity that would have significant impact on how children came to understand the world, and reinforcement of parental authority, especially that of fathers. On the other hand, all of these changes must be viewed within the context of life in the sixteenth century. Throughout the period of the Reformation, life remained uncertain in even more ways than it is today. After several centuries of outbreaks of the plague, climatic changes, and civil wars, the Reformation might be seen broadly as an attempt to bring stability and order to society and perhaps to gain some slightly increased confidence about one's status in the eyes of God. From this standpoint we might see Protestant efforts regarding children in a more positive light. From a religious point of view, reforming theologians argued that children were an important part of the "family of God" from the time of their birth and, for that very reason, deserved faithful nurture and care from their parents. In the best situations, children experienced these teachings in the diligence and care that their parents applied to raising them. In other instances, church and civic authorities intervened in attempts to guide wayward parents in their duties to their children.

ORPHANS AND ABANDONED CHILDREN

Of course, not all children were raised by their own parents. No amount of reforming zeal or idealism could entirely solve the problem of child abandonment, much less the realities of disease and unexpected death that eluded the medical techniques of the time. One well-established social change hastened, if not initiated, by the Protestant Reformation was the shifting of responsibility for the care of the poor from church institutions like convents and confraternities to centralized civic organizations like city poor funds, or poor chests, as they were commonly called. While this transition was already under way in many parts of Europe, once the Reformation began to spread, the transformation of poor relief services, including the care of poor children and orphans, was often incorporated into broader changes in church and society.

During the Middle Ages, poor relief had been provided by church institutions; collecting alms and dispensing aid to the poor had been part of the missions of confraternities, hospitals, convents, and monasteries. Sometimes parents abandoned their babies at convent doors anonymously; other times they turned to confraternities or parish "poor tables" for temporary assistance. As Protestant authorities closed down these Catholic institutions, they had to develop new means of dealing with those in need. During the course of the sixteenth century, the care of poor or abandoned children increasingly became the responsibility of the government; at the same time, it became closely tied to particular confessions. In areas such as France and the Netherlands, where Protestants and Catholics coexisted in the same towns, the city authorities might provide relief specifically to "deserv-

ing" adherents of the official city religion; members of the minority religion received relief from their own church authorities.[18]

While Catholic charity continued to depend more on a decentralized system of church institutions rather than on a city poor chest, Catholic and Protestant reformers shared new ideas about what precisely poor relief should provide to children in need. These changes had a significant effect on poor, orphaned, and abandoned children. In Geneva, church and city authorities focused on identifying the parents of abandoned children in order to hold them responsible for their children's upbringing. In the cases of orphans, the children of faithful church members were cared for either by appointed guardians or, in extreme cases, at the city's hospital. But children whose fathers had left Geneva

for Catholic places or had been exiled were most often sent out of the city with their mothers, to be cared for by their fathers. In Scotland, in contrast, the children of banished parents were more likely to be kept and "fostered in the town" by church members committed to raising the children as faithful Christians.[19]

Most important, as a result of both the Protestant and the Catholic Reformations, the provision of care for children in need became intimately tied to religious beliefs and practices. Both Protestants and Catholics distinguished between the "deserving" and the "undeserving" poor. Children whose parents had been faithful church members qualified as deserving (as did, by default, children whose parents were

Fig. 5.3. Even the poorest children could symbolize innocence and goodness, as seen in their expressions here. *Beggar Boys Playing Dice*, Bartolomé Esteban Murillo (1618–1682), Alte Pinakothek, Munich, Germany. Photo: Scala / Art Resource, NY.

unknown). Poor relief, whether it consisted of financial assistance to a family or of lodging and board for an orphan, was dispensed with certain expectations. Children generally received schooling—at the least, religious instruction—along with financial assistance. And increasingly, as the sixteenth century wore on into the seventeenth century, Catholic and Protestant officials acted on the conviction that the care of poor or orphaned children should include apprenticeships and other forms of job training to ensure that they would be able to support themselves as adults. This was intended not only as an act of compassion toward children in need but also as a means to guarantee the future stability of the Christian community.[20]

THE IMPACT OF RELIGIOUS DIVISIONS ON CHILDREN

As we see in these changes in official systems of poor relief, the new religious divisions of the Reformation directly affected how and from whom needy children received support. In times of intensified religious conflict or competition, children might find themselves caught directly in the midst of power struggles between Protestants and Catholics. This was the case for the three daughters of the Huguenot Magdelaine Bergerand, living in France in the 1670s, the decade before the Edict of Nantes was revoked. The girls were sent to live with their paternal grandfather as their widowed mother struggled to earn a living as a house servant. When their grandfather converted to Catholicism, he enlisted aid from fellow Catholics to support his granddaughters. In response, Magdelaine sought the support of her local consistory, accusing her father-in-law of kidnapping her daughters and demanding that he send them back to her. The girls returned to their mother when a provincial court ruled that they were too young to choose their own faith and that their mother was the only one who could make such decisions for them.[21]

When families were split over religion, children were perhaps the first to feel the effects. Through catechism and grammar school education, as well as participation in church services and other religious practices, children learned from the earliest ages to think of themselves as a particular *kind* of Christian—the "correct" kind, so long as they learned their prayers and scripture lessons properly. In some parts of Europe, this definition of oneself, one's family, and one's community as "true" Christians helped to shape and delimit relations with other Europeans, both individuals and communities. This self-understanding undoubtedly provided a sense of stability to many children during the Reformation period. But during that same time, religious wars ravaged parts of Europe, including the Holy Roman Empire and France. Children could not help being affected by these battles, fought in the name of Christian doctrines and practices.

The successive waves of nominally religious wars in Europe—including wars in the Holy Roman Empire from the 1530s until 1555, the French Wars of Religion from 1562 to 1598, and the Thirty Years' War from 1618 to 1648—left thousands of children hungry, orphaned, and either prepared to die for their religion or appalled at the violence justified by religious convictions. Even in places like the Netherlands, where Catholics and Protestant were more likely to exist peacefully in the same civic communities, the goal of church leaders of any confession was to raise children according to "true" beliefs. In times of peace and of war, an important result of such efforts was that children would come to define themselves by religious tenets and practices. While their predecessors in the fourteenth and fifteenth centuries had learned to identify themselves by town and family, and perhaps by the fact that they were not Jewish or Muslim, Christian children raised during the Reformation faced a newly divided world around them, in which they learned to define themselves in opposition to other children raised according to the "wrong" Christian teachings.

During the sixteenth and seventeenth centuries, Protestant and Catholic reformers sought to teach children how to be faithful Christians, responsible offspring, and dutiful members of the church and civic communities. Some young people appear to have taken those lessons to heart, including the Protestant Georg von Grumbach, who wrote to his mother: "I intend to devote myself in every way to carrying out your will and [my tutor's], so that I learn something, to the honor of God and the benefit of myself and my neighbor, for I know very well that no one is born for the sake of himself alone."[22] This did not guarantee that these children would always *act* according to Christian teachings. But there is no doubt that the Protestant and

Catholic Reformations helped to shape how adult society and children themselves viewed children's relationship to God, their need for education, their relationship to their parents, and their place in society. Over time, the reformers' increased focus on families, children, and parental responsibility contributed to a growth in literacy among children, greater church and civic oversight of parents' care and treatment of their children, strict expectations regarding grown children's obligations to their parents, and new self-understandings based on confessional definitions of Christianity. In these important ways the Reformation changed the way that European children interacted with and experienced the world.

FOR FURTHER READING

Bunge, Marcia J., editor. *The Child in Christian Thought: Religion, Marriage, and Family.* Grand Rapids: Eerdmans, 2001.

Cunningham, Hugh. *Children and Childhood in Western Society since 1500.* London: Longman, 1995.

Fletcher, Anthony. "Prescription and Practice: Protestantism and the Upbringing of Children, 1560–1700." In *The Church and Childhood,* edited by Diana Wood, 325–46. Cambridge, Mass.: Blackwell, 1994.

Haas, Louis. *The Renaissance Man and His Children: Childbirth and Early Childhood in Florence, 1300–1600.* New York: St. Martin's, 1998.

Luke, Carmen. *Pedagogy, Printing and Protestantism: The Discourse on Childhood.* Albany: State University of New York Press, 1989.

McCants, Anne E. C. *Civic Charity in a Golden Age: Orphan Care in Early Modern Amsterdam.* Urbana: University of Illinois Press, 1997.

Ozment, Steven, *When Fathers Ruled: Family Life in Reformation Europe.* Cambridge: Harvard University Press, 1983.

Safley, Thomas Max. *Charity and Economy in the Orphanages of Early Modern Augsburg.* Studies in Central European Histories. Atlantic Highlands, N.J.: Humanities, 1997.

Tudor, Philippa. "Religious Instruction for Children and Adolescents in the Early English Reformation." *Journal of Ecclesiastical History* 35, no. 3 (July 1984): 391–413.

Watt, Jeffrey R. "Calvinism, Childhood, and Education: The Evidence from the Genevan Consistory." *Sixteenth Century Journal* 33, no. 2 (2002): 439–56.

WOMEN AND MEN, TOGETHER AND APART

MERRY E. WIESNER-HANKS

CHAPTER SIX

Sometime in the late sixteenth century, in a Swiss Reformed Protestant village, the adult men who are heads of household gather in the village square for their annual oath swearing. Along with swearing to defend the village if it is attacked, serve honorably as an official if called upon, and pay any assessed taxes, the men also swear to uphold Reformed Protestantism. The oath swearing this year has an additional special order of business—the pastor of the village church has just died, and, as they have since the fourteenth century, the men must elect a new pastor. Instead of seeking the advice of local Catholic bishops about likely candidates, however, they now look to the academy established by John Calvin in Geneva. After they have sworn their oath and agreed on a candidate for pastor, the men gather in a village tavern.

In a north German evangelical (or "Lutheran") Protestant city, about forty days after giving birth, a new mother is met at her home by the midwife who attended the delivery and other relatives and friends who had been present. They go with her to church for a regular service, which includes the ritual of churching (Kirchgang in the German spoken in north Germany) for the new mother. After the sermon, the pastor calls the group of women to the altar, where the new mother kneels. He says a prayer over her, highlighting Eve's sin as the source of "great anxiety and labor pains," but also commenting that "a woman is blessed with the fruit of her body . . . and made happy with the joyous sight of a happy, living fruit."[1] The women leave the church when the rest of the congregation does, and they return to the mother's house for a meal that is as elaborate and festive as she can afford, with special cakes and drinks.

In a Catholic Italian city, men gather at the regular meeting of the confraternity (literally "brotherhood") devoted to the Holy Sacrament in their parish, established through the actions of a reforming bishop such as Carlo Borromeo of Milan. They decide who will take the eucharist to sick parishioners, who will carry the host around the city when they all march in the annual Corpus Christi parade, and who will organize a Forty Hours devotion in their parish church, during which believers pray before the host for that period. Some members of the confraternity discuss their upcoming pilgrimage to Rome, which will also include a dramatic procession, with penitential flagellation. The members debate whether to spend money hiring an artist to decorate one of the chapels in the parish church or instead hold a feast in honor of their chosen saint. They decide on the latter, as the saint is especially venerated by carpenters, the occupation of most of the men.

In a French Catholic city, a small group of single women and widows who live in the same neighborhood decide to dedicate themselves to serving the poor, the ill, orphans, and war victims. They are inspired by the example of the Jesuits to devote themselves to an active life of service to the needy, and they have heard about similar groups of laywomen dedicated to charitable service springing up in Italy, Spain, the Netherlands, and other parts of France. They discuss whether to affiliate themselves with one of the religious orders with a similar mission, such as the Franciscans,

Fig. 6.1. German women rake in the hay after the harvest. Daily tasks as well as religious activities were often divided by gender. Sigmundt Heldt, sixteenth century. Kunstbibliothek, Staatliche Museen zu Berlin, Germany. Photo: Bildarchiv Preussischer Kulturbesitz / Art Resource, NY.

but decide that remaining informal would be best. Seeking approval for their group from the local bishop or from a religious order would draw attention to it, and then they might be ordered to enter a convent, where they would be cut off from the people they hope to help.

These scenes describe religious activities of four types of people in post-Reformation Western Europe: Protestant men, Protestant women, Catholic men, and Catholic women. The Reformation split Western Christianity, creating distinctions between Protestants and Catholics in terms of theology, church structure, religious institutions, and devotional practices. What the Reformation did not do was end differences between male and female Christians. The religious lives of Reformation-era people, whether Catholic or Protestant, were shaped by their gender. Thus, though there were many differences between religious denominations—termed "confessions" in early modern Europe—men and women shared certain things across confessional boundaries.

CITIZENSHIP

The impact of gender can be seen in each of the scenes described above. Switzerland was religiously divided after the Reformation, with each canton deciding whether it would be Protestant or Catholic and then defending that decision, sometimes militarily. The process was different in each canton, but the decision was always made by men, just as it was men in many parts of Switzerland—both Catholic and Protestant—who elected the parish priest or pastor. Women who ruled territories in Europe often had the power to appoint priests and bishops, just as male rulers did; this secular control of church personnel had existed since the time of the Roman Empire and persisted despite many efforts by the papacy and other high church officials to end it. During the Reformation, female rulers, just like male rulers, also changed their realm's confessional allegiance. Queens Mary and Elizabeth of England are the most famous examples of female rulers who did this, but several countesses and duchesses ruling the smaller territories of the Holy Roman Empire also changed the confession of their territories, from Catholic to Protestant or from Protestant to Catholic. If the appointment of a pastor or the choice about confessional allegiance was made by a group of people, however, rather than a single individual, that group was always a group of men. The Twelve Articles of the Peasants, issued in 1525 and laying out social and religious demands of south German and Swiss peasants, asserted, "we ought to have the authority and power for the whole community to elect and appoint its own pastor."[2] Though the language just says "we," what was clearly meant was "we men" speaking "*for* the whole community." Women who were nuns had often voted for their abbesses in the Middle Ages, and continued to do so after the Reformation. In terms of all other religious matters, however, voting—what is often termed "democracy"—marked a division between men and women.[3]

Gender restrictions in electing clergy were eased in a few congregations among some Baptists, Independents, and other radical Protestant groups in seventeenth-century England, where women as well as men raised their hands to approve or disapprove a new pastor. Even in congregations that allowed women to vote, however, positions as pastor or elder were reserved for men. Only groups that did not have formal clergy, such as the Quakers, allowed women to preach, and even among the Quakers this was debated.

Fig. 6.2. In this depiction of Dutch city life around 1600, women spin the wool, while the men weave it. Spinning was not only a common task of women, but was a symbol of the good woman, who kept her hands busy to support her family and avoid temptation. Photo: Erich Lessing / Art Resource, NY.

Choosing a Pastor

Electing a pastor was sometimes done directly, with representatives from a village or parish approaching an approved candidate themselves. Sometimes this was handled through regional church officials. The following is a 1606 petition from the (male) villagers of Ebsdorf parish in central Germany to a superintendent, asking that he approve a new pastor. The villagers always refer to the superintendent politely and indirectly as "your honor," but they are very clear about their wishes.

We respectfully affirm the following: One of our neighbors, Balthasar Fischer, sent his son, whose name is Heinrich Fischer, to study at great expense. By God's grace he continued until he had learned all the duties of the pastoral office well, and was given a position as the regular pastor in the congregation of Altenhassell in the duchy of Hanau. We then fervently asked that he would be given to us as a pastor because he was the son of one of our neighbors. . . . But because of his duties there, the above-mentioned Heinrich Fisher could not be freed from his position, so we asked your honor if there was another person who would be suitable. We came to an agreement, which your honor approved, that the pastor of Walgern should give a sermon at our church, so that we could see if we approved of him. Not only was this to happen, but the village mayor was to order every citizen in each village of this parish, man for man, to attend this service and listen to the sermon. After the end of the service, the mayor was to speak with each man individually to get a clear idea of whether each of them was happy with this pastor or not. This then happened as it was supposed to. Not only did everyone individually say yes, but the whole parish did communally as well. In addition, the parish said that they were also satisfied with the other actions that their elected representatives had already taken in regards to this matter, as well as actions that they would take in the future for the good of this poor parish. So we ask, both as a group and individually, that you appoint this pastor as a teacher and pastoral shepherd. Hopefully, it will honor God, be of good to you, and yield the most good to us poor people.

—From Stadtarchiv Marburg 4i 153, quoted in David Mayes,
*Communal Christianity: The Life and Loss of a Peasant Vision
in Early Modern Germany* (Leiden: Brill, 2004), 102,
translation by Merry Wiesner-Hanks.

Annual oath swearings of all male citizens (*Schwörtag*) were not limited to Switzerland but took place in many towns and villages in the Holy Roman Empire; male citizens' adolescent sons were also expected to participate, in the same way that male adolescents in England were sworn into a tithing. Women were designated as "citizens" in medieval and early modern cities, which gave them rights of residence and legal advantages over noncitizens. They swore oaths of loyalty on first becoming citizens and were otherwise obligated to perform most of the duties of citizenship, but they did not participate in the annual oath swearing; the reasons for this are never stated explicitly in the sources. With the Reformations, the annual oath swearing created a distinction not only between male and female citizens but also between male and female Christians. (The vast majority of Europe's population was Christian, of course, and there was never any discussion of granting citizenship to non-Christians such as Jews or Muslims during this period.) Faith was a ritualized civic matter for men—but not for women.

This situation led to uncertainty about how to handle the citizenship status of certain women. In Protestant cities one of the key political effects of the Reformation was the integration of the male clergy into the citizenry, ending the distinction between clerical and lay status. In most cases, these priests also married, but this was not a requirement for obtaining citizenship. For nuns, however, it was. The only way they could become citizens was to marry, which meant, of course, they were no longer nuns. A priest could be both a citizen and a priest, but a nun could not be a citizen and a nun. Thus both the public political community and the public religious community— which were regarded as the same in sixteenth-century Europe—were for men only, a situation reinforced in the highly gendered language of the reformers, who extolled "brotherly love" and the religious virtues of the "common man." We might think that the phrase "common man" included women, but it did not.[4]

WIFELY OBEDIENCE

Along with the relationship between clerical status and citizenship, intermarriage between spouses of different Christian denominations, or the conversion of one spouse and not the other, also posed a problem for religious reformers and political authorities. What should take pre-cedence, a woman's faith or her duty to obey her husband? Continental Protestants generally urged the wife to obey her husband; she could pray for his conversion but, in Calvin's words, "should not desert the partner who is hostile."[5] Some radical Protestants, such as the Anabap-tists in the German city of Münster, allowed—and a few even encour-aged—believers to leave their unbelieving spouses, but they expected the women who did so to remarry quickly and thus come under the authority of a male believer. In their sermons and printed household guides, English Puritans also put wifely obedience over a woman's religious convictions, though they did suggest that their female fol-lowers could try to be "domestic missionaries" and attempt to convert their children, servants, and husbands. Many Catholic authors agreed, supporting women working to convert their Protestant or indifferent husbands, or even daughters converting or inspiring their parents. "Young girls will reform their families, their families will reform their provinces, their provinces will reform the world," went a saying taught to Catholic schoolgirls.[6] Religious differences were not a valid ground for separation in Catholicism, however, nor could married women enter a convent unless their husbands agreed.

During the first decades after the Reformation, marriages between spouses of different confessions were more common than they would be later when the lines of confession hardened. Such mixed marriages occasioned less comment than one would assume, given the violence of religious disagreements in general, because for the nobility and gentry, and even for middle-class city people, economic considerations and family politics could outweigh religious concerns when choosing a spouse. By the seventeenth century, intermarriage across religious lines was less common, with some cities and states issuing explicit prohibi-tions, often in gender-specific terms. In 1631 in Lutheran Strasbourg, for example, any female citizen who married a Calvinist was to lose her citizenship "because she would let herself easily be led into error by her husband and would be led astray," while a man who married a Calvin-ist would not "because he can probably draw his spouse away from her false religion and bring her onto the correct path."[7]

Sometimes a woman's duty of obedience toward her husband cre-ated opportunities rather than restrictions. In 1559, Queen Elizabeth ordered everyone in her realm to attend services in the Church of

England or be penalized with fines and imprisonment. Many English and Irish Catholics outwardly conformed, but others did not, becoming what were termed "recusants." Among these was a large percentage of women, who posed a special problem for royal officials trying to enforce the law. A single woman or widow found guilty of recusancy could be fined, but a married woman, according to English common law, had no legal identity separate from her husband—she owned and controlled no property. Imprisoning her would disrupt family life, and fining her would harm her husband, who might not even share her religious convictions. The Crown tried a variety of tactics to solve the problem, but only the most adamant Protestant men were willing to back measures that would allow a wife to be responsible as an individual for her religious choices and put her husband's property at risk. If Catholic wives became legally independent property owners, might their own wives do the same? Most Protestant members of Parliament were horrified at the prospect.

A few women, such as Margaret Clitherow and Anne Line, were executed for their Catholic faith, but most recusant women were able to avoid strict punishment. Their husbands often did outwardly conform, attending services to avoid punishment, leaving their wives to arrange for private masses or even to shelter illegal Catholic missionaries. These recusant women became a new kind of Catholic heroine—capable, benevolent, intelligent, and even somewhat crafty in the way they dealt with authorities. They were able to use ideas about a husband's God-given authority over his home and family to the advantage of their religious beliefs, carving out a space for Catholic worship in the privacy of their own households.

CHURCHING

Catholic women in England and Ireland were in an unusual—and sometimes dangerous—situation, but some aspects of their experiences were shared by women elsewhere in Europe. When women participated in public ceremonies or rituals affirming their faith, these were usually tied to their families, not to their cities or communities. The ceremony of churching described above for Lutheran Germany was one such ritual. Churching was shared by Lutheran mothers throughout Germany and elsewhere, and by Catholic and Anglican mothers. Churching had its origins in the Jewish ritual of postnatal purification (Lev. 12:1-8), which the Virgin Mary herself underwent, as described in Luke 2:22-39.[8] By at least the fifth century, Mary's purification was being celebrated as the feast of Candlemas (February 2 in the Latin church, February 14 in the Greek church), and by at least the eleventh century new mothers were being given a special blessing.

Official Christian theology declared that women who had given birth were not ritually unclean, and canon law does not discuss churching in much detail. Whatever the view of learned theologians and church officials, however, it is clear that churching was an important ritual for more ordinary people, and especially for women. By the fifteenth century, churching was common in many parts of Europe, and even mothers who had died in childbirth were brought by their families to be churched. Churching could be denied to those who gave birth out of wedlock, so the ritual marked the reintegration of a new mother into the community of honorable women and of publicly worshiping Christians.

Martin Luther did not oppose churching, as it had a clear New Testament basis, and in some Lutheran areas churching was required of all married mothers and forbidden to unmarried ones. In England unmarried women who had given birth were only to be churched if they named the father and wore a white sheet signifying their penitence

---

Prayers for Churching

Manuals for priests and pastors often provided sample prayers for all church rituals, including the churching of women after childbirth. A prayer from pre-Reformation Germany begins:

Lord God, who through Your servant Moses commanded the people of Israel that when a woman had borne a son, she should refrain from entering the temple for forty days, consider this your servant worthy to be strengthened from every pollution of the flesh so that with a clean heart and pure mind she may serve to enter into the bosom of [our] mother, the church. . . .

After the Reformation, references to the new mother's impurity were lessened. A Lutheran prayer from 1569 begins:

On account of sin this curse went out to all the daughters of Eve: "I will increase your labor and your groaning, and in labor you shall bear children"—which still remains as a reminder that children are conceived and borne in sin. All the same it is a special work of grace of God's creation, that a woman is blessed with the fruit of her body, that a little child is formed in the mother's body and is nourished and maintained, that the mother is delivered with great anxiety and labor pains, and is made happy with the joyous sight of a living, healthy fruit. . . .

—From a translation quoted in Susan C. Karant-Nunn, *The Reformation of Ritual: An Interpretation of Early Modern Germany* (London: Routledge, 1997), 77, 80.

during the service. Churching was violently opposed by English Puritan men in the seventeenth century as a Catholic holdover, but many Puritan women continued to demand it, as did English women well into the twentieth century even if they never attended other church services. We may view churching and similar ceremonies as stemming from clerical hostility toward the female body and childbirth, but there is evidence that early modern women rejected this interpretation and instead regarded churching as a necessary final act of closure to a period of childbirth.

A woman attended her churching in the presence of the women who had been with her during the birth, including the midwife. Such women were called her "gossips" in England, a word that was originally also used for godparent, and, as a verb, to describe the socializing that took place after a churching. Women objected when pastors sought to change the ritual in any way; one report from Abingdon in England in 1668 noted that "women refuse to be churched because they have not their right place, and midwives are excluded . . . from their women, who always used to sit together."[9]

BAPTISM

Churching was a ritual for women only—except for the priest or pastor—but many religious rituals marking family events, such as baptisms, weddings, and funerals, were shared by kin of both sexes. Gender still shaped these rituals in significant ways, however. Late medieval baptism manuals specify that the priest was to ask the sex of the baby and to say different prayers and exorcisms for boys and girls. If two or more children were baptized at the same time, boys were to come first and were usually held on the priest's right; girls came second and were held on the left. Lutheran baptismal manuals end gender distinctions in prayers, but boys may still have been held on the right and girls on the left.

Both Catholics and Protestants saw unbaptized children as under grave threat from the devil, so baptisms were held quite quickly after birth. This was before the mother's churching, so she was generally not present at the baptism. The child was carried to the church by the midwife, who sometimes served as a godparent. Before the Reformation, and in Catholic areas after the Reformation, midwives could also conduct emergency baptisms if they thought the child might die before a regular baptism could be arranged. Lutheran theologians and officials debated whether this was proper, and they allowed it under very limited circumstances; they examined midwives during church visitations to make sure they were conducting the ceremony properly and issued instructions as part of church ordinances. In the sixteenth century, the Church of England permitted any Christian to conduct a baptism "when great need shall compel them," and admonished pastors to "instruct parishioners, and especially the midwives, the essential manner and form how to christen a child in time of need."[10] Parish records indicate that baptism by a midwife was not uncommon. By the seventeenth century, this had changed. Puritans saw baptisms by anyone who was not a pastor as a popish abomination, and both Church of England prayer books and parish records make no mention of baptism by women. Calvinist leaders on the continent also banned it completely, noting, as did English Puritans, that God in his mercy might still allow the unbaptized to enter Paradise.

Most people were not as convinced as Calvinist divines that unbaptized children could be saved, and relatives or godparents sometimes presented infants who had died during childbirth for baptism. Officially baptism may only be performed on a living person, however, so certain chapels became known

Boys and Girls at Baptism

Many late medieval baptism manuals provide slightly different prayers for the baptisms of boys and girls. They do not contain much gender-pertinent language but demonstrate that right from the start male and female Christians were put into separate conceptual categories. Here is the prayer for boys from the Salisbury manual:

God of Abraham, God of Isaac, God of Jacob, God who didst appear to thy servant Moses on Mount Sinai, and didst lead the children of Israel out of the land of Egypt, appointing for them the angel of thy mercy, who should guard them by day and by night, we beseech thee, Lord, that thou wouldst vouchsafe to send thy holy angel from heaven, that he may likewise guard this servant N., and lead him to the grace of thy baptism.

The prayer for girls reads:

God of heaven, God of earth, God of angels, God of archangels, God of patriarchs, God of prophets, God of apostles, God of martyrs, God of confessors, God of virgins, God of all that live good lives, God whom every tongue confesses and before whom every knee bows, of things in heaven and things on earth and things under the earth, I invoke thee, Lord, upon this thy handmaid N. that thou mightest vouchsafe to lead her to the grace of thy baptism.

—From John D. C. Fisher, *Christian Initiation: Baptism in the Medieval West* (London: SPCK, 1965), 160–62.

as places where deceased infants were miraculously brought back to life for a few minutes to allow them to be baptized. Archaeological excavations around the site of one such chapel in rural Switzerland have recently uncovered hundreds of infant corpses, dating from over several centuries. From the state of the remains, it is evident that in some cases the trip to the chapel took several weeks, for the infants had died long before they were buried.

Among poor families, the midwife might be the only godparent, but most families chose other people as well, sometimes quite a few. Godparentage was a way to cement alliances among family members and between families. Godparents held the child during baptism and announced its name to the officiating priest or pastor; they were expected to provide a gift and to serve as the child's patron in later life. In England, boys customarily had two godfathers and one godmother, and girls the reverse, though any combination was possible. Many areas, both Protestant and Catholic, tried to limit the total number of godparents and prevent people from delaying baptism while they sought godparents with high social standing. Such rules were difficult to enforce, however, for they went against people's desire for godparents who could provide the greatest social benefit for their child.

Fig.6.3. In this famous sixteenth-century painting of a peasant wedding by Pieter Bruegel the Elder, the calm bride sits in the middle, with an older couple, probably her parents, to her left. The whole village joins the couple to enjoy the simple food, drink, and music. Kunsthistorisches Museum, Vienna, Austria. Photo: Scala / Art Resource, NY.

MARRIAGE

Marriage ceremonies elaborated on the distinctions made between men and women in baptism rituals and godparentage practices. Marriage had been defined as a sacrament—a ceremony that provides visible evidence of God's grace—in the thirteenth century in the Western church, though theologians differed about exactly what was needed to make a marriage valid. Most regarded freely given consent as the only absolutely necessary requirement, though some included the presence of a priest or witnesses, consummation, or very specific words of consent to make a marriage fully valid (and thus indissoluble). In southern Europe and among the well-to-do everywhere, weddings often took place in people's homes, while in northern Europe, they frequently took place at the church door, with only a few family members. Manuals for priests suggest specific readings, prayers, and blessings, which emphasize God's institution of marriage and its indissolubility, the dangers of sexuality, the bearing of children, and the duties of the wife toward her husband. "May she be as amiable toward her husband as Rachel," went the final blessing set out in the fourteenth-century handbook for the diocese of Breslau in Germany, and "may she fortify her weakness with vigorous discipline."[11] The service itself was very brief, and the duties of the husband were spelled out less often.

Luther and other Protestants broke with Catholic teachings about the sacramentality of marriage, but the actual wedding ritual changed only slowly, and remained varied, even within Lutheran areas. By the middle of the sixteenth century, weddings in Germany were longer and generally held at the main church altar in front of a larger group of people or even the entire congregation. In Lutheran Denmark, however, after a 1582 marriage law stipulated that a priest and five witnesses were required for a valid betrothal, many rural people never had an actual wedding, as they believed the betrothal was ceremony enough. Protestant weddings generally included a sermon or homily, which reiterated the principles laid out in the readings and prayers; wedding sermons were frequently printed, with less gifted preachers just reading a printed version. Protestant rituals and sermons went on at greater length about the duties of the husband than had Catholic rituals, but these were still very different from the duties of the wife.

Fig. 6.4. Protestant reformers tried to limit the drinking and dancing at weddings to make them serious and sober religious ceremonies, but as this painting by Pieter Brueghel the Younger, son of Pieter Bruegel the Elder, demonstrates, that was easier said than done. Museum voor Shone Kunsten, Ghent, Belgium. Photo: Scala / Art Resource, NY.

According to a 1561 "Wedding Booklet for the Simple Pastors in Mark Brandenburg," the groom was to swear that he would exercise reason in his dealings with his wife, "treat her in a friendly manner . . . faithfully attend to your vocation . . . so that you may . . . nourish yourself [and] feed your wife." The bride was to "do with a glad heart everything he says, and everything that he forbids you to do you should leave alone . . . be obedient to him in all godly matters."[12] The Tudor homily on marriage laid out both the physical dangers and restraints on freedom that marriage brought to women: "Truth it is that they [women] must specially feel the griefs and pains of matrimony, in that they relinquish the liberty of their own rule, in the pain of their travailing [i.e., labor and delivery], in the bringing up of their own children, in which offices they may be in great peril, and be grieved with many afflictions, which they might be without, if they lived out of matrimony."[13] It is very difficult to find information about what men or women sitting in the congregation thought about these statements, but as weddings became more public, and wedding homilies more frequent, we do know that they heard them over and over again.

Husbandly authority and wifely obedience were enjoined not only in wedding ceremonies, but in household guides, devotional literature (especially that given to young people), and even in law codes. A 1526 law code from the territory of Salzburg in Austria is typical in this:

The husband shall not spend away the dowry or other goods of his wife unnecessarily with gambling or other useless frivolous pastimes, wasting and squandering it. . . . If there is no cause or she is not guilty of anything, he is not to hit her too hard, push her, throw her or carry out any other abuse [but] act appropriately toward her. For her part, the wife should obey her husband in modesty and honorable fear, and be true and obedient to him. She should not provoke him with word or deed to disagreement or displeasure, through which he might be moved to strike her or punish her in unseemly ways.[14]

Marriage manuals written by pastors also discuss physical coercion, noting that it might be necessary in order to enforce husbandly authority—the metaphor used most often was breaking in a horse—but should always be measured. Law codes in some places specify the limits to this; in Germany the husband was allowed to beat his wife only "until the blood flows" and in England only with a stick thinner than his thumb. (This is the origin of the phrase "rule of thumb.")

INHERITANCE, PROPERTY RIGHTS, AND OTHER LEGAL ISSUES

As they neared the end of life, Christians in early modern Europe prepared for their deaths in ways that were both practical and spiritual. They wrote out wills bequeathing their property to family members, relatives, and friends, and they were advised to make their souls ready, for "death keeps no calendar." An individual's ability to bequeath property as he or she wished was limited in many parts of Europe by laws that required heirs to be granted a minimum amount, although in England both women and men had relative testamentary freedom. Most legal systems limited a wife's ability to bequeath property without the express approval of her husband, but widows and unmarried women were not restricted in their disposition of movables, and women's wills include bequests not only of clothing and household goods, but also of books, art objects, and in parts of Western Europe where there was slavery, such as Italian and Portuguese cities, slaves. Women were more likely than men to pass property to other women, and they tended to specify a wider circle of relatives and friends for specific bequests. They also generally included members of both their birth and marital families in their wills, and they often contributed to the dowries of nieces from both birth and marital families with grants of property or cash while they were still alive.

In many parts of Europe, women made more and larger donations for religious purposes than did the men of their families, leading in at least one instance to laws that restricted their testamentary freedom. In 1501, the Strasbourg city council limited the amount of money a woman could donate or deed to a convent when she entered, claiming that this unfairly disinherited her relatives and decreased the city tax base. The preacher and moralist Geiler of Kaisersberg, normally no great friend of women, opposed this move, commenting that "widows who are responsible and sensible persons" should be able to handle their own financial affairs, and that "it is a mockery of God, a haughty service of the devil to forbid a pious person to give everything that she owns for the will of God."[15] Geiler's arguments were unsuccessful, the law stood, and the city council further declared that all widows and unmarried women should be assigned guardians for their financial affairs. Such gender-based guardianship was increasingly adopted across much of Europe as jurists who were educated in Roman law revised and reformed city and state law codes in the sixteenth century. Justinian's Code, the basis of Roman law, clearly prescribed a dependent legal status for women because of their "fragility, imbecility, irresponsibility, and ignorance." Roman law also called for fathers to have absolute rights over their children (*patria potestas*), and in many parts of Europe widows lost the right of guardianship over their own children if they remarried.

CONFRATERNITIES

The first two scenes with which this essay began—choosing a pastor and participating in a religious ritual marking a family event—and many of the developments we have discussed so far would have been common to both Protestants and Catholics. Both Protestants and Catholics in Switzerland and some parts of Germany chose pastors, and both Protestants and Catholics throughout Western Europe were baptized, married, churched, and buried. The second two scenes, of men organizing a religious confraternity and women a more informal group of unmarried women devoted to charity, were limited to Catholic Europe, but the notions of gender we have already examined shaped them as well.

Male confraternities expanded rapidly with the growth of the mendicant orders such as the Franciscans and Dominicans in the thirteenth century. Voluntary lay confraternities, organized by occupation, devotional preference, neighborhood, or charitable activity, grew up in larger cities and many villages. Venice had 120 confraternities

Plate A. Cheese was a basic item in people's diet. Here we see a peasant couple on their way to market to sell their cheese. Despite his ragged garments both the man and his wife seem assured and confident. He carries a sword, and there is something dashing about his hat and feather. She appears to be keeping him in line! Ordinary folk featured prominently in the work of poets, writers, and artists in the early 1520s in Germany. This 1521 woodcut is attributed to Hans Weiditz.

Wie sälig ist der ackerman
Der mit dem pflüg sich neren kan
Er schlaft mit rüw auff baider seit
Die weil der reych in sorgen leit

Der wasser krüg geit jm gut tranck
Er achtet nit der herzen zanck
Kain frümmer volck geborn was
Wiechs vntrew nit bey jn als gras

Plate B. Off to the dance! This very romantic portrayal of the simple pleasures of the poor is accompanied by a rhyme that contrasts the ploughman, who works hard, nourishes himself and others, and sleeps soundly as a result, with the wealthy, whose life is dogged by anxiety and conflict. The Peasants' War was soon to give the lie to such idealization. Hans Weiditz, c. 1521.

Plate C. (above) Monk and Donkey. Crude anti-clerical polemic coursed throughout Europe in the early sixteenth century. This satirical drawing by Leonhard Beck from 1523 compares a monk to a donkey. The latter, dressed in fool's costume, is trying, ludicrously, to spin, rather like the nun on the monk's back, also spinning, but losing the thread. The verse mocks good-for-nothing clerics who wander the land, clutching their money-bags. The wise owl is attacked by magpies, whose black and white livery again symbolizes the monastic orders.

Plate D. (right) A miraculous divine intervention! This 1706 "ex voto," from Saint Leonard's Church in Inchenhofen in Württemberg, indicates gratitude for Saint Leonard's help. The kneeling woman, at bottom right, had successfully called upon the saint when her husband and son were about to be massacred by the occupying Austrians. Note that the eyes of the latter have been gouged out of the painting by outraged worshippers. Pilgrimage shrines were full of such "ex votos," which generally testified to dramatic healings.

Plate E. The Peasants' War. The tragic defeat of the peasants at the battle of Frankenhausen in 1525, portrayed here, is part of a remarkable panoramic mural at Bad Frankenhausen, completed in 1989. The artist Werner Tübke makes the radical preacher, Thomas Müntzer, whose five hundredth anniversary it was, the central figure. Despite the promise of the rainbow, his flag is lowered, for he is soon to be captured, tortured, and executed. Below him stand Luther with other reformers, around his emblem, the Luther rose. Panorama Museum, Bad Frankenhausen, Germany. Photo: Panorama Museum/Werner Tübke; VG Bild-Kunst, Bonn. Used by permission.

Plate F. The Koberger Bible. Published in 1483 in Nuremberg by Anton Koberger. This beautifully printed and illustrated two-volume Bible was one of fourteen German Bible editions that appeared before the Reformation. Contrary to widespread belief, vernacular Bibles did not originate with Luther, though the translations tended to be rather wooden, and only the wealthy could afford such magnificent folio volumes. Here we see the creation of Eve and the sufferings of Job.

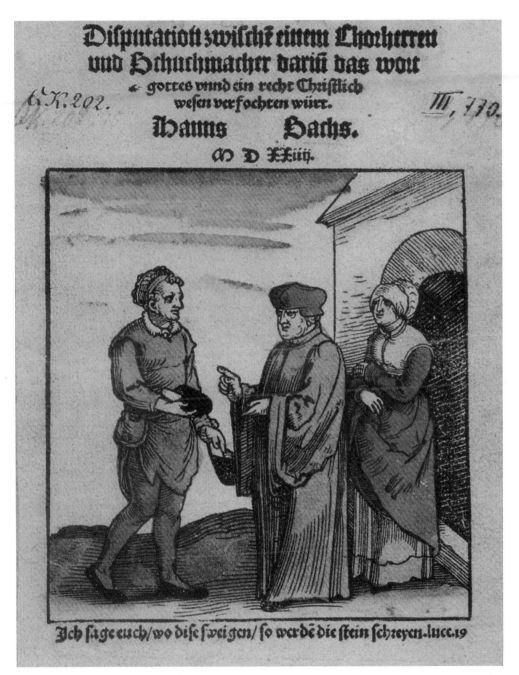

Dispntation zwischt einem Chorherren und Schuchmacher darin das wort gottes vnnd ein recht Christlich wesen verfochten würt.

Hanns Sachs.

M D XXiiij.

Ich sage euch/wo dise sweigen/ so werdē die stein schreyen.luce.19

Plate G. Lay people know best! Dialogues in which peasants or artisans got the better of the clergy were common during the early Reformation. This woodcut, by the popular Hans Sachs of Nuremberg (1494–1574), himself a shoemaker, shows a cobbler taking on a cathedral canon and fronts a pamphlet which went into ten editions in 1524 alone. Note the cleric's "cook" in the background. The Lucan verse reads: "I tell you, if these be silent, the very stones will cry out."

Plate H. The sacred city. This oldest known depiction of Nuremberg, which depicts the Saint Lawrence Church towering over the city, stands above the Krell altar within the church itself. It reminded worshippers that their worship had to do with the whole of their life and that the life of the city was accountable to God. The sixteenth-century Reformations inherited this profound conviction.

in about 1500 and almost 400 by about 1700. They held processions and feasts; engaged in penitential flagellation; handed out charity to the poor; conducted funerary services for their members; purchased candles, furnishings, and art for churches; administered hospitals and orphanages; and supported local shrines and altars. Some confraternities specialized in praying for souls in purgatory, either for specific individuals or the anonymous mass of all souls. Some were established by and associated with specific craft guilds. In England they were generally associated with a parish, so are called parish guilds, parish fraternities, or lights; by the late Middle Ages, they were financially responsible for keeping their parish church clean and repaired and for supplying it with candles and other liturgical objects.

Membership in a confraternity gave a man spiritual, social, and charitable benefits—and in some cases political ones as well, for some confraternities were limited to and thus connected to members of the elite. Before the Reformation in the English town of Coventry, for example, only men who were members of the Trinity Guild could hold an office in the city government. In sixteenth-century Portugal, nobles and other wealthy men were often members of the Misericordia confraternities supported by the monarchy. These groups were free of control by the bishops, and they monopolized most charitable activities. Jesuits relied on confraternities organized under their auspices, called Marian sodalities, for financial and political support in their charitable, educational, and missionary activities. Some of these, such as the French Congregation of the Holy Sacrament, were secret bodies of courtiers and officials who provided support for the monarchy as well as engaging in devotional and charitable activities. Most men in confraternities were not members of the elite, of course, but the groups still gave them regular opportunities to reinforce their devotional life, express their faith outwardly, assist others, and socialize with their peers.

Across Europe, women had fewer opportunities to establish, join, or lead confraternities than did men. Some confraternities did allow female members, but women could not become officers in mixed-sex groups. There were a few all-female confraternities, often dedicated to the Rosary, the Virgin Mary, Saint Anne (the mother

Confraternities

In 1547, a group of women in Bologna, Italy, staged a public protest against their exclusion from the confraternity of S. Maria della Pietà, which supervised a very popular public shrine that held an image of the virgin Mary. The women practiced their devotions at the shrine but wanted to be allowed to join the confraternity as well. Their protest achieved this to a degree, because they gained their own subordinate company within the confraternity. But it was a hollow victory. From the thirteenth through the fifteenth centuries women had been fully integrated as members into Bolognese confraternities (though without authority to hold office). In the fifteenth century, they were shut out as "temptresses." After the Pietà protest, women were brought back into many confraternities, but always in these "separate but equal" subgroups. The general statutes of the confraternity give one version of the events, and the separate statutes for the women's company give a slightly different version.

The men's version reads:

Our company was formed under the emblem of . . . the Madonna della Pietà in 1502, under the pontificate of Julius II [sic], in our city of Bologna. . . . The image was found in an old ruined house by the city wall by some young girls, and from them it was bought by some pious and devout men. They fixed it here with highest devotion, whereupon a great devotion began, with infinite favors, miracles, and good deeds that Christ performed here for them in order to ensure that this holy place would be visited by many. For which reason the devotion grew with great alms . . . such that in the shortest time there was built the oratory and the portico to the amazement and wonder of all. A little afterwards Francia, a most famous painter in those times, made the picture of the middle altar with beautiful ornament. And because the Blessed Virgin in this place demonstrated gracious favor as much to one as to the other sex, many honored and celebrated it. Many women by their particular devotion gathered together and demanded

Continues on next page

of the Virgin), or another female saint. The best studied of these have been women's parish guilds in England right before the Reformation. These groups—often specified as the "wives' guild" or the "maidens' guild"—held dances, ales, and collections to raise money to repair church buildings and altars, dressed statues and images in special clothing or jewelry for feast days, and kept the church supplied with clean rushes and altar cloths. They were led by a warden picked from among their own members, who was often from one of the more prominent families in the parish. Service as a guild warden did not lead to higher offices for women the way it often did for the young men who headed the parish "younglings guilds" for unmarried men, but it was still a way for women to demonstrate both their piety and their administrative skill. Women's parish guilds often disappear from the records when lights and images were prohibited in English churches in 1536, as they no longer had a reason to collect money, and they were suppressed, along with other similar groups, by the Chantries Act of 1547.

On the continent, women more often appear as beneficiaries of the confraternities' welfare measures than as members. Many confraternities provided dowries that would allow poor girls to marry or enter a convent. (Convents generally required a payment upon entrance, though this was usually less than a woman was expected to provide as a dowry on marriage.) Alms for the deserving poor were often targeted to aged, ill, or poverty-stricken widows, who were the poorest group in any city. Confraternities in Italian cities opened institutions for repentant prostitutes (*convertite*), and also asylums for women who were felt to be at risk of turning to prostitution or losing their honor, such as orphans, poor unmarried women and widows, or battered wives. In Catholic theory marriage was indissoluble, but in practice such asylums offered women who had been abandoned or victimized by their husbands a respectable place to live, an alternative that was unavailable in Protestant areas.

Continued from previous page

that they too be numbered among those of the confraternity in service of the Madonna. This was graciously granted by a public vote of the whole confraternity, as it appears in their books. . . .

—From the Prologue to the 1600 Statutes of the Confraternity of S. Maria della Pietà (Bologna), Archivio di Stato di Bologna, Fondo Demaniale, 10/7696, #4, fol. 3r.

The women's version reads:

The above mentioned women with proper permission entered the oratory, and in order to make their petition elected Mona Lucia, wife and consorte of M. Guaspare Bolza. They gathered together before Daily Office, and Mona Lucia on behalf of all her sisters demanded first of God on high, and then of the officials and men gathered, that they also be counted under the mantle of the virgin Mary, and that they be able to gather in this holy place to her service, honor, and glory, and to do all that the statutes commanded of them. And hearing all this, the men put it to a vote and all the votes were in favor, and so they accepted them as good mothers and sisters. The women then asked the men to give them a head and guide to keep them from error, and after prayer and by the will of God, they elected and confirmed the above mentioned Lucia for the whole of the following year of 1548. . . .

—From the Prologue to the 1600 Statutes of the Women's Company of the Confraternity of S. Maria della Pietà (Bologna), Archivio di Stato di Bologna, Fondo Demaniale, 10/7696, #3, fol. 2r. Translations by Nicholas Terpstra.

WOMEN'S RELIGIOUS ORDERS AND CONGREGATIONS

Along with confraternities, new religious orders were established and older orders reinvigorated during the Catholic Reformation. Catholic men and women felt God had called them to oppose Protestants directly through missionary work and to carry out active service to the world in schools and hospitals. Older religious orders like the Franciscans and Dominicans and new orders like the Jesuits provided opportunities for men to engage in one or both of these kinds of activities, and women attempted to do this as well. Angela Merici, for example, founded the Company of Saint Ursula, a group of lay single women and widows dedicated to serving the poor, the ill, orphans, and war victims, earning their own living through teaching or weaving. Merici received papal approval in 1535; the pope saw her group as a counterpart to the large number of men's lay confraternities and societies that were being founded in Italy as part of the movement to reform the church.

Similar groups of laywomen dedicated to charitable service began to spring up in other cities of Italy, Spain, and France, and in 1541, Isabel Roser decided to go one step further and ask for papal approval for an order of religious women with a similar mission. Roser had been an associate of Ignatius Loyola, the founder of the Jesuits, in Barcelona. She saw her group as a female order of Jesuits that, like the Jesuits, would not be cut off from the world but would devote itself to education, care of the sick, and assistance to the poor, and in so doing win converts back to Catholicism. This was going too far, however. Loyola was horrified at the thought of religious women in constant contact with laypeople, and Pope Paul III refused to grant his approval. Despite this, Roser's group continued to grow in Rome and in the Netherlands, where they spread Loyola's teaching through the use of the Jesuit catechism.

The Council of Trent, the church council that met between 1545 and 1563 to define what Catholic positions would be on matters of doctrine and discipline, reaffirmed the necessity of cloister for all women religious that had first been stipulated in the papal bull *Periculosa* in the late twelfth century. Enforcement of this decree came slowly, however, for several reasons. First, women's communities themselves fought it, ignored it, or subverted it; as in the fourth example with which this chapter opens, they remained informal groups and did not affiliate themselves with any religious order. Followers of Isabel Roser, for example, were still active into the seventeenth century, for in 1630, Pope Urban VIII published a bull to suppress them, reporting that they were recruiting members and building communities despite the lack of papal approval. Second, church officials themselves recognized the value of the services performed by such communities, particularly in the area of girls' education and care of the sick. Well after Trent, Carlo Borromeo, a reforming archbishop in Milan, invited in members of the Company of Saint Ursula and transformed the group from one of laywomen into one of religious who lived communally, though they still were not cloistered. From Milan, the Ursulines spread throughout the rest of Italy and into France and began to focus completely on the education of girls. Gradually, the Ursuline houses were ordered to accept cloistering, take solemn vows, and put themselves under the authority of their local bishop, however. They were allowed to continue to teach girls, but now only within the confines of a convent. No nuns were sent to the foreign missions for any public duties, though once colonies were established in the New World and Asia, cloistered convents quickly followed.

Beginning in the seventeenth century, Catholic laywomen in some parts of Europe were slowly able to create what had been so forcibly forbidden to religious women—a community of women with an active mission out in the world. In the parts of the Netherlands that became Protestant, convents were generally closed, their assets liquidated, and the nuns who had lived in them given a small pension from these funds. Though some returned to their families, others continued to live together in small, informal domestic groups of five or six. Because Catholic ceremonies and organizations were banned, these women, called *kloppen* or *geestelijke maagden* (holy maidens), kept their religious life private. From land-ownership records and family genealogies, however, we know that they lived together or near one another long after areas became officially Protestant and that new women joined the groups. They supported themselves from family money or the production of lace or embroidery, and they devoted themselves to charitable activities, such as care for the ill and orphans.

Many were members of wealthy and prominent upper-class families who had only slowly accepted the Reformation, so they were supported by their families in their decision to remain unmarried.

Kloppen may have thought of themselves as women religious, but they were officially laywomen, so were not required to follow rules about cloister. The same was true with the Daughters of Charity, a much larger group begun by Vincent de Paul and Louise de Marillac (Mademoiselle de Gras) in the 1630s. Though both founders privately thought of the group as a religious community, they realized that outwardly maintaining lay status was the only thing that would allow them to serve the poor and ill. The Daughters took no public vows, did not wear religious habits, and constantly stressed that they would work only where invited by a bishop or priest. This subversion of the rules was successful, for the Daughters of Charity received papal approval and served as the model for other women's communities that emphasized educating the poor or girls; by 1700, numerous teaching and charitable "congregations" were found throughout Catholic Europe. They explicitly used the Virgin Mary as their model, stressing that she, too, had served as a missionary when she had visited her cousin Elizabeth during Elizabeth's pregnancy with John the Baptist, revealing to Elizabeth that they would both give birth to extraordinary sons.

The Daughters of Charity and similar congregations came to be financially supported by expanded and reinvigorated women's confraternities, in the same way that men's confraternities backed the Jesuits. Through a confraternity, wealthy women supported a congregation financially and sometimes engaged in charitable works themselves. By 1700, then, congregations and confraternities provided women as well as men in Catholic areas with opportunities for companionship, devotional practices, and charitable service. The women's confraternities were less tied to politics than were men's, but membership in some of them was linked to social prominence and family standing just as it was for men. By 1700, well-to-do Protestant women in some areas also engaged in charitable activities as members of a group, such as the female regents of the old men's home in Haarlem portrayed so vividly by the Dutch painter Frans Hals.

Letter from Louise de Marillac (Mademoiselle de Gras) to Vincent de Paul, April 1650

Louise de Marillac and Vincent de Paul founded the Daughters of Charity, a women's community dedicated to service of the poor. In this letter, de Marillac discusses some of the issues facing the Daughters and describes a meeting she has just had with the Procurator General, an appointee of the king, explaining why she wants the Daughters of Charity to be a secular company and not a religious order.

My Most Honored Father, . . .

Yesterday I had an opportunity to see the Procurator General. He did me the honor of receiving me most courteously. He immediately asked me if I was there concerning some business he had at hand. I told him that I had come to refresh his memory on the matter. He asked me if we considered ourselves regular or secular. I told him that we aspired only to the latter. He told me that such a thing was without precedent. I cited for him Madame de Villeneuve's Daughters [the Daughters of the Cross, another secular congregation founded earlier] and pointed out to him that they go everywhere. He said many good things about the Company and added that he did not disapprove of our plan. However, he said that something of such importance merited much thought. I expressed my joy that he felt as he did about the matter, and I begged him, if he thought that the Company was unworthy to be, or for some reason should not be continued, to destroy it entirely. But if he considered it good, I said that we begged him to establish it on a solid foundation. I explained that it was this thought that had motivated us to give it a trial for at least 12 or 15 years, and that during this period, by the grace of God, no insurmountable obstacles have appeared. He replied, "Let me reflect on this, I do not say for months, but at least for a few weeks." He took the trouble to escort us to our carriage and showed us great cordiality in the courtyard. He asked us to extend his very humble greetings to you. He added that he would consider himself a usurer if he accepted the very humble gratitude that we offered him for the honor he shows to all our sisters when they dare to approach him with their needs for the poor galley slaves or for the little children.

—From *Spiritual Writings of Louise de Marillac: Correspondence and Thoughts,* ed. and trans. Sr. Louise Sullivan, S.C. (New York: New City Press, 1991), 317–18.

SIMILARITIES AND DIFFERENCES

This essay has highlighted ways in which men's and women's experiences as Christians differed from one another in Reformation Europe. Over the last thirty years, historians have focused their attention on the lives of women far more than they did in the preceding centuries of historical study, and they have found that there is no historical development in which the experiences of men and women are the same. Research has also made clear, however, that social class, urban or rural location, age, and personal characteristics interacted with gender to shape people's experiences, in the realm of religion and in every other area of life. Thus, though they were both Catholic, a wealthy recusant woman in England and a poor peasant woman in southern Italy had very different spiritual lives. The recusant woman read religious texts, celebrated Mass regularly, and perhaps discussed her faith with the well-educated priest she was hiding, while the peasant woman attended church sporadically with a priest who knew no Latin and worked in his own fields the rest of the week. Similarly, Protestantism was a very different matter for a prosperous Lutheran or Anglican merchant, sitting in a family pew surrounded by his wife and children listening to a pastor he had helped pick extol obedience to earthly authorities from what it was for a poor Anabaptist weaver whose family had been driven from place to place by religious persecution, worshiping secretly in a barn.

This variety in experience makes it impossible to generalize about the impact of the Protestant or Catholic Reformation on all women, or on all men. It is also much easier for us to assess what people were told or ordered to do, or how they expressed their religious ideas outwardly, than it is for us to understand the inner beliefs of ordinary Christians, the vast majority of whom could not read and write. What we can safely say, however, is that any expression of those beliefs was shaped by ideas and norms about the proper roles of women and men. With only a tiny number of exceptions, those norms prescribed a superior role for men and an inferior role for women, a hierarchy that was understood to be rooted in Christian scripture, along with other types of authorities, such as Greek philosophy and Roman law. The Reformation shattered the institutional unity of Western Christianity, but it did not seriously challenge this hierarchy of gender. It would take at least another five hundred years for the egalitarian possibilities of Christianity to begin to be explored, and it is hard to say when, or if, Christians will ever agree on exactly what the proper balance between equality and difference should be. The power of the pope, the balance between faith and works, and the proper age for baptism—all issues that led sixteenth-century Christians to kill each other—seem, by contrast, very minor concerns.

FOR FURTHER READING

Blickle, Peter. *From the Communal Reformation to the Revolution of the Common Man.* Translated by Beat Kümin. Leiden: Brill, 1998.

Carlson, Eric Joseph. *Marriage and the English Reformation.* Oxford: Blackwell, 1994.

Crawford, Patricia. *Women and Religion in England: 1500–1720.* New York: Routledge, 1993.

Cressy, David. *Birth, Marriage, and Death: Ritual, Religion, and the Life-Cycle in Tudor and Stuart England.* Oxford: Oxford University Press, 1997.

Diefendorf, Barbara. *From Penitence to Charity: Pious Women and the Catholic Reformation in Paris.* New York: Oxford University Press, 2004.

Harrington, Joel. *Reordering Marriage and Society in Reformation Germany.* Cambridge: Cambridge University Press, 1995.

Karant-Nunn, Susan C. *The Reformation of Ritual: An Interpretation of Early Modern Germany.* London: Routledge, 1997.

Mayes, David. *Communal Christianity: The Life and Loss of a Peasant Vision in Early Modern Germany.* Leiden: Brill, 2004.

Rapley, Elizabeth. *The Dévotes: Women and Church in Seventeenth-Century France.* Montreal: McGill-Queen's University Press, 1990.

Roper, Lyndal. *The Holy Household: Women and Morals in Reformation Augsburg.* Oxford: Clarendon, 1989.

Terpstra, Nicholas. *Lay Confraternities and Civic Religion in Renaissance Bologna.* Cambridge: Cambridge University Press, 1995.

Wiesner-Hanks, Merry E. *Christianity and Sexuality in the Early Modern World: Regulating Desire, Reforming Practice.* London: Routledge, 2000.

LEAVING THE WORLD

CHAPTER SEVEN

The Reformations of the sixteenth century changed much about people's lives, but they could not alter one inexorable fact: everybody dies. For the peoples of late medieval and early modern Europe, Death was a much more frequent visitor than he has since become, at least in the developed West. What historians have termed the "mortality regime" of premodern Europe translates into human experience as a regular sequence of bereavements and as uncertainty about one's own prospects for extended time on this earth.

Average life expectancy was barely thirty, a figure dragged sharply down by the heart-wrenching incidence of infant mortality: one in four children failed to make their first birthday, and one in two died before their tenth. Surviving children were quite likely to come under the authority of a stepparent; marriages were dissolved by death as frequently as they are today by divorce, and remarriage was common and expected. In a world without antibiotics or reliably effective sanitation, influenza, smallpox, typhoid, and dysentery were regular and lethal callers (particularly in towns). Yet more frightening was the plague, never quite as calamitous as during the first major outbreak of 1348–1349, but bad enough. A quarter of London's population died in 1563, and nearly as many did so in 1603 and again in 1665. In such visitations contemporaries could not help seeing the hand of God. The impact of disease was periodically exacerbated by harvest failure and resultant famine. Across Europe the rich did not starve, but the poor did in the "hungry" decades of the 1590s and 1660s.

In the face of sometimes almost unimaginable suffering, how did ordinary people cope? Some historians have suggested they did so by hardening their hearts, making little emotional investment in relationships with spouses or with young children, until the rigors of the mortality regime began to ease in the eighteenth century. Not just common sense but a wealth of surviving evidence work against this view. It was precisely because grief could be so intensely felt that making religious sense of death was both a cultural and psychological necessity. The medieval Church had spent a long time getting its answers prepared. It could not prevent or stave off death, but it did provide lay Christians both with a "map" for navigating the realms beyond death and with detailed sets of instructions for how to die and how to remember the dead. Yet over the course of the sixteenth century, parishioners throughout Protestant Europe (and in many areas that remained Catholic) would be taught that most of this guidance was wrong, indeed literally damnable. If theology matters to ordinary people at any time, it must surely do so here, in the act of contemplating the fate of loved ones after their death or of peering through the veil to try to catch a glimpse of one's own eternal destiny. The aim of this chapter is to survey the prescriptive advice offered to laypeople in the Reformation era about how they should approach the business of death and dying, and also (a much harder task) to attempt to gauge their responses to it—the degree to which such teachings were "internalized," and whether some spoke louder than others to laypersons' aspirations and concerns. We will begin by attempting to reconstruct the approach to the "management" of death that the reformers so resolutely rejected.

THE GOOD DEATH BEFORE THE REFORMATION

It is 1500, or thereabouts. We are in northern France, midland England, or southwest Germany, where a man (note that the rituals were the same for men and women) lies in bed waiting for death. He is at home, not in a hospital. He has lain there some weeks already and sees a regular string of visitors from among neighbors and kindred. If he is a person of any substance, he has already summoned a scribe, most likely the local priest, to take down his last will. There are matters to be settled—the jointure, or sum out of his estate to be paid to his widow; the disposal of domestic animals or trade tools; arrangements for the education or wardship of his children. But the will is by no means a purely secular document; it opens with an invocation of the name of God or the Trinity, and the first item to be bequeathed is the testator's own soul, typically commended to "God my creator, to the very mild and glorious Virgin Mary his mother, to Saint Michael the archangel, to Saint Peter and Saint Paul, and to all the blessed company of heaven."[1] The will also contains detailed instructions for helping the soul on its way to these recipients. We will return to this shortly.

As the man's condition worsens, the priest is summoned again; he sets off from the church accompanied by an acolyte bearing crucifix and candle. Passersby fall to their knees at the priest's approach, not out of respect for the clergy, but because they know that in the box he carries is the true body of Jesus Christ under the form of bread. The church bell may also be set ringing, to encourage all in the vicinity to pray for the dying man in the hour of his approaching death. On arriving at the deathbed the priest's responsibility is to lead the dying person through the performance of the "last rites," though these might equally be termed "last rights," for they are the entitlement of any faithful Christian.

The Church offered no less than three of its sacraments to men and women at the very end of their lives, in extremis. One of these was the ritual anointing ("extreme unction") of the sick. Oil was placed on eyes, ears, nostrils, mouth, hands, and feet as a dedication of the senses to God. Here we might suspect a lack of perfect fit between the understanding of the man receiving the anointing and the authorities who had prescribed it. Many laypeople seem to have viewed extreme unction itself as an irrevocable crossing of the boundary between the world of the living and the dead. If (as sometimes happened) the recipient subsequently recovered, popular opinion doubted whether the sacrament could be administered again; the authorities had to insist that it could and that such a person was not barred permanently from the consumption of meat or bound to a life of chastity.[2]

The other deathbed sacraments were a last confession of sins and the administration of communion, here called the *Viaticum* (literally "that taken on a journey". Props were employed to assist the dying to make a good end. The crucifix is held up before our dying man as a comforting reminder that Christ had died for his sins, holy water is sprinkled on his body, and a lighted candle is placed in his hands. The comfort is requisite rather than routine, for the hour of death is a moment of tense drama when salvation can be won or lost. Here a sinful life could be redeemed by full and heartfelt penitence; conversely, a failure to confess or a giving way to feelings of despair could cast the most hitherto pious Christian into the jaws of hell. We must presume that our dying man is able to answer the priest's questions and to show and feel remorse for his sins. It could be touch-and-go. A London woman, Alice Gysby, dying in 1538 with a ruptured tumor on her neck was unable to receive the *Viaticum* or even look upon it. Her female friends gathered round the bedside, calling out, "what, will ye die like a hellhound and a beast, not remembering your maker?" In the end, she was able to knock herself on the breast and hold up her hands. It was enough to reassure her friends that she had died a good death.[3]

The presence not just of the priest but of such (supportively) hectoring neighbors reminds us that the bedchamber was a busy, public place rather than a haven of quiet reflection. It was crowded in another sense too, as it was universally believed that a parallel set of spectators and protagonists participated in the deathbed struggle, unseen by the humans present or visible only to the dying themselves. The pain and anxiety that were an inescapable part of the business of dying rendered humans particularly susceptible to the wiles of the devil. He would be present in person, or would dispatch some of his demons, to tempt the dying to despair and thus win possession of their departing souls. But ranged against him were a small army of heavenly helpers: saints (especially the Blessed Virgin Mary); angels, particularly Satan's ancient foe Saint Michael; and the guardian angel who had been watching over the person from his or her birth.

This struggle was the theme of the *ars moriendi* (art of dying), a how-to handbook that enjoyed an extraordinary diffusion in the fifteenth and early sixteenth centuries, translated into all the main European languages. Here the deathbed was the site of a cosmic struggle between forces of good and evil, the angels encouraging the dying to overcome the temptations of the devil, and contending with Satan's forces for custody of the soul. The impact of the text was undoubtedly strengthened by a dramatic set of accompanying woodcuts, depicting angels and devils in tense confrontation with each other across the body of *moriens* (the dying one). These culminated in a scene depicting the final rout of the demons and the reception of the soul (invariably portrayed as a small naked person) by attendant angels (see fig. 7.1).

Our protagonist has successfully negotiated the hazards of the deathbed; his soul is saved and destined for heaven. His body meanwhile is carried in procession from his home to the church and thence (after the celebration of a requiem Mass) to the grave. If he is a man of real importance, he might expect burial within the walls of the church itself; more likely he will be interred within the consecrated ground of the churchyard, where his body will lie until it is reunited with his soul at the time of the last judgment. But these rituals of the deathbed and of the disposal of the body are only the first steps in confronting and negotiating the challenges of death. There is the not-so-small matter of purgatory to overcome.

Purgatory was one of the great imaginative achievements of the medieval mind. It was a scholastic doctrine but not a remote or aloof one. Indeed, in a very real sense theological thinking about purgatory had crystallized precisely because of a strong popular intuition that God would not condemn the great bulk of humankind to eternal torment in hell, just because they were not good enough to merit immediate entry into heaven. Purgatory fitted into the late medieval calculus of sin and salvation something like this: Christ's atonement on the cross (collectively) and the sacrament of baptism (individually) freed humans from the taint of Adam and Eve's "original" sin and made it possible for people to gain access to heaven. Their continuing propensity to commit serious ("mortal") sins, however, created a further barrier. Fortunately, the Church on earth was delegated authority to forgive these sins via the sacrament of penance (hence the concern with confession on the deathbed). But medieval authorities drew a distinction between the guilt attached to a mortal sin and the penalty or satisfaction that was still due to God when the guilt had been removed. Such penances as the priest might impose in confession constituted only a fraction of the satisfaction due; the remainder

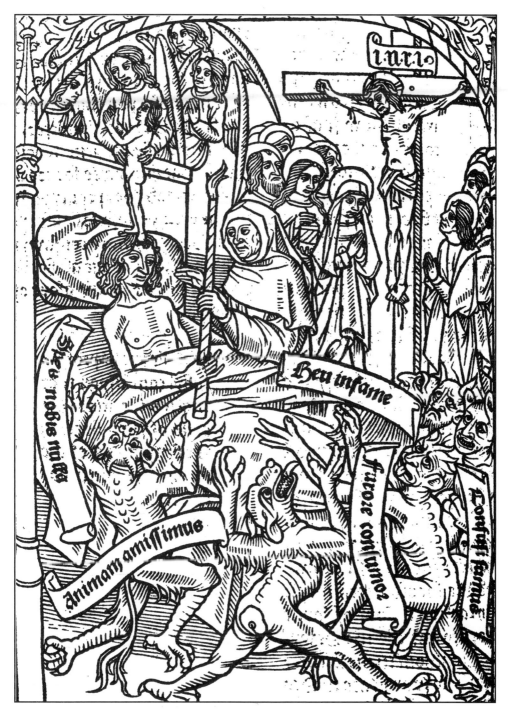

Fig. 7.1. The deathbed struggle is won. From *The Art of Good Lywyng and Good Deying* (1503).

(along with the punishment for less serious or "venial" sins) would have to be paid off after death in purgatory.

Official Church formulations (such as that supplied by the Council of Florence in 1439) were remarkably nonforthcoming about what sort of place purgatory was and what exactly souls could expect to find there. But the vacuum was filled by a flood of vernacular preaching and popular devotional books. It is ironic that to us the most familiar late medieval depiction of purgatory should be the one in Dante's *Divina Commedia*—a stately, almost liturgical ascent up the slopes of Mount Purgatorio. Overwhelmingly, preachers and writers projected a different image: purgatory was a place of intense fiery torment, hardly distinguishable from hell and often imagined as in physical proximity to it under the earth (see fig. 7.2). Theologians' qualifications about the nature of "time" in purgatory were too

Fig. 7.2. Souls in Purgatory. From *This Prymer of Salisbury Use* (1535).

abstruse even for many churchmen to master, and there is little doubt that most Christians expected the tariff due in the "prison" of purgatory to be measurable in tens, hundreds, or thousands of years. Indeed, by issuing indulgences (certificates remitting part or all of the satisfaction due for sin) and expressing them in terms of "days" and "years" equivalent to earthly penance, the authorities themselves encouraged the perception that the experience of purgatory was a recognizably temporal one.

Indulgences (which were first made available to assist souls in purgatory by a papal bull of 1476) had, of course, a central role to play in the unraveling of Catholic understandings of death in the early and middle decades of the sixteenth century, but here they serve as a reminder that Christians were not helpless or friendless before the prospect of their fiery postmortem purgation. In conjunction with its theology of penance and purgatory, the medieval Church had elaborated the notion of a "communion of saints," the compelling idea that all Christian souls, whether saints in heaven, sinners on earth, or suffering in purgatory, were inextricably linked to each other, and that the living had the ability, and the duty, to ease the sufferings of the dead.

The Florentine decree stressed the importance of "the sacrifice of the Mass and prayer and alms and the other works of piety." But more vivid testimony to the necessity of intercession for the souls in purgatory might be provided by the dead themselves. Late medieval Europe was awash with stories of ghosts appearing to describe the sufferings they experience in purgatory and to request masses and prayers. One such work, *On the Appearance of Souls after Death*, by the fifteenth-century German monk Jacob of Jüterbog survives in over eighty manuscripts and thirteen printed editions from before 1520.[1] Cynical historians might suggest that the Church had a vested interest in publicizing, if not inventing, these tales as a means of buttressing its doctrinal and practical authority (a charge made by Protestants during the Reformation). Yet the evidence suggests that the "exempla" or illustrative stories in preachers' sermons were usually at the end of a chain of transmission starting with an experienced supernatural event. Church teaching about purgatory and ancient folklore about the activity of ghosts came together and reinforced one another.

Small wonder, then, that if we return to our dying man's will, we encounter a distinct concern with the "health" of his soul. There are stipulations about the funeral and where alms are to be distributed to the poor (almsgiving was in itself a meritorious work, and the poor would be expected to pray for their benefactor). There are

The Pope Makes Indulgences Available to the Dead (1476)

Our aim is that the salvation of souls may be secured above all at that time when they most need the intercession of others and are least able to help themselves. We wish by our Apostolic authority to draw on the treasury of the Church and to succour the souls in purgatory who died united with Christ through love and whose lives have merited that such intercessions should now be offered through an Indulgence of this kind. With the longings of such great paternal affection . . . we grant by concession and indulgence as follows:

If any parents, friends or other Christians are moved by obligations of piety towards these very souls who are exposed to the fire of purgatory . . . let them during the stated period of ten years give a fixed amount or value of money, as laid down by its dean and chapter or by our own collector, for the repair of the church of Saints, paying either in person at the Church or by duly accredited messengers. . . .

—From Sixtus IV's bull *Salvator Noster*, quoted in *Martin Luther*, ed. E. G. Rupp and Benjamin Drewery, Documents of Modern History (London: Edward Arnold, 1970), 14.

also payments for masses to be said, either for a set period or, if he is very wealthy, in perpetuity as the result of an endowment of land or property. The resultant institution, sometimes located in a separate chapel, was in English called a chantry, and its incumbent a chantry priest.

Perhaps our man was what we would today term an informed consumer, weighing up the claims made by various groups within the Church for the special power of their own intercessions. Thus the services requested might be masses focusing devotion on the Five Wounds of Christ or masses of the Virgin Mary. Or he might have turned to the friars, who made claims for the efficacy of so-called trentals—a sequence of thirty requiem masses to be said in the month after death. Some religious orders encouraged the idea that to be buried wearing their habit or cowl was a sure passport to Paradise. A sensible testator, however, did not put all his faith in such quick-fix solutions. The surest way to shorten the pains of purgatory was to secure the prayers of the living on a long- rather than short-term basis. In other words, it was vital to be "remembered."

Memorial services were often repeated on the anniversary of death in order to help fix the departed person in the memory of the community. Gifts to churches—of chalices, vestments, or stained-glass windows—were inscribed with the donor's name for precisely the same purpose. Those who could afford it sought to leave behind them a permanent memorial in stone or brass, not so much for vainglory (though that may have played its part) as to retain a claim on the memory, and prayers, of the living community. Such monuments were invariably inscribed with "*ora pro anima* . . ." ("pray for the soul of . . ."), and some tugged at the heartstrings with depictions of a once-proud knight or merchant as a helpless rotting cadaver (see fig. 7.3). The very poor rested content with an annual collective

Fig. 7.3. The tomb of John Baret (c. 1450), St. Mary's Church, Bury St. Edmunds, England. Photo: St. Mary's Church / V&A Images.

commemoration on the feast of All Souls, when the churchyard would be blessed, the bells rung, and, in some places, food laid out on the graves to succor dead ancestors.

Not just funerals, then, but a great deal of pre-Reformation religious practice was driven by a "commemorative impulse." It has been said that late medieval Catholicism was essentially "a cult of the living in the service of the dead." It may be more accurate, however, to think in terms of a mutual exchange between the living and the dead, a circular flow of favors in which the former offered spiritual assistance in return for the material benefits of alms and well-equipped churches. This pattern was found across Europe, but not identically replicated. It may be significant that we have made our notional testator into a northern European: based on the surviving evidence of wills, concerns about negotiating one's way out of purgatory seem to have been more intensely felt in Germany, France, and England than in Italy and Spain. Conceivably, this has implications for how the Reformation itself was received by the people in these different territories.

So far, so good. But the "good death" we have outlined—from the appropriate demeanor on the deathbed, through the correct performance of funeral rituals, to the devout intercession of those passing by an engraved monument—was an ideal and an aspiration, whose full performance was not always possible. In times of plague, of course, there was no sustained deathbed "performance," and bodies would be dumped unceremoniously in a collective pit. Some scholars indeed have argued that the elaborate concern with individual memory developing in the later Middle Ages was itself a reaction to the horrors of the Black Death.

But even in more settled times, the shadow of the "bad death" might hover over a community. Sudden, accidental death, without the opportunity to confess and repent, was widely feared—a glimpse into pre-Reformation mentalities on this score is provided by the poignant scene in *Hamlet* where the Prince determines not to kill his uncle when he comes upon him at his "orisons" (prayers), but to wait until such time as his soul is unprepared. Priests, who through negligence or absence from their cure failed to attend the dying, aroused the sharpest resentment. Given the high incidence of postnatal mortality, it was also imperative that they be on hand to baptize infants within a day or two of their birth. Church teaching held that in an emergency, lay, even female, baptism was valid, but people had understandable doubts. In a Devon (England) parish in the mid-1530s, a child was reported to have died "unchristened except that which the midwife did to it."[6] Anxieties over the salvation of infants exacerbated the grief of bereaved parents, and the Church was able to offer comfort, of a sort. Children who had died unbaptized but without the capacity willfully to sin were not in hell but in limbo, a place without God but also without pain. Unbaptized infants did not return as ghosts, but it is striking how many medieval ghost stories begin with a "bad death."

Indeed, it is hard to avoid the conclusion that to many of the laity one of the prime functions of a "correctly" performed death was to ensure that the soul would be at rest and not return as a potentially dangerous revenant. There was a strong popular belief, not supported by official teaching, that ghosts sought to seize a companion to bring back with them into the realms of the dead. These concerns are particularly in evidence around the ultimate bad death, that of the suicide, someone who by definition had despaired of God's mercy. Suicides were denied burial in consecrated ground and were usually interred face down (so that they would not rise at the day of resurrection), with a stake through the body (to prevent the soul from wandering), and often at a crossroads (to confuse it if it did escape).

There was, in other words, an element of fear as well as compassion characterizing the relationship of the living with the dead. Some scholars would go further and, again echoing contemporary Protestant claims, be prepared to assert that the whole edifice of purgatory and intercession was built upon an unhealthily intense fear of punishment in the life to come. Caution is required. The exact motivations with which laypeople endowed masses, left alms to the poor, and gave instructions for funeral monuments are usually opaque to us. It is probably safest to assert that belief in purgatory, and the possibility of effective intercession, allowed most people to approach death along a narrow path perched between anxiety and hope, fear and confidence. The overscrupulous, however, might easily lose their footing, and it is possible to find examples of overwrought testators demanding to have thousands of masses performed immediately "it may be perceived that my soul should be from my body separate."[7]

How might people of this frame of mind react to the suggestion that purgatory was all a fraud and a fantasy? To see the peoples of early sixteenth-century Europe as in some sense waiting to be "released" from the psychological burden of penance and purgatory would be both tendentious and anachronistic. But it would be equally partial not to recognize that the late medieval "way of death" imposed a price, and one that was material and economic as well as spiritual. The living had obligations to the dead that were both time-consuming and, in the form of Mass endowments, depletive of their own inheritances. Without bearing all these perspectives in view, it is difficult to understand the complex reactions of ordinary Christians to the revolutionary assault on traditional mortuary culture that exploded in the 1520s.

THE REJECTION OF PURGATORY

Martin Luther's 1517 broadside against the papal abuse of indulgences ensured that from the outset the question of purgatory would be intimately bound up with the protest against the Church. As in much else, Luther proved himself on this issue a rather cautious conservative, not feeling his way to a complete rejection of the concept of purgatory until 1530. By this point his disciples in Germany, the Netherlands, England, France, and Switzerland had already moved to make purgatory a main focus of their attack on traditional religion. At the head of the indictment sheet was the charge that purgatory was profoundly unbiblical and therefore, according to the principal of *sola scriptura,* unnecessary for salvation. The English reformer Simon Fish insisted that there was "not one word spoken of it in all holy scripture," while the Frenchman Guillaume Farel described it as "but an invention of the devil." Worse, the notion of purificatory suffering in purgatory suggested that people played some role in their own salvation, seeming to imply that the sacrifice of Christ was inadequate.

Believers in justification by faith alone asserted that the blood of Christ was the only true purgatory. But the most compelling arguments against purgatory were not always the finely calibrated theological ones. The English Lutheran William Tyndale coined the powerful catchphrase ("purgatory-pickpurse") to underline the mercenary motives of the Church in promoting the doctrine. Meanwhile, German propagandists like Pamphilius Gengenbach and Nicholas Manuel satirized the Catholic clergy in poems and plays as *Totenfresser* (feeders upon the dead). The spiritual condition of the dead could not be ameliorated by the imprecations of the living. To pray for the dead was at best useless, at worst blasphemous—a message reinforced in the second, Calvinist or Reformed wave of Protestant theology, with its insistence that God's decree had preordained all human souls to either salvation or damnation before the world was created.

As the Reformation became institutionalized across large swaths of northern Europe in the middle decades of the sixteenth century, urban and national governments acted upon these imperatives, confiscating the monasteries, chantries, and Mass endowments that had sustained prayers for the dead. Some of this wealth was reallocated for desirable civic purposes—education, care of the sick, poor relief—but much of it disappeared into government or other secular coffers, as it did in England after 1547, when parliament declared Purgatory to be a "fond" (that is, stupid) opinion.

In some parts of Europe, there was pressure to move the bodies of the dead away from the places of worship of the living, so that the latter would not feel tempted to offer intercessory prayer. Luther and other reformers pointed to the biblical practice of burial outside the city walls and, supported by public health considerations, had some success in persuading German and Swiss municipal authorities to relocate churchyards away from their traditional proximity to the church. Burial inside churches, which originally stemmed from a desire for closeness to the relics of saints and to the altars where masses were said, was viewed

---

A Protestant Satire on Catholic Intercession (1523)

Church Offerings, weekly, monthly and
, annual masses for the dead
Bring us more than enough.
Pity the hardship it inflicts upon the
    children of the givers! . . .
Indulgences lend a hand
By making men fearful of penance.
We also put a lot of stock in purgatory
(Although scripture doesn't have much
    to say about it).
The reason is that we must use every
    chance)
To scare the hell out of common
    folk. . . .
So let us plague and punish the world
For wine, grain, meat and cash
And be thankful to the dead
Who make it possible for us to fleece
    the living.
    —From Nicholas Manuel's play,
Die Totenfresser [Feeders upon the
Dead], quoted in Steven E. Ozment,
*The Reformation in the Cities: The
Appeal of Protestantism to Sixteenth-
Century Germany and Switzerland*
(New Haven: Yale University Press,
1975), 112–13.

with some suspicion throughout the Protestant world. Hostility to the practice was most marked in Calvinist Scotland, where regular enactments against it were passed at the Kirk's General Assemblies.[9] Everywhere that Protestantism took hold, the rituals of the deathbed were radically simplified: crucifix, holy water, anointing with oil were all swept away. Comportment on the deathbed remained important, but it was no longer principally an occasion for the salvation-bringing ministrations of a priest. At the same time, burial services and funeral liturgies were rewritten to remove any suggestion that participants were interceding with God on behalf of the departed.

Taken together, this package of reforms represented a remarkably revolutionary assault on deeply ingrained cultural habits. The doctrinal certainties of theologians and preachers here touched on the lives of the faithful in an unavoidably direct fashion, affecting the most intimate of relationships within the family, as well as the allocation of personal and communal resources. How did people feel on hearing that their parents were not after all in purgatory, and that they themselves were dupes for having wasted time and money believing they could help them through it? Did they react with relief and with anger at the representatives of the old Church for having deceived them so cruelly? Or were they incredulous and traumatized to discover they were now forbidden to offer the suffrages that would bring relief to their loved ones? One historian, contemplating the dissolution of the chantries, has invited us to imagine in our own society "the forcible closure of all hospices for the terminally ill."[10]

There were, of course, immediate and enthusiastic converts, demonstrating their contempt for the old order in iconoclastic words and actions. There are reports from German towns in the early 1520s of people wiping their backsides with the indulgence letters they had purchased only a short time before. A Yorkshire schoolmaster shocked the parish clerk in 1537 with the vehemence of his disavowal of traditional, familial pieties: "Thy father was a liar and is in hell, and so is my father in hell also." Even some reformers were alarmed by the incidence of radical indifference to funeral ceremony of any kind in the early years of the Reformation.

But alongside this there is much evidence of slow and grudging compliance with the new ordinances and sometimes of outright resistance. In Calvin's Geneva it was felt necessary to require pallbearers to swear an oath to avoid "superstitious" practices contrary to the Word of God. The rebels who rose in the English southwest in 1549 demanded that "every priest at his Mass pray specially for the souls in purgatory" and for good measure insisted that christenings be celebrated on weekdays as well as Sundays: they distrusted the new Protestant perception that baptism was not absolutely and formally necessary for salvation. Through to the last decades of the sixteenth century and beyond, we find English (and especially Welsh) bishops, Calvinist inspectors in Germany, and Reformed ministers in the Netherlands reciting a similar litany of abuses: wooden crosses placed on graves, use of candles at funerals and around the coffin, kneeling and praying in the presence of the corpse, excessive ringing of bells, either at the funeral or on the eve of the abrogated feast of All Souls. The relocation of burial sites was often controversial and sometimes resisted: the moving of a cemetery at Lübeck in 1629 provoked one citizen to experience an angelic vision condemning the plan.[11]

Yet to view changes to the "mortuary culture" of European peoples in the century and a half after Luther's protest against Rome solely in terms of acceptance or rejection of top-down initiatives is to adopt too rigid a framework. Lay parishioners responded to new teaching and new rituals in a variety of ways, sometimes creatively appropriating them for their own purposes. Conversely, and rather in spite of themselves, pastors often took into account the needs and capacities of the people in both the formulation and the presentation of Reformed teaching. The result was the gradual emergence of a highly variegated Protestant culture of death and commemoration, one that was obliged to address the same fundamental questions as its Catholic predecessor and that did so in sometimes strikingly similar ways.

MANAGING DEATH IN THE PROTESTANT WORLD

In Germany, England, Switzerland, and other parts of the Protestant world, the experience of the deathbed was reformed but not transformed over the course of the sixteenth century. In the first place, the aspiration to making a "good death" retained its hold over elites and common people alike. The *ars moriendi* underwent a Protestant makeover, and tracts on how to make a good end achieved the status of an art form in the hands of English Calvinist authors like Thomas Becon and William Perkins. Here the emphasis was not on any form of deathbed ritual but on the edifying—and often implausibly extended—statements of faith the dying were expected to make.

We might be inclined to regard such texts as embodying a literary ideal, remote from the experience or priorities of ordinary people. Yet some features suggest the hold of tradition and a genuine engagement with popular concerns. Protestant authors generally downplayed the notion that salvation could be won or lost on the deathbed, and some of them explicitly denied that spiritual meaning should be read into the ravings and convulsions of the terminally ill. But there was nonetheless an underlying presumption that a "good death" was the corroboration of a pious Christian life, and vice versa. If anything, the diffusion of Calvinist theology tended to heighten the significance of the dying person's demeanor—

Fig. 7.4. A Lutheran death scene. From Martin Luther, *Ain sermon vo[n] der Beraitung tzüm sterbe[n]* (1520).

courageous confrontation with death was likely a "sign" of election to eternal life; impiety or despair an indication of damnation. Another familiar note was struck by the continued presence of spiritual forces in and around the bedchamber. Protestants rejected any intercessory role for the saints, but writers on death from Luther onwards took for granted that the devil and the angels would be present to perform their accustomed roles (see fig. 7.4). When pious Englishwomen called out in extremis that they saw visions of angels coming to carry them to heaven, their words were eagerly reported by Puritan writers.[12]

In fact, the *ars moriendi* literature tends to understate the extent to which the Protestant clergy maintained a crucial role in the management of death. Most Protestant churches developed orders of worship for the visitation of the sick, and reformers like Luther and Friedrich

Myconius composed treatises instructing the clergy in how to care for the dying. In England an interest in hearing confessions of the sick, and administering communion to them (both permitted by the Prayer Book of 1559), tended to be the prerogative of a "high church" wing of the clergy, but throughout Lutheran Germany absolution and communion on the sickbed came to be the hallmark of approved pastoral practice. The inclusion in Lutheran formularies of prayers against dying unprepared, as well as official instructions to pastors to withhold the communion from those who seemed unrepentant, suggest that the fear of "sudden death" remained strong and that the authorities were prepared to work around it. But theological probity and pastoral comfort did not always neatly dovetail: a number of ministers in late sixteenth-century Saxony were ordered to administer communion to the house-bound sick, even though laypeople regarded the ritual in the way their forebears had seen extreme unction, as a portent of imminent death they were eager to defer.[13]

Offering comfort to the dying, whether with familiar ritual or with assurances about the redemptive power of Christ's death, was only one part of the pastoral equation. How were the survivors to be consoled for their loss? It is clear that the practice of intercessory prayer possessed a positive therapeutic function, allowing the bereaved to feel that they were *doing* something for the deceased and keeping them usefully occupied at the time of sharpest grief. At the same time, belief in purgatory, despite its undoubted terrors, offered an effective guarantee that the great majority of Christians were saved and would live with Christ in heaven. Could the new Protestant churches do as much?

The most pertinent question, then, was what would actually happen to the souls of the dead. There were, initially at least, no uniform answers about this from official Protestant teaching. Martin Luther proclaimed the "sleep of the soul," the idea that the dead would remain insensible and unconscious until the last judgment and resurrection of the dead. But Calvin condemned the doctrine, and most mainstream reformers gradually fell into line, particularly as "psychopannichism" (soul-sleeping) came to be associated with radical Anabaptists. But if souls went immediately to their reward, were most destined for heaven or for hell? The logic of Protestant teaching, and especially Calvinist emphasis on the elect as a favored "remnant," seemed to imply the latter. Reformed writers regularly condemned the presumptuous view that all would be saved, something they associated with ignorant country dwellers. But, then as now, preaching damnation had a limited popular appeal. In pastoral situations, even Calvinist ministers seem often to have leaned toward optimism, and an accommodation with the anxieties of the people. Clergymen seem to have been asked, as Jesus himself was, whether people would recognize their loved ones in the next life and whether there would be marriage in heaven. Christ's response that "they neither marry nor are given in marriage" (Matt. 22:30) was usually glossed over to imply that there would indeed be joyful reunions and recognitions in the afterlife. One Reformed minister in sixteenth-century Switzerland spoke of friends in heaven gathering again around their *Stammtisch* (pub regulars' table).[4]

Arguably, it was such positive assurances about the likely fate of the dead that made the loss of purgatory bearable. In practice it was implied, if seldom openly stated, that the majority of Christians could expect to be saved. The needs of the bereaved were also addressed through the retention of a fair amount of funeral ritual and ceremony, Protestants reassuring themselves with Saint Augustine's dictum that funereal pomp was rather a comfort to the living than a help to the dead. In general, the Lutherans and the outlying branches of the Reformed family in England and Eastern Europe seem to have been more hospitable to elaborate funeral ceremony than the Calvinist churches of Switzerland or Scotland. Processions, a moderate quantity of bell ringing, almsgiving to the poor, the wearing of mourning black, and, with varying degrees of official acquiescence, communal feasting were features of post-Reformation as of pre-Reformation funeral practice.

In all societies, the wealthy had a vested interest in funeral display as a public reaffirmation of the social order, something with which the church was usually ready to collude. But there was a powerful sense that even the poorest were entitled to an "honest" funeral: in many English parishes a communally owned bier and cloth covering was made available for pauper burials. The decent burial that was the "due" of the dead also continued to involve interment in the consecrated ground of the church precincts, despite the limited experiments with the relocation of urban cemeteries and the official insistence that no place on God's earth, intrinsically, was holier than any other. Burial inside churches carried on, even in Reformed territories where the religious authorities disapproved. Scottish landowners skirted the ban by erecting elaborate "burial aisles" on the side of churches, and in the Netherlands, where responsibility for the church fabric lay with the parish community not the Reformed consistory, "intramural" burial went on as before.

In confessionally divided communities, burial could become a fraught issue. French Catholics were apt to regard their cemeteries as "polluted" by the presence of the bodies of heretics; they sometimes disinterred Huguenot corpses to throw them into ditches. The Edict of Nantes (1598), which ended the first round of religious wars, assigned to the Reformed their own burial places, yet interestingly, many Huguenots seem to have retained the desire to be buried with their ancestors. Recusant Catholics in Protestant England felt the same way, burying their dead secretly at night within the parish churchyard. Before and after the Reformation, the village churchyard was the preeminent symbolic and practical communal space. Only partially encumbered with grave markers, it was a site for regular sports, fairs, and festivities, activities of which the Church authorities often disapproved but were powerless to prevent.[15]

If Protestant culture displayed a rather traditional care for the reverent disposal of the remains of the dead, it showed itself equally concerned with preserving their honorable memory among the living. It is perhaps too neat a substitution to see a pattern of *intercession* replaced by one of *commemoration* in post-Reformation Protestant Europe, but as a rough shorthand for a complex process of cultural change it has some merit. Catholic polemicists charged that Protestantism exhibited a callous disregard for the memory of the dead. Protestants denied this and often recognized that to seek to remember the departed was a natural human impulse. The challenge was to channel this into theologically acceptable directions.

One of these was the institution of the funeral sermon. Despite the fact that there was relatively little preaching at burials before the Reformation, the Swiss Reformed churches distrusted funeral sermons as a form of surrogate prayer for the dead. In England, however, even Puritan clergy rapidly came to see their utility as a means of instruction, and growing numbers were printed through the early decades of the seventeenth century. The numbers pale in comparison with Lutheran Germany, where pastors were expected to preach at every funeral, and some three hundred thousand texts survive from the early modern era. The preachers wished to edify their congregations; the congregations wished to hear the dead well spoken of. The result was the inclusion of biographies presenting the deceased as exemplars for the living. Significant numbers of these were for women, and reports of pious exhortations delivered from the deathbed had the effect, momentarily at least, of inverting the passivity and religious subservience traditionally expected of their sex.[16] A form of memorialization that continued unabated across the Reformation divide was the placing of epitaphs on tombs and monuments in churches. In Protestant lands these lost their clamorous calls for intercessory prayer but compensated with ever more detail about the virtuous life of

---

Continuity and Change in English Church Epitaphs

Brass of Thomas Gray and wife Benet, All Saints' Church, Cople, Bedfordshire, 1520:

We trust to be had in memory
As long as the parish of Cople shall last
For our benefits done to it largely,
As witness £20 with other gifts many,
Wherefore all Christian men that go by this way,
Pray for the souls of Benet and Thomas Gray.

Brass of Joanne Goddard, St. Mary's Church, Carlton, Bedfordshire, 1610:

Here lyeth her corpse entombed, which was ever from infancy to age a dying liver; her body here doth lie. No massive stone entombs her soul, her soul is Godward gone, who Godward lives with God shall live and rest; Then is her soul entombed in Abram's Breast.

Brass of Christopher Strickland, St. Mary's, Yielden, Bedfordshire, 1628:

Here lyeth the body of Christopher Strickland, gent; who lived in this parish a long time and was a very good benefactor. He died the 12th of Jan. 1628; being of the age of 80 years.
    —From G. Isherwood, *Monumental Brasses in the Bedfordshire Churches* (London: Elliott Stock, 1906), 18, 21–22, 68.

---

the deceased and, for wealthy landowners, about their lineage and titles. English epitaphs were often unashamed to assert that the soul of the departed was undoubtedly in heaven. The mass of the people, however, bore witness to a continuity of a different sort: after the Reformation as before, most graves had no permanent marker.

The suggestion is sometimes made that the Reformation severed the ties between the quick and the dead. That is too bald an assertion. What we have seen is rather a process of renegotiation of the terms of coexistence and a refashioning of the claims the dead could make on the memories and consciousness of the living. Those in the process of passing from one stage into the other still faced the ultimate ordeal and continued to be offered practical advice and ritual support in confronting it. Whether, in the end, the Protestant deathbed offered more or less comfort to the dying than its Catholic predecessor is a simply unanswerable question. In all these areas, theological and liturgical imperatives—the preoccupations of an educated elite—drove the changes and opened new questions. In practice, however, the solutions could not be arbitrarily imposed but had to work with the grain of popular sentiment in this most sensitive of pastoral arenas.

This point is illustrated by the fate of the wandering dead. Despite the abolition of purgatory, there remained, right across northern Europe, "a thick sub-stratum of Protestant popular belief about spirits, ghosts, poltergeists, restless souls."[17] The insistence of the pastors that any such apparition could only be a deceiving devil from hell or (much less likely) a messenger angel from heaven failed to convince their hearers. In the end most of the Protestant clergy came around to accepting the possibility of ghosts, even recording their appearances as anti-atheistical evidence for the immortality of the soul. In this they provided a striking example of the victory of popular intuition and deep-rooted cultural expectation over the rationalizations of intellectuals.

FOR FURTHER READING

Ariès, Philippe. *The Hour of Our Death*. Translated by Helen Weaver. London: Penguin Books, 1981.

Gordon, Bruce, and Peter Marshall, editors. *The Place of the Dead: Death and Remembrance in Late Medieval and Early Modern Europe*. Cambridge: Cambridge University Press, 2000.

Houlbrooke, Ralph. *Death, Religion and the Family in England, 1480–1750*. Oxford Studies in Social History. Oxford: Clarendon, 1998.

Koslofsky, Craig M. *The Reformation of the Dead: Death and Ritual in Early Modern Germany, 1450–1700*. Early Modern History. New York: St. Martin's, 2000.

Marshall, Peter. *Beliefs and the Dead in Reformation England*. Oxford: Oxford University Press, 2002.

FINDING THEIR VOICE

Part 3

Fig. 8.1. Title page from *To the Assembly of Common Peasantry*. The pope is depicted with his tiara on a wheel of fortune, being turned from a group described as "Romanists and Sophists" onto the waiting lances of "peasants, good Christians." Beneath the picture is the rhyme, "Who makes Switzerland grow? The greed of the lords." Image from Horst Buszello, *Der deutsche Bauernkrieg von 1525 als politische Bewegung* (Berlin: Colloquium 1969), 152.

THE DREAM
OF A JUST SOCIETY

JAMES M. STAYER

CHAPTER EIGHT

JUSTICE DIVINE AND HUMAN

In his lectures on Galatians (1516), Martin Luther set forth a central belief that sustained him in his struggle for a trusting relationship with God: justice is faith in Jesus Christ. So conceived, "justice" is not something that human beings, great or small, can struggle for; rather, it is something freely bestowed to them by their all-powerful God. Also referred to as *iustitia dei* (divine justice), this was a major concept promoted by the Reformation. Nevertheless, the Christianity of the Reformation, which made divinely bestowed justification by faith its watchword, was troubled by the obvious fact that, for whatever reason, justice was not equitably distributed among human beings. Hence, at the beginning of the Reformation, there was a struggle for divine justice, understood as *social justice*.

This struggle for justice only lasted two decades. It was correctly observed by traditional historians that the Reformation could only succeed in institutionalizing itself with the support of established political powers. These powers knew that the struggle for equitable justice was extremely disruptive. In describing the struggle for justice among Reformation Christians, I will try to combine three perspectives that are often thought to be antithetical. The first is the insistence of East German Marxist historians that, although the European Reformation as a whole cannot be labeled "revolutionary," the first stages of the Reformation in Germanic Europe did contain revolutionary elements.[1] The second is Heiko A. Oberman's conception of a "gospel of social unrest," which antedated the Wittenberg Reformation and must be distinguished from it but was nevertheless undoubtedly of a religious character.[2] The third perspective is that of the historians of "confessionalization," such as Heinz Schilling:[3] in the later sixteenth century, magistracies of all major forms of Western Christianity undertook to direct and elevate the lives of their subjects by a process of "social disciplining."

Reformation Christianity burst forth in two waves—the first beginning about 1520 and affecting Germanic Europe, the second beginning about 1550 and affecting the Dutch Republic, France, England, Scotland, and Eastern Europe. This chapter concerns itself with the first wave only. The Reformation in Germanic Europe initially enjoyed broad social support from aristocrats and commoners, townspeople and villagers. After the echoes of the German Peasants' War became muted, certainly by the end of the 1530s, the support of rural commoners for the Reformation diminished, but the Reformation continued its territorial advance with the support of some rulers and a significant minority of aristocrats and townspeople. Expressing the values of superior estates, aristocrats, and townspeople, rulers imposed social discipline and thus replaced initiatives to secure social justice by unprivileged commoners, particularly villagers. What follows will be devoted to presenting this interpretation. It is also my impression that the situation that prevailed in the Germanic Reformation from the 1540s onward applied to the second wave of the Reformation generally. This interpretation is disputed by some historians of the Scottish Reformation, who point to the national reconstruction programs of the Books of Discipline of 1560 and 1578 as having a definite appeal to ordinary people.[4]

Minimizing the connection of the German Peasants' War and the Reformation, Günther Franz has stressed that the slogans of the laced peasant boot and "divine justice" antedated the Reformation, indeed that they had roots in the Lollard and Hussite heresies of earlier centuries. These same points have been made by Heiko Oberman and Tom

> **Martin Luther on Galatians 2:16 (1516)**
>
> A wonderful new definition of righteousness! This is usually described thus: "Righteousness is a virtue which renders to each man according to his due" (*iustitia est virtus reddens unicuique quod suum est*). But here it says: "Righteousness is faith in Jesus Christ" (*fides Jhesu Christi*)!
>
> —Quoted in Alister E. McGrath, *Luther's Theology of the Cross: Martin Luther's Theological Breakthrough* (Oxford: Basil Blackwell 1983), 112.

Scott, and they cannot be ignored. The heresies of the late Middle Ages did not enjoy the success of Protestant established churches precisely because they combined religious and social radicalism. Moreover, Franz and Peter Blickle, the outstanding Peasants' War historians of the past century, have stressed that, aside from its religious appeal, "divine justice" was a slogan made to order for the legitimation of peasant revolt. It freed the peasantry from the problematic nature of the appeal to traditional custom that they otherwise had to use against the exploitation of landlords, priests, and rulers. Rural traditions were always specific to a limited territory and its subjects, but when divine justice was the rallying cry, rebels could be recruited everywhere without regard to the many small jurisdictions into which the medieval world was divided.

THE HAPSBURG FEAR OF SWISS AND *BUNDSCHUH*

The battle for "divine justice" began in southwest Germany in the aftermath of the Hapsburg emperor Maximilian I's disastrous failure to provide masters for the "peasant Swiss" in the unsuccessful war he waged against them in 1499. The outcome of this war prompted Basel to join the Swiss Confederation in 1501, continuing a process of unrelenting Swiss expansion into the Holy Roman Empire of the German Nation that had been going on for two centuries and was expected to continue. That same year, the young serf Joß Fritz began a conspiracy centered in one of the ecclesiastical territories, the Bishopric of Speyer. His banner, designed in Basel, displayed a *Bundschuh*, the traditional laced boot of the peasantry, together with the slogan, "Nothing but divine justice," placed over the image of the crucified Christ. He tried to recruit not only peasants but "Landsknecht" mercenary soldiers unemployed from the recent war. It was no accident that the conspiracy began in an ecclesiastical territory seething with economic anticlericalism; its other slogan was "We cannot rid ourselves of the plague of priests." Its radical aims were to get rid of all intermediate authorities between peasants and the empire (as the Swiss had supposedly done), abolish all temporal and ecclesiastical taxes, and restore common use of waters, forests, and meadows to the peasantry.

Contemporary chroniclers claimed that Fritz had twenty thousand followers in the territories of Speyer before his plans were betrayed.

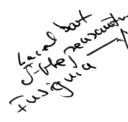

The semi-legendary Fritz escaped in 1502, to plot two further *Bundschuh* uprisings: in Lehen in Breisgau in 1513 and on both the Alsatian and Baden banks of the Upper Rhine in 1517. The chroniclers give discordant descriptions of these conspiracies, both of which were discovered before anyone acted upon them, just as was the case in 1502. The paucity of sources makes the extent of the plots' support difficult to reckon. The Breisgau scheme was for a relatively moderate program including religious objectives, but the 1517 plot aimed at only temporal (no religious) goals and was spread about by wandering beggars, jugglers, patent medicine quacks, and other "highway people" without fixed abode. A good dose of skepticism is needed for conspiracies that were never carried out and for fascinating conspirators like Joβ Fritz; all we have to go on are crackdowns by nervous rulers and chronicle accounts that depict Fritz's numerous changes of tactics and invariable escapes. In 1525, Fritz was certainly no major player; we are told that he made a curtain call in the Hegau, on the borders of Switzerland, as a man with "an old gray beard," "who would not die before the *Bundschuh* ran its course."[5]

However, the years 1510–1513 saw widespread unrest against urban oligarchies, as Heiko Oberman says, "from Deventer to Regensburg and from Swabia to Saxony."[6] The actions against the *Bundschuh* in the German southwest were probably, as Thomas Brady argues, due to a justified fear by the Hapsburgs and their allies that the unprivileged commoners in towns and villages were looking to Switzerland both for aid and as a model for their aspirations. But the calls upon "divine justice" in the rural areas were probably, as Oberman thinks, patterned on the "civic righteousness" of the towns that had for a century or more connected *iustitia coram deo* with *iustitia coram hominibus* (that is—in opposition to the later tenets of Luther's theology—there is an intrinsic connection between "justice before God" and "justice before human beings"). The chartered towns of the empire saw themselves as each "a church in miniature"—*corpus christianum* in microcosm. Therefore they provided preacherships and morals legislation for their citizens and secured a degree of administrative control over their church institutions that would hobble the bishops in their later attempts to reassert their administrative control against the Reformation.

THE KNIGHTS' REVOLT

Thus, before Martin Luther's theology burst upon the awareness of the Germanys a "gospel of social unrest" was already in the field—in the German southwest but elsewhere as well—that had an entirely different notion from Luther's about the relation between the gospel of Jesus Christ and the human struggle for justice. The cross-pollination of Luther's theology and the struggle for justice in Germany set in only subsequent to Luther's appearance before the emperor and the princes at the Diet of Worms in April 1521. Before that, the Luther issue was a strictly theological controversy. But during the period that Luther was in hiding in the Wartburg, from May 1521 to March 1522, the implementation of the Reformation became a topical issue. In general, princes and town councils tried to avoid committing themselves to support of or opposition to Luther's theology—this applied even to his protector Frederick the Wise, Elector of Saxony. The first open choices for the Reformation were made by the lesser nobility, especially imperial knights subject to no one but the emperor. Not all of them supported the Reformation, but some of them did and, further, pledged themselves to protect it.

This brings us to the case of Franz von Sickingen, lord of the Ebernburg in the Rhineland and one of the most famous imperial knights in Germany. Franz had mobilized his troops to support the election of Charles V in 1519. It was the special claim of the knightly estate to seek justice for the oppressed by direct military action through the "feud." The feud was of doubtful legality since the imperial reforms of 1495 had declared an end to private warfare and established a supreme court—the Imperial Chamber Court—to settle disputes. However, it was well known that the great princes, whose judges dominated the Imperial Chamber Court, would not submit their own disputes to its decisions. Feuds continued; in many respects the Peasants' War can best be understood as a series of feuds by the peasantry, seeking direct justice from their overlords. In July 1519, Sickingen declared a feud in defense of the humanist Hebraist Johannes Reuchlin against the German Dominicans, who were oppressing him by legal action in the Roman curia. The next year, in the same spirit he offered Luther protection at the Ebernburg and actually gave it to Johannes Oecolampadius and Martin Bucer, the future reformers of Basel and Strasbourg, respectively.

> **Johannes Schwöbel,**
> **Reformer of Pforzheim**
>
> No man in orders, however spiritual . . . nor any theologian, however learned, could speak so discerningly . . . in praise of God and with regard to salvation as this group of noblemen. The game has been turned completely upside down. Formerly one learned the laws of God from the priests. Now it is necessary to go to school to the laity and learn to read the Bible from them. The nobility now seek the honor and love of God instead of power and wealth.
>
> —Miriam Usher Chrisman, *Conflicting Visions of Reform: German Lay Propaganda Pamphlets 1519–1530* (Atlantic Highlands, N.J.: Humanities, 1996), 69.

There can be no doubt of Sickingen's sincere commitment to the Reformation, although he was not a trained theologian and did not understand all of Luther's ideas. Some thirty pro-Reformation pamphlets were published at the Ebernburg, advocating the use of German in worship and communion in both bread and wine for the laity, opposing prayers to the saints, and championing the word of God against papal customs.[7] In August 1522, Sickingen organized six hundred knights of the Upper Rhine into a "Christian Confederation" that attacked the powerful ecclesiastical territories of Trier, Würzburg, and Bamberg on behalf of the Reformation. The confederates declared that these ecclesiastical lands, which were ruled by clerics, had been extorted from their ancestors by trickery and false religion. Once these lands had been repossessed, there would be enough for all estates, even the peasantry. Some of the prince bishops, particularly the archbishop of Trier, turned out to be effective warriors. They mobilized the Swabian League, the Hapsburgs' instrument for maintaining peace and order in the German southwest. Princes, whether Lutheran or anti-Lutheran in religion, refused to permit imperial knights to dispossess their fellow princes. The fortunes of war turned against Sickingen and the knights, and he was killed defending one of his castles. Whatever Luther's viewpoint in 1520, by 1523 and the collapse of the Knights' Revolt, he had made it clear that he regarded the territorial rulers, the princes, as the proper authorities to maintain law and order in Germany.

TITHE RESISTANCE

However strange to contemporary notions of class conflict this may appear, the Knights' Revolt acted as a prelude to the Peasants' War. The notion among imperial knights that church lands and revenues, particularly monastic lands and revenues, had been procured through fraud from their ancestors spread in 1523 to the other rural estate, the peasantry. There was widespread refusal to pay the customary ecclesiastical tithe, particularly when it had become the property of cathedral chapters and monasteries. These tithe refusals occurred in the Franconian and Rhenish territories that were the locale of the Knights' Revolt, as well as in rural villages subject to centers of the early Reformation, such as Nuremberg and Zurich. The ecclesiastical corporations that had enriched themselves by appropriating village tithes assumed the responsibility for seeing that Mass was performed in dependent villages. This system, even when diligently applied, was ill suited to providing pastoral care for new centers of rural population, and it was even less workable for evangelical villages, where the preaching of the gospel replaced the reading of the Mass. Hence tithe resistance was a genuinely religious—and at the same time a social and financial—issue.

Like Sickingen's feud against the ecclesiastical territories, village resistance to tithes was accompanied by a pamphlet campaign. Ulrich von Hutten wrote on behalf of the knights and was a protector of Otto Brunfels, who wrote the tract *On Ecclesiastical Tithes* in 1524. Brunfels stressed that the ecclesiastical tithe was not commanded by Christ in the New Testament. It was an alms that properly belonged to the poor, to preachers of the Word, and to the community as a whole for useful public works. Evangelical governments would not tolerate peasant villagers taking this matter into their own hands, creating, in one particular case, a source of friction between the Zurich government and future Anabaptists. Nevertheless, the campaign against monasteries and cathedral chapters that misappropriated the tithe led in one of two directions. Either town governments confiscated these institutions for their own programs of education and poor relief in the spirit of the Reformation, or the monasteries became the first objects of plundering and sacking at the beginning of the Peasants' War. The "recommunalization of the tithe" became the theme of the second article of the *Twelve Articles*, the most widely circulated summary of the insurgents' demands.

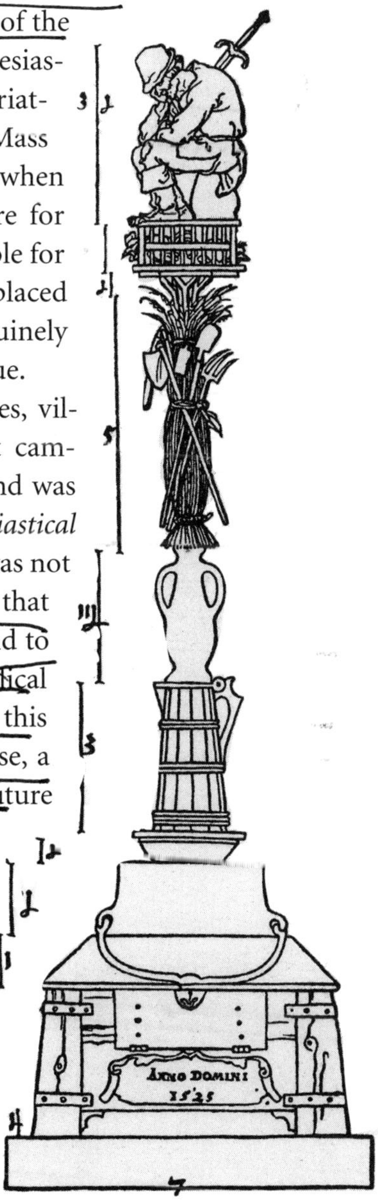

Fig. 8.2. Albrecht Dürer, satirical sketch of a memorial column for the Peasants' War, from Dürer's *Unterweysung der Messung* (Nuremberg, 1525), 164. Image made available by Hans-Jürgen Goertz.

RADICAL PASTORS: MÜNTZER AND HUBMAIER

The diverse theological emphases and reform agendas of major preachers leading the Reformation in the Germanys had a great impact on the Peasants' War. Nowhere was this clearer than in the relation between Martin Luther and Thomas Müntzer. Attending lectures in Wittenberg in 1517–1519, Müntzer was appointed to a pastorate in Zwickau with Luther's support. While there, he developed a style of prophetic biblicism that began a gradual estrangement between him and the Wittenberg theologians. Luther seems to have regarded the prophetic writings in the Old Testament as the outcome of prophets such as Isaiah and Jeremiah devoting themselves to theological study of Moses; by 1521, in a manifesto he published in Prague, Müntzer denounced theologians who claimed to find the Word of God through mere scriptural study and called upon the church not to worship a mute God but a living and speaking one.

These differences intensified when Müntzer became pastor of the isolated Electoral Saxon territory of Allstedt from April 1523 to August 1524. Attracting the peasants of surrounding Catholic lands to his new German liturgy in Allstedt, Müntzer had to concern himself with defending his growing flock against imprisonment and exile by their overlords. This was his motive in delivering a sermon at the Allstedt castle in July 1524 to the two Saxon princes, John and John Frederick, calling on them to take up arms in support of the Reformation. That same month, Luther wrote a letter to the Saxon princes denouncing Müntzer's tendency to resort to force. The chain of events that followed led to Müntzer's flight from Allstedt in August and to his securing a role in the ongoing Reformation of the Thuringian imperial city of Mühlhausen. In his sermon in July, Müntzer had warned the Saxon

> **The *Twelve Articles*: Article 2**
>
> Second, although the obligation to pay a just tithe prescribed in the Old Testament is fulfilled in the New, yet we will gladly pay the large tithe on grain—but only in just measure. Since the tithe should be given to God and distributed among his servants, so the pastor who preaches the word of God deserves to receive it. . . . The remainder should be distributed to the village's own poor, again with the community's consent and according to need. What then remains should be kept in case some need to be called up to defend the country; and then the costs can be met from this reserve, so that no general territorial tax will be laid upon the poor folk.
>
> —From Peter Blickle, *The Revolution of 1525: The German Peasants' War from a New Perspective*, trans. Thomas A. Brady Jr. and H. C. Erik Midelfort (Baltimore: Johns Hopkins University Press, 1981), 196–97.

princes that if they did not do their duty to defend the Reformation, their power would be taken from them and handed over to the common people. But Müntzer's enemies at Allstedt were also the princely protectors of the militarily weak imperial city of Mühlhausen. They threatened his new position, so he must have regarded the uprising of the Thuringian peasantry in April 1525 as a heaven-sent deliverance.

A rather different path into the Peasants' War was taken by Balthasar Hubmaier, the pastor of Waldshut and future Anabaptist leader. In December 1523, the government of Austrian territories in the Black Forest and Alsace noted with alarm that he had become a partisan of the Reformation, with strong connections to Zwingli in Zurich. The council of Waldshut rejected efforts to arrest Hubmaier, saying that he proclaimed the Word of God purely and clearly. Some radical supporters of the Zurich Reformation, with connections to the future Anabaptist movement, garrisoned Waldshut in 1524. Zurich would gladly have extended its military and religious influence over Waldshut but avoided a direct confrontation with Austria. What most protected evangelical Waldshut was the uprising in the summer of 1524 of Black Forest peasants, who refused feudal dues and services. A band that combined the traits of a strike and a public demonstration marched around the area under the leadership of a former mercenary, Hans Müller from Bulgenbach. Waldshut was one of their assembly points.

Hubmaier, who thought that he had an agreement with Zwingli that "children should not be baptized before they were of age," was distressed by the rupture between Zwingli and the first Anabaptists in January 1525. He used the disorder of the Peasants' War in April 1525 to introduce believers' baptism in Waldshut with broad congregational support. He also became the most eloquent and theologically schooled defender of believers' baptism against infant baptism

> **Thomas Müntzer, A Protestation concerning the Situation in Bohemia**
> Anyone who does not hear from the mouth of God the real living word of God, and the distinction between Bible and Babel, is a dead thing and nothing else. But God's word, which courses through heart, brain, skin, hair, bone, marrow, sap, might and strength surely has the right to canter along in a quite different way from the fairy tales told by our clownish, testicled doctors. Otherwise no one can be saved; otherwise no one can be found.
> —From *The Collected Works of Thomas Müntzer*, trans. and ed. Peter Matheson (Edinburgh: T & T Clark, 1988), 368.

Figs. 8.3 and 8.4. Parallel maps of the incidence of Anabaptism in Central Europe, 1550, and of the spread of the German Peasants' War, 1524–1525, showing that the two movements touched some, but not all, of the same regions. Maps by Lucidity Information Design. Maps from *The German Peasant War of 1525: New Viewpoints*, ed. Bob Scribner and Gerhard Benecke, adapted by permission of Unwin Hyman Ltd., and by Jan Gleysteen in *An Introduction to Mennonite History*, ed. C. J. Dyck, adapted by permission of Herald Press, Scottdale, Pennsylvania.

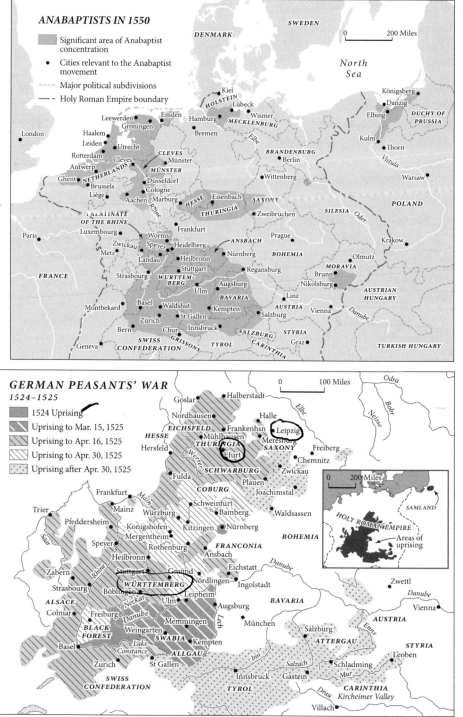

in an exchange of polemics with Zwingli. The collapse of the Peasants' War caused Hubmaier to flee Waldshut just before the arrival of Austrian troops in December 1525. Arriving with the occupiers was Johannes Faber, humanist vicar general of the bishop of Constance and a major enemy of the Reformation. He found in Hubmaier's abandoned papers two pro-peasant declarations: the Constitutional Draft and the Letter of Articles. According to Faber, Hubmaier edited the Constitutional Draft, which justified the deposing of established rulers and outlined a procedure for their replacement. We know of the Constitutional Draft only through Faber, but there is independent authentication of the Letter of Articles, which was used by the Black Forest band.

The Letter of Articles, apparently composed by Hubmaier, imposed a boycott patterned on ecclesiastical excommunication on opponents of the creation of a Swiss-type confederation in the Black Forest. This new government would remove the financial and legal burdens resting on the towns and villages of the region "without any fighting or bloodshed." Castles and monasteries were to be boycotted immediately; their owners could escape the boycott if they withdrew from their strongholds and permitted them to be disarmed or dismantled. Otherwise, the commoners' weapon against their feudal superiors was total social and economic ostracism. Hubmaier's contribution to the peasant resistance was partly opportunistic, making use of the protection it extended to the Waldshut Reformation, and aimed at nonviolent achievement of justice for Waldhut's rural allies. Nevertheless, his entanglement with the Peasants' War in the Black Forest was the main justification the Austrians used for hunting him down in his Moravian refuge and executing him in 1528.

The Letter of Articles of the Black Forest Peasants, Before May 8, 1525

All those who are in this Christian union shall, by the honor and highest obligations which they have undertaken, hold and practice no communion of any kind with those who refuse and oppose admittance to this Christian union and the furthering of the common Christian weal, to wit, by eating, drinking, bathing, milling, baking, ploughing, reaping, or by supplying or letting others supply them with food, grain, drink, wood, meat, salt, etc., or by buying from or selling to them. In those matters which do not promote, but rather retard, the common Christian weal and public peace, they shall be treated as severed and dead limbs.

—From *The German Peasants' War: A History in Documents*, trans. and ed. Tom Scott and Bob Scribner (Atlantic Highlands, N.J.: Humanities, 1991), 136.

CHRISTOPH SCHAPPELER AND DIVINE JUSTICE

The primary outbreak of the Peasants' War occurred in the first months of 1525 in Upper Swabia, leading to the assembly of the leaders of the Baltringen, Allgäu, and Lake Constance bands in the first week in March in the imperial city of Memmingen.[9] The Baltringen leader Ulrich Schmid declared that "divine justice" legitimated peasant demands, and he involved the evangelical leaders Sebastian Lotzer and Christoph Schappeler in drawing up the program of the Upper Swabian peasantry. They became the most important spokesmen of the Peasants' War as the presumed drafters of the *Twelve Articles*, which received the endorsement of all rebel bands except those of northern Switzerland and the Alpine territories of Tirol and Salzburg. Lotzer was a layman, a citizen of Memmingen, literate in the vernacular, a furrier who had been writing pamphlets endorsing Lutheranism from the spring of 1523. Schappeler, Swiss by birth and education, had been a priest in Memmingen since 1513. From 1521, he was a supporter of the Reformation; he participated in the Reformation disputations in Zurich, and in 1524 he became an outspoken opponent of the tithe.

Lotzer was chosen by Ulrich Schmid as secretary of the Baltringen band and is generally thought by Peasants' War scholars to have edited three hundred grievances from the region into the famous *Twelve Articles*. Assuming Lotzer as author of the *Twelve Articles*, scholars sometimes credited Schappeler with being the source of the biblical legitimation of the articles, appearing in the margins of the printed edition.[10] If only one of the two drew up the *Twelve Articles* and the *Federal Ordinance*, the case for Schappeler now appears better, because of the strong presumption that he was the anonymous author of the pamphlet *To the Assembly of Common Peasantry*. Lotzer would not have been able to supply the numerous classical allusions that are sprinkled throughout that pamphlet.

A major reason for the popularity of the *Twelve Articles* was that it was regarded as part of the Reformation's own programmatic literature. The prologue defended the new evangelical teaching against the accusation of its enemies that it undermined spiritual and temporal authority. It declared that all demands of the peasantry were based on the aspiration "to hear the gospel and live accordingly." Since the gospel taught Christ and peace, any violence and disorder that accompanied the peasant movement was the fault of ecclesiastical and temporal lords who denied justice to their subjects. The first two articles of the twelve gave villagers the right to choose and dismiss their pastors, and adopted the program of tithe resisters that the tithe should be reserved for local purposes, support of the pastor, alms for the poor, and defense of the land. The uncustomary small tithe on meat products was to be totally abolished. Article 12 established the Bible as the standard for all the others; any article shown to be inconsistent with the Bible would be withdrawn, but new demands could be advanced as the commoners' insight into the Bible became greater.

The organization of the *Articles* illustrates the belief of Schmid, Lotzer, and Schappeler that the concerns of the Upper Swabian commoners were in harmony with the Reformation. Articles 1, 2, and 12 were seen as validating the social, economic, and legal demands of the other nine articles. Article 3 rejected serfdom, arguing that it was unseemly for people to hold other people as property, since Christ had died for people in all estates from the most humble shepherd to the greatest lord. Articles 4, 5, and 10 protested against the peasants not having free access to the common resources of the village, forests, waterways, and meadows. Here we have the very general grievance of the peasantry about being excluded by aggressive landlords and officials from sources which had traditionally supplemented the income from their crops—wood and game from the forests, fish and irrigation from water sources, as well as grazing space for their cattle. Articles 6, 7, 8, 9, and 11 brought together labor services, rents, and dues, as well as legal penalties that the commoners regarded as untraditional, unjust, and infringing upon their livelihood.[11] These demands tended especially to reflect the interests of the upper strata of the villages, peasants with lifetime or hereditary leases, who made up the

> **The *Twelve Articles*: Article 3**
>
> Third, it has until now been the custom of the lords to own us as their property. This is deplorable, for Christ redeemed and bought us all with his precious blood, the lowliest shepherd as well as the greatest lord, with no exceptions. Thus the Bible proves that we are free and want to be free. Not that we want to be utterly free and subject to no authority at all; God does not teach us that. We ought to live according to the commandments, not according to the lusts of the flesh. But we should love God, recognize him as our Lord in our neighbor, and willingly do all things God commanded us at his Last Supper.
>
> —From Blickle,
> *Revolution of 1525*, 197.

local authorities supervising the common agricultural life. It appears that in the Peasants' War these village leaders defined the "common good" and controlled the attitudes of their poorer neighbors who did not have farms, the cottagers, landless laborers, and servants.

If the *Twelve Articles* reflected the problems and aspirations of villagers at the local level, the Upper Swabian program for common governance, which Peter Blickle describes quite reasonably as "republican," emerges in the *Federal Ordinance*. This second major document of the Peasants' War, printed in early March 1525 in Memmingen, was probably also drawn up by Christoph Schappeler. This document aimed at creating a "Christian union and league," "for the praise and honor of the almighty, eternal God, to call upon the holy Gospel and the word of God, and to protect justice and the divine law."[12] Its goal was to transform Upper Swabia into a permanent Swiss-type confederation of "towns, villages, and rural regions." Had this plan been realized it would have created a smaller Swiss-type confederation bordering the greater one. Just twenty-five years previously, the Swiss victory over the Austrians in the Swabian War had led to the annexation of a similar confederation, Graubünden. In 1525, the expansion of Switzerland appeared as an inexorable historical process. The Swiss recognized the Holy Roman emperor as a shadowy overlord, which in no way interfered with their practical independence. This Swiss connection lends special interest to the contention of Peter Blickle and other prominent Peasants' War historians that Swiss-born Christoph Schappeler was the author of a third important printed pamphlet of the Peasants' War, *To the Assembly of Common Peasantry*, published in Nuremberg in May.[13]

If we assume Schappeler's authorship, *To the Assembly of Common Peasantry* provides the key to the precarious balance between nonviolent resistance and self-defense that has puzzled interpreters of the *Twelve Articles* and the *Federal Ordinance*. It must have been written in late March or early April, when it became evident that the army of the Swabian League under the Upper Swabian landlord George of Waldburg had opted for a military solution of the dispute with the peasantry. The substance of the pamphlet concerned the source of rulers' legitimacy, how rulers can lose their legitimacy, how to get rid of an illegitimate ruler, and with whom to replace him. It amounted to a rationale for resistance to tyranny and an argument for replacing hereditary lords with republican authorities directly responsible to the emperor, in the manner of imperial cities, as the pamphlet explicitly stated.

The author wrote in an Upper Swabian dialect, laced with Swiss expressions, and made various allusions to the republican experience of the Romans and of the Swiss when they were oppressed by tyrants. The substance and the phraseology of the *Twelve Articles* and the *Federal Ordinance* recur throughout the pamphlet, particularly the insistence upon "freedom," so that common people could not "be sold like cattle." Its content suggests a close acquaintance with the theology of Zwingli. Luther's doctrine of two kingdoms, from his *On Temporal Power* (1523), was explicitly rejected: "Again and again people speak of two commands: the divine, which concern the soul, and the political, which concern the common good. But God knows these commands cannot be divided, for the political commands which genuinely promote the common good are also divine." On the title page is an illustration that identifies the peasants as "loyal Christians" in opposition to "Romanists and sophists," as well as the jingle "*Wer meret Schwyz, Der herren gytz*" (Who makes Switzerland grow? The greed of the lords). The connection of the Upper Swabian Peasants' War with the Swiss traditions of resistance to tyranny—indeed, to the theme of southwest Germany "turning Swiss"—could hardly be more explicit.[14]

After the Peasants' War, Lotzer disappeared, and Schappeler took refuge in his native Saint Gall, where he served as a Reformed pastor until his death in 1551. In his later reassessments, Schappeler concluded that the struggle began as a religiously motivated effort at liberation but that the peasants' violence and greed ended by turning south Germany into a Sodom and Gomorrah. "We pray for forgiveness and ask that we who started because of faith will not perish without it."[15] Luther's total rejection of Schappeler's notions of justice appeared in print in *Admonition to Peace: A Reply to the Twelve Articles of the Peasants*, before the publication of *To the Assembly of Common Peasantry*.

> **Christoph Schappeler, To the Assembly of Common Peasantry**
>
> And to say nothing of the old histories: what great and ineffable deeds have so often been performed by that poor little band of peasants, your neighbors the Swiss? ... The majority of their enemies have been put to flight, and king, emperor, princes and lords held up to mockery, the more powerful and the greater the armed might that was used against them. And as often as the aforesaid Swiss fought for themselves, for their country, their wives and children, and had to defend themselves against arrogant powers, they have mostly been victorious against the odds and earned great honor. All that without doubt occurred through the power and providence of God.
>
> —From Scott and Scribner, *German Peasants' War*, 275.

THE NEW ORDERS OF GAISMAIR AND MÜNTZER

The moderate conceptions of evangelical justice voiced by Hubmaier or Schappeler pale when compared to the aspirations of Michael Gaismair or Thomas Müntzer. In May 1525, when the peasant bands were being suppressed elsewhere, Gaismair shocked the Tirol by seizing the treasure of the archbishop of Brixen, hiring mercenaries, and mounting a temporarily effective resistance against the Hapsburgs. During the leisure afforded by his refuge in Switzerland in early 1526, he imagined the constitution for a liberated Tirol, a semi-utopian version of the struggle for justice in the Peasants' War. Gaismair's Tirol was to be a Reformation territory with the Mass outlawed, images destroyed, books of scholastic philosophy and canon law burned, the scriptures the sole basis of university instruction, and the Word of God preached everywhere. All privileges, whether those of aristocrats, townspeople, or merchants, were to be abolished. The mines that distinguished the Tirolian economy were to be expropriated from the big south German companies (denounced as "monopolies") and used to finance the Tirolian government. This would have been a land on the Swiss model, purged of lordship—far more radically egalitarian than Switzerland was in reality.

In Müntzer's case, the extent of his aspirations is more difficult to determine. In his final interrogation he said that Mühlhausen aimed to secure itself from the neighboring princes by controlling a territory of fifty-mile radius around the city. He had obviously given up hope of just rule from any princes, whether or not they presented themselves as supporters of the Reformation. His oft-quoted watchword was: "The people will become free,

---

Michael Gaismair's Territorial Constitution for the Tirol, Composed Early in 1526

You should root out and expunge all godless men who persecute the word of God, burden the common man, and hinder the common good. You will spare no effort to establish a wholly Christian constitution, which is founded in all things on the word of God alone, and live wholly according to it. All privileges shall be abolished, for they are contrary to the word of God and pervert justice, so that no one will have advantage over another. All fortifications around towns and all castles and fortresses should be demolished so that henceforth there should be no more towns, but only villages, in order that all distinctions between men will be abolished, from which disruption, pride and disturbance may arise in the land, but rather there will be a complete equality in the land. All images, wayside shrines and chapels which are not parish churches should be abolished throughout the entire land, along with the mass, for it is an abomination before God and wholly unchristian.

—From Scott and Scribner, *German Peasants' War*, 265–66.

and it is the will of God that he alone shall be their lord." This statement has been interpreted by Hans-Jürgen Goertz as at once democratic and theocratic, but what does it mean? There is a consensus among contemporary scholars that, unlike Luther, Müntzer did not expect an imminent end of the world or an immediate second coming of Christ. He was a prophetic revolutionary, presenting himself in the personae of Gideon, Elijah, or John the Baptist. The value he placed on the prophetic "church" of the Old Testament weighs his theocratic democracy toward theocracy. He seems to have seen his time as experiencing a new Pentecost initiating a Spirit-led Reformation church in succession to the Old Testament prophets and the church of the apostles—a veritable third age of the church. This was to have been the dawn of a new world, not the end of the world. Ultimately, like Schappeler, Müntzer rejected the material objectives of the peasant bands and concluded that they were not cut out for the high mission he had imagined for them.[16]

> **Confession under Torture of Thomas Müntzer (May 1525)**
>
> The articles which they held and sought to put into practice were: All things are to be held in common and distribution should be to each according to his need, as occasion arises. Any prince, count or gentleman who refused to do this should first be given a warning, but then one should cut off his head or hang him. . . . If things had turned out as he had hoped and planned he had meant—and that had been common knowledge among all the members of his covenant—to appropriate all the land within a forty-six mile radius of Mühlhausen and the land in Hesse, and to deal with the princes and gentry as described above.
>
> —From *Collected Works of Thomas Müntzer*, 437.

THE ESTABLISHED CHURCHES AND THE ANABAPTIST PROTEST

The aftermath of the Peasants' War was that the princes and theologians grew to disdain the rural majority of the Germanic lands. In the pre-1525 pro-Reformation pamphlets a typical spokesman was Karsthans, "the evangelical peasant," who understood the gospel better than the monks and the scholastic university professors.[17] After 1525, Karsthans disappeared. It is hard to know how deeply the pro-Reformation message of a Hubmaier or a Schappeler, or even a Gaismair or a Müntzer, was absorbed into the consciousness of the rural-people. But certainly the interest of the villagers who flocked to Allstedt to experience Müntzer's new German ritual was not an isolated occurrence. Peter Blickle writes of the post–Peasants' War

Germany. "Now the princes had to take over the Reformation. Only if they could bring it under political control could revolt be eliminated root and branch."[18] That was surely the meaning of the decision of the Imperial Diet of Speyer in 1526 that from henceforth the individual estates should regulate religion as their consciences dictated, recognizing that they would have to justify what they did to God and the emperor. The consequence of this was Luther's approval, (with whatever mental reservations) of the Saxon Visitation of 1528, which organized the territorial church as a branch of the government. This became the model for the organization of the churches that followed the Lutheran Augsburg Confession. From now on godly princes, devout burghers, and aristocrats became the mainstay of the evangelical faith and the support of the new pastorate that imposed their version of "social disciplining" on the rural populace.

What remained of a bottom-up struggle for justice in the Reformation after 1525 expressed itself in the nonconformist sects, the Anabaptists, and, more equivocally, the "civic righteousness" of some of the German and Swiss towns. Socially, the Anabaptists were in the majority persons from villages and small towns, but a strong minority lived in cities in Switzerland and south Germany and in the Netherlands and Hanseatic north Germany. In the first two or three years, they were led by highly educated humanist laypeople, but as these first leaders were eliminated by persecution, urban and rural artisans became the characteristic Anabaptist leaders. Vernacular literacy rather than Latinity shaped an anti-elitist notion of justice among these sectarians. Later, in the seventeenth century, doctors became the first trained professionals to assume leadership roles among Dutch Mennonites.

The Anabaptist sects, which began to appear in 1525, were in some cases led by men who had been able to spread their message under the protection of the peasants' uprising, as we have noted of Hubmaier, or, like Hans Hut and Melchior Rinck, had an earlier close association with Müntzer. More general than their leaders' association with the Peasants' War, however, was their preoccupation with the community of goods ascribed to the early church in Acts 2, 4, and 5. Felix Mantz, a major leader of the earliest Anabaptists in Zurich, stated that, immediately after he baptized people, he "taught them further about love and unity and community of all things, as in Acts 2." Although an early Swiss Anabaptist congregational ordinance prescribes the community of goods, this principle was assumed to be compatible with the maintenance of separate household economies and amounted in practice to generous sharing with needy brothers and sisters in the congregations. The Swiss Anabaptists, particularly, disapproved of people living from invested property. Everyone, they believed, should support himself from his own work, and anyone who had more than he needed had a Christian obligation to put it to the use of the poor.

Within the Anabaptist groups that arose from onetime followers of Thomas Müntzer the stress was on *Gelassenheit*, a mystical breaking free from material attachments. When heavy persecution in 1528–1529 drove many Anabaptists from Switzerland and south Germany to take refuge on the estates of tolerant aristocrats in Moravia, sectarian disputes about the community of goods became a major issue. These quarrels were exacerbated by the tensions between Anabaptists in the settled Moravian population and indigent refugees. The years 1534–1536 became a crisis for the Anabaptist community of goods for several reasons. In Münster in Westphalia, an Anabaptist congregation came into control of the city and adopted an apocalyptic militancy. In the course of a sixteen-month siege of the city by Catholic and Protestant princes, the Münster Anabaptists set up a "Davidic" kingdom that aspired to world domination, pending the return of Christ, and practiced polygamy and the community of goods (the community of goods was more theoretical than real, given drastic inequalities of condition during the siege). At the same time, King Ferdinand prevailed upon the Moravian aristocracy to expel the Anabaptists.

The only Anabaptist sect that was able to maintain itself through the Moravian persecution was the Hutterite group, which in later years systematized the community of goods in large multifamily dwellings, living from the profits of

> **Swiss Anabaptist Congregational Ordinance (1527)**
> Of all the brothers and sisters of this congregation none shall have anything of his own, but rather, as the Christians in the time of the apostles held all in common, and especially stored up a common fund, from which aid can be given to the poor, according as each will have need, and as in the apostles' time permit no brother to be in need.
> —From *The Legacy of Michael Sattler*, ed. and trans. John H. Yoder (Scottdale, Pa.: Herald Press, 1973), 45.

craftsmanship and controlled in all details of their lives by a rigid hierarchy of elders. In the aftermath of the crisis in Münster and Moravia, most Anabaptist leaders, like Menno Simons and Pilgram Marpeck, abandoned the early church of Acts 2, 4, and 5 as a norm. They instead regarded the New Testament church as compatible with the holding of private property and insisted only that Anabaptists should assist each other generously with mutual aid. This general abandonment of the community of goods, along with internal Anabaptist revulsion against the excesses of the Anabaptist rule in Münster, marked a decline of the radical hostility of the Anabaptists to the surrounding persecuting society. The Anabaptists put their stress on personal holiness of life, an emphasis of the movement from the beginning, and achieved the status of tolerated nonconformists later in the sixteenth century, a situation that continued until the Thirty Years' War in Moravia and permanently in the Dutch Republic.[19]

CIVIC RIGHTEOUSNESS

Mass support for Lutheranism continued in north Germany into the 1530s. It did result in a democratizing expansion of the ruling group in some Hanseatic cities such as Hamburg, as burgher committees supervised, and eventually amalgamated with, the established councils.[20] In southwest Germany and Switzerland medieval traditions of "civic righteousness" continued the Reformation aspirations for communal justice, and the ideal of a godly life held some balance over against Lutheran justification by faith alone. For instance, Zurich's Reformation ordinance on alms for the poor was in the tradition of essentially medieval ideals of morality, piety, and social hierarchy and conformity. The poor were to be assisted only if they behaved worthily and deferentially and if they were authentic residents of Zurich. Poor relief was connected with the dismantling of the ostentatious cult of the old church. The images that had previously decorated the churches were "images of man," while the poor were a "true image of God."

Zwingli came to the Reformation from Erasmian biblical humanism, and there were deep-seated differences between him and Luther. After Zwingli's death in 1531, however, Martin Bucer's diplomatic facility negotiated a merger for the south Germans, uniting them with the Lutherans in the Wittenberg Concord of 1536. Pastors in Basel and Bern gave their support to the Wittenberg Concord, but they lost out in their struggles with Heinrich Bullinger, who soldiered on as leader of a doctrinally distinct Reformed Protestantism in Zurich. The jump of the Reformation over the linguistic frontier between German- and French-speaking Europe did not work to the benefit of Lutheranism. Calvinism became the primary vehicle for the spread of the Reformation to France, the Netherlands, England, Scotland, and Eastern Europe. In this way a Swiss republican model added a tincture of anti-tyrannical "freedom," in the tradition of William Tell, to the further history of the Reformation. But it was the freedom of an elite of burgers and aristocrats who conceived of themselves as God's elect. In some respects the struggle for justice among people continued in the later Reformation of northern and western Europe and made its way across the ocean to the Americas, but it subsisted on a slighter social foundation than Hubmaier, Schappeler, Gaismair, and Müntzer had hoped for in the early months of 1525.[22]

FOR FURTHER READING

Blickle, Peter. *The Revolution of 1525: The German Peasants' War from a New Perspective.* Translated by Thomas A. Brady Jr. and H. C. Erik Midelfort. Baltimore: Johns Hopkins University Press, 1981.

Matheson, Peter, translator and editor. *The Collected Works of Thomas Müntzer.* Edinburgh: T & T Clark, 1988.

Scott, Tom, and Bob Scribner, translators and editors. *The German Peasants' War: A History in Documents.* Atlantic Highlands, N.J.: Humanities, 1991.

Scribner, Bob, and Gerhard Benecke. *The German Peasant War of 1525: New Viewpoints.* London: Allen & Unwin, 1979.

Stayer, James M. *The German Peasants' War and Anabaptist Community of Goods.* Montreal: McGill-Queen's University Press, 1991.

THE EMERGENCE
OF LAY THEOLOGIES

ELSIE McKEE

CHAPTER NINE

I know that it will be considered shameful or worthless for a woman to dare to answer such big guys. . . . [But] I know that Christ said to me as much as to all bishops: "Whoever confesses Me before men, that one I will confess before My Father who is in heaven; whoever denies My Word before men I will deny before My Father" Matt. 10[:32-33]. . . . I will not cease doing what I am obligated to do; God will require an accounting from all of us.[1]

If there is one thing which can be said about all lay theologians in the sixteenth century, it is that they expressed themselves with amazing confidence in their right to be heard and taken seriously as Christian voices. For most, the basis of this confidence was the priesthood of believers, the conviction that all Christians have equal access to God by faith and therefore all have the right and obligation to be responsible religious actors. Whatever their specific doctrinal stance, lay theologians claimed and exercised a voice and a choice with an assurance that was historically unprecedented, at least in scale if not in kind.

In this chapter I distinguish theology, that is, speaking about God, from piety, the practices of devotion. Piety is less dependent on mind than on heart, while theology by definition involves the capacity to think and articulate religious ideas. Most who sought actively to speak about God for themselves were people who were not satisfied with their situation, and so this discussion gives greater weight to changes in lay thought than to continuities.

THE LAY CHRISTIAN WORLD IN THE LATE MIDDLE AGES

The huge majority of Europeans in the early modern world considered themselves good Christians. Precisely because they were devout, laity were bound to the clergy, who were the ministers of the church's sacraments, *the* means of grace. Salvation was all-important, overriding even desires for power and pleasure, if not all the time, at least when disaster or death (which always hovered on the horizon) closed in on the hapless/helpless man or woman or child, prince or beggar.

Laypeople were far from dumb: they thought and they spoke. Perhaps they could not understand all the doctrine they heard; much of it was in a foreign language, while some of it relied on esoteric philosophical distinctions. However, they certainly recognized when teacher and teachings contradicted each other, something they did not allow to pass without critical (and often ribald) comment. Many priests also called on their fellow clergy to keep the church's clear standards. All who vowed celibacy should keep their vows. Clergy with cure of souls should be resident in their parishes or dioceses, willing and able to preach as well as to give the sacraments; they should not use their offices for material gain. Lay Christians did not expect, or even want, to do without clergy, but they demanded that the latter do their jobs properly, something even the least educated peasant could see was not always the case. Scrupulous parishioners worried that contradictions between teaching and practice might threaten their salvation. Rather than improving the lives of those for whom they were responsible,

> ### Utz Rychsner on Christ's Universal Call (1524)
>
> Weaver: Dear Merchant.... In Mark 16[:16] Christ said, "Go into all the world..." and afterward on Pentecost He anointed them with the Holy Spirit.... It was certainly not just the eleven disciples; many more received this "anointing," namely Christ's mother and perhaps also the seventy-two disciples.... In Mark 13[:37] He says "What I say to you, that I say to all," which I understand to mean that what He said to the apostles He has also said to everyone.
>
> —From Utz Rychsner, *Ain gesprech buochlin von ainem Weber und ainem Kramer* (Augsburg, 1524), C4v–D1r.

these priests set a bad example—which (as some laity recognized) the laity, their neighbors, and especially their princes were only too happy to follow. So the whole community was infected.

Lay Christians also frequently worried about their personal access to God's forgiveness and salvation. How do I fulfill the known commands? How do I face sufferings that are punishment for my sins?

Is there some (other) means to deal with the unbearable? For many people the church's sacraments were a great comfort, but for many others the church's teaching left them suspended in uncertainty and confusion. The all-powerful and just God would someday judge everyone according to the church's teaching—such a long list of rules! The devout layperson did her best to follow them. (Sometimes she supplemented official practices with means that the church did not approve but which from the lay viewpoint did not seem much different from miracles done by the saints.)

Ordinary Christians could not know all about God's will. Clergy cited scripture and church councils; great theologians like Saint Augustine, Saint Bernard, and Saint Thomas; canon law, papal bulls, and decrees; and more. Even educated city citizens could not master enough theology to debate the church on most doctrinal matters. Moral lapses were easier to identify: a fat and lecherous monk obviously contradicted his vows of poverty and chastity. But how to determine the religious value of a vow of celibacy when the priest manifestly did not keep it? The church says that the life of a monk or nun or priest is more holy than that of a king or a mother or a baker (even if some clergy have concubines or live in luxury!), but how does it all fit together?

SOMETHING NEW IN THE SIXTEENTH CENTURY

Devout Christian laity in early modern Europe possessed an intellectual capacity to judge church teaching when teaching and practice contradicted each other. They also had a growing sense of the inadequacy of the church to satisfy their need for assurance of salvation, because the more educated the laity became, the more apparent it was that not all church teaching was coherent. The sources of theology, however, were generally not accessible to ordinary people, so they could not fully evaluate the teaching.

Theological Questioning

Laity were not alone in seeing problems with theology and expressing impatience with the complexity of its sources. Quite traditional churchmen publicly disputed about aspects of church teaching; for example, Franciscans and Dominicans fought (literally!) over the Immaculate Conception of the Blessed Virgin Mary. The fact that this had not yet been defined as a dogma that must be believed was not immediately obvious, but the violent dispute among learned clergy suggested that church teaching was uncertain. Furthermore, humanist clergy like Desiderius Erasmus were heaping scorn on hairsplitting disputes about obscure points of doctrine and urging everyone: "Go 'back to the sources! Strip away all those glosses that have been added and get at the original texts of Jesus and the apostles!" Then there were more radical priests like Martin Luther, preaching at the top of their voices: "The only means of justification before God's judgment throne is sheer trust in *Christ alone,* that is, *faith alone,* which is *solely God's grace;* we know this from the *Bible alone.*" Both humanist and radical clergy said that the Bible ought to be put into the language and hands of the people.

Now lay Christians could clearly identify the only source for knowing God's will, and they were even invited to read it themselves. All had known the Bible as one basis of theology, but what it said had not been differentiated from the rest of the church's teaching. In addition, access to the Bible had been limited. Usually it was available only in Latin, which most laity could not read or comprehend orally, even if they certainly understood the meaning of some phrases and could recite the Pater Noster and Ave Maria (Lord's Prayer and Hail Mary). Even when vernacular translations were to be had, and clergy did not discourage or prohibit their use, only the rich could afford copies. Some parish priests themselves had little more than the selected Gospel and Epistle readings needed for Mass. By the beginning of the sixteenth century, however, things were changing. The combination of two factors—the printing of and humanist attention to original texts and the idea of the Bible as the unique source of the knowledge of God to which everyone should have access in her or his own language—was revolutionary for lay theology.

Knowledge and Confidence

Lay Christians now had a new confidence in their theological knowledge. They could check out for themselves what was necessary for salvation, share it with others, and argue with clergy on the basis of the one source all must acknowledge. Both their new confidence and their new knowledge had significant consequences for lay theologians, although these were not always what modern observers might anticipate.

For one thing, neither confidence nor knowledge automatically meant individualism. It is true that for some people the conviction that all can have access to God without human mediators led to claims for individual illumination and disengagement from structured church life. For the great majority, however, confidence in their right to address God directly and to study scripture did not require rejecting clergy or church as such. Most laity were in fact happy to acknowledge the value of evangelical preachers like Luther because as intelligent Christians they recognized that they needed teachers—at least at first.

Fig. 9.1. Argula von Grumbach, Bible in hand, rebukes the professors of the University of Ingolstadt. Her title explains: "The Account of a Christian Woman of the Bavarian Nobility whose open letter, with arguments based on divine Scripture, criticises the University of Ingolstadt for compelling a young follower of the gospel to contradict the word of God." Argula von Grumbach, *Argula von Grumbach: A Woman's Voice in the Reformation*, ed. Peter Matheson (Edinburgh: T & T Clark, 1995), 72. The image comes from the edition published in Erfurt by Matthew Maler, 1523; in the Köhler Microfiche 1002/2543.

Hearers are supposed to test and prove sermons by the Bible and to maintain a critical judgment. They should be eager to learn and also ready to correct their teachers according to the only rule to which all must be faithful: the Bible. Without rejecting gospel preachers, laity also quickly began to assume the role of teachers themselves, citing scripture to educate others and reform the church.

At first virtually all who "discovered" the wonder of a single source for the knowledge of God thought that everyone would agree. It soon became evident, however, that people often drew different conclusions about what the Bible means, and clergy were inclined to dispute about this at length. Lay Christians were suspicious that extrabiblical influences might lead people astray from the clear words of the Bible. Thus, whether facing traditional clergy and Roman doctrines or their Protestant counterparts, lay theologians tended to trust common sense and literal interpretations of scripture. For some, this was explicitly grounded in an appeal to the Holy Spirit as the immediate source of illumination; Joel 2:28 was a favorite proof text.

Such illumination gave laity the ability to understand and explain the Bible without formal study, and it was consistent with *sola scriptura* because it did not add content. However, a few individuals claimed actual new revelations from the Spirit.

DIVERSITY AMONG LAY CHRISTIANS

A wide variety of lay theologies developed in the early modern world, shaped by the different political, religious, cultural, geographic, social, and economic factors in which their authors lived.

The People in Context

Perhaps one of the most significant divisions between lay theological viewpoints is that between parts of Europe that remained loyal to Rome and those that did not. It is suggestive to contrast the Alumbrados of Spain and the Spirituali of Italy with the lay theologians of Germany or England. (*Alumbrados* ["Enlightened"] is the common name for Spanish mystics who tended to substitute Spirit for church; the Spirituali were loosely organized small groups in Italy who sought a more spiritual life for the church and themselves and advocated justification by faith.)

In Protestant lands, official church teaching affirmed the Bible as the sole authority for faith and salvation and made its text accessible to all. All theologians had to argue on the basis of the same content. By their own principles (they also believed in the priesthood of believers), clergy had to acknowledge lay voices. Varied interpretations of the same scripture meant that there was plenty of disagreement about practical reforms, but the basic ground of theology was more generally shared and circumscribed than in the medieval tradition. Roman clergy, however, claimed sole religious authority; thus Catholic laity could not establish an equal access to the sources of theology. Logically, then, Spanish or Italian lay theologians emphasized the Holy Spirit and inward spiritual life as much as or more than the Bible and outward reform of the church.

Gender, economic status, and social location also contributed to differences among lay Christians. Almost without exception, men had access to more education than women of their own rank. Nobles and wealthy merchants could buy books or engage a tutor or pay the entrance fee to a religious order more easily than gardeners or herdsmen. City dwellers had more avenues for education and professional diversification than rural peasants (although both contexts included a spectrum of levels, from patrician to solid artisan to servant to vagrant, from substantial farmer to day laborer). People with a degree of power or responsibility in the public realm usually had more confidence in their own judgment than those who had never been free to decide anything for themselves.

Access to education and tools for self-expression, along with sufficient time or energy to reflect and the imagination and courage to explore new things and take risks—all play roles in the practical development of thinkers. Naturally, therefore, among the lay theologians of the early modern world there were more men than women, more urban than rural people, more comfortably established citizens than members of the lowest social ranks. Lay theologians were also likely to be individuals who were already in some measure "untraditional" or "extreme" because of some outward experience (such as the Peasants' War) or an inner crisis of faith. Thus there was no one "lay theology" in early modern Europe any more than one "Protestant" or one "Anabaptist" or one "Roman Catholic." However, a single chapter can only outline some of the significant features.

Lay Theologians in View

Since they were probably more numerous and certainly are more accessible, we will take those who broke with Rome as our main focus in examining lay theology of the period. Although Dutch, Italian, English, and French examples are included (and one Polish reference), many of the primary sources are German-language because those are early and abundant and may have had collectively more influence than others. Concentrating on the beginning of a movement is logical because that is precisely when enthusiastic and dedicated converts who do not have formal credentials may be able to assume leadership roles. We will center on the first part of the sixteenth century, before the process of confessionalization (in all its dimensions) again reduced the public role of laity in religious discussions—at least for the great majority who were not princes.

Given the range of laity, from kings to beggars, it is not possible even to consider all lay voices. In addition, evidence for conscious articulate reflection on theological issues—as distinct from matters of piety—is not equally available for all. In hopes of coming as close as possible to the religious thought of the majority of people in the pews (an item of church furniture developed by and characteristic of Protestants, who made preaching central to public worship), the lay theologians presented here were mostly common people. That is, they were literate in their vernaculars but not in Latin; they usually came from an urban background; most of the men were of middling or lower social ranks, although some of the women (excluded by sex from anything except private "higher education") might be members of the aristocracy. While the theologians discussed here were in general better educated than many of their contemporaries, each one was firmly rooted in the language and identity of his or her locale; they made no pretensions of belonging to the academic discourse practiced in the universities. As a rule they were very down-to-earth, regarding the biblical characters as their contemporaries and appropriating the biblical stories through their own experience. In general, although they did not hesitate to address clergy in polemic, lay theologians regarded other laity as their primary audiences. Whether relatives, acquaintances, or the general public, these were the people they felt compelled to teach.

Fig. 9.2. The weaver Rychsner talks with a friend about testing a priest's writing by the Bible. His title explains: "A little book about a conversation between a Weaver and a Merchant concerning the Booklet of Dr. Matthis Kretz about private Confession which he preached in Augsburg in the Cathedral of Our Lady in 1524" (Augsburg, 1524). The merchant holds the printed sermon, the weaver is pointing to a text in the Bible which lies on the table. The image comes from Köhler, Microfiche 253 / 707.

Lay thinkers differed considerably among themselves. While possessing a similar access to scripture and other vernacular texts, they varied significantly in the sophistication of their ability to use these sources and to make their arguments. Some voices are scarcely different from their formally illiterate friends who faithfully attended sermons and listened to a neighbor read a pamphlet or the moral story explaining a woodcut. At the other end of the spectrum are lay theologians who were in regular contact with educated clergy. Their religious knowledge was circumscribed by their inability to read Latin, but they could nevertheless learn or teach themselves a facility with theology that many a pastor—then and now!—might envy.

BECOMING THEOLOGIANS

To be a Christian theologian does not require producing original ideas. In fact, for most of history doing that would come closer to heresy than true theology. For early modern Europeans "innovative" was not a term of praise; on the contrary, in religious matters only God may "be creative," and even in earthly matters the authority of antiquity could always trump a claim for novelty. Thus the purpose of theology was not to say something new but to explain God's will better than it had been understood before. The Roman church had long maintained the sole right to teach, claiming a monopoly on the knowledge of God's will. When challenged about some apparently "new" dogma, clergy unhesitatingly answered that the point was part of the unwritten tradition in the keeping of the church.

Finding the True Faith

The great majority of those who broke with Rome, as well as those who did not, were not even interested in having a "new" theology;

what they wanted was God's *true* teaching, which many believed Rome had betrayed. One way early modern Europeans differed from their medieval predecessors was in the sheer numbers of those who now felt compelled and able to judge for themselves what God's true teaching was and then to articulate that for anyone they could persuade to listen. The process of determining "true teaching" might involve drawing on various teachers or explicitly rejecting any human sources. The point was that the lay theologian, like her or his clerical counterpart, was consciously formulating and explicating his or her (if not *the*) understanding of God's will. However, many intellectual influences contributed to these lay theologies—traditional catechetical texts (for example, the Lord's Prayer, familiar parables); apocalyptic ideas of war between God and the devil or attempts to identify the Antichrist; belief in magic and the supernatural; late medieval mysticism and more esoteric sources like the Jewish Cabbala; Roman doctrines like transubstantiation and new "heretical" teachings such as justification by faith alone.

> **Katharina Schütz Zell on Divine Comfort (1558)**
>
> Since I have experienced so many afflictions in myself and in others, and also God has given me again much comfort, I have thought about your affliction and Paul's words: "God afflicts us that we may believe the afflicted, and He comforts us again so that we can comfort the afflicted out of our experience." [2 Cor. 1:4] So I wanted to share these two Psalms with you in writing. While I hope that God will give you more teaching and comfort in bearing your cross than I can do here, nevertheless love does not cease to be concerned for others.
> —From Katharina Schütz Zell, *Church Mother: The Writings of a Protestant Reformer in Sixteenth-Century Germany*, ed. Elsie Anne McKee (Chicago: University of Chicago Press, 2006), 133–34.

Various Patterns of Lay Activity

In an effort to find the true teaching, different people combined these influences in their own ways. Sometimes individuals produced virtually new religions. Carlo Ginzburg has made the fascinating (or bizarre) cosmology of an Italian miller famous, setting out Menocchio's views of creation as "the cheese and the worms." Anselm Schubert is completing a study of the remarkable (or mad) German weaver-furrier Augustine Bader, who shaped his secondhand acquaintance with the Cabbala into a new religion in which first he, then his infant son, was to be the Messiah.[2]

At other times lay theologians worked within their institutional churches to renew the religious spirit, but chose or were driven to a separatist mode. Camilla Russell has shown how, without officially leaving Rome, the Italian noblewoman Guilia Gonzaga led the dissidents of the Spirituali movement shaped by the learned layman Juan de Valdès. One might call Gonzaga "a nursing mother" to this elite lay spirituality more than an original voice, but her initiative is clear. Not only was she committed to Valdès's teaching of justification by faith alone; she also felt qualified to choose his successor. When she asked Marcantonio Flaminio to write for her circle, Gonzaga was acting as a kind of lay bishop and theologian, able to identify good doctrine and confident to provide it for herself and others—quietly defying Rome but avoiding open conflict.[3]

Most often lay theologians sought not only to reshape doctrine but also to reform the institutional church as they knew it, particularly in the interests of bringing assurance of salvation to people's souls and justice to their lives. They now had new grounds to continue old anticlericalism. Especially clear are attacks on pastoral abuses such as demanding alms (payment) for sacraments or excommunicating the poor for debt, and sharp rejection of a double standard such as withholding the communion cup from the laity. Beyond traditional anticlerical issues, the positive answers to old problems often sounded like ideas that earlier "heretics" had espoused, but sometimes they also went (much) further.

SOME CHARACTERISTICS OF LAY THEOLOGIES

The teachings characteristic of lay theologians were ones that touched them most closely; that is, they were practical, not abstract.

The Bible, the Church, and the Nature of Holiness

Among the most important "new" ideas was the insistence on testing everything by "the Word of God" and rejecting anything that could not be found in the Bible. Appeal to scripture could be sharp in polemic or gently persuasive when laypeople shared their discoveries with each other. Virtually everyone agreed that the church is necessary for salvation, but the church was now both subordinated to the Bible and tightly bound to it. The true church is where God's Word is known and preached and obeyed. True Christians follow the Bible, and for most lay theologians, that meant turning the traditional idea of holiness upside down. Not only were the clergy's abuses wrong, but the basic idea of celibacy was unbiblical and a denigration of baptism, the common vow of the whole people of God. Instead of celibacy, life "in the world" as honest married folk working to support their families now became the model of holiness.

Sacraments and Ministers

In the Roman church, by virtue of their special rank as privileged intercessors, the clergy maintained exclusive control over most sacraments, which had been *the* means of grace. Penance, one of the two sacraments laity experienced frequently, had suffered from financial abuses and had also required the greatest lay subordination. The situation changed with the introduction of the priesthood of believers: every believer has equal access to God in prayer, so all are priests. Forgiveness comes from Christ alone, not any human intercessor, but any believer may serve as priest to others because James says "to confess to each other" and each one who knows "the Gospel" can pray for others and tell them Christ's forgiveness (5:16). The Mass, traditionally the main source of grace, became as controversial as penance. Laity often attacked Rome for teaching people to trust in a "breaden god" that would quickly become moldy if left uneaten, and making the Mass into a way to "buy heaven." Others demanded to know where transubstantiation is found in the Bible or expressed outrage at the "idolatry" that would

---

Ursula Weyda on Biblical Authority (1524)

If you can show us our error with the scriptures we will gladly repent and change our confession, but if not. . . . Unless God's Word is there, the people must certainly be heathens even if they appear holy before the world—so holy that they could raise the dead. So then . . . it follows necessarily that nothing should be preached in the church except God's own Word without any addition; for the Word of God alone makes people citizens of heaven.

—From Ursula Weyda, *Wyder das unchristlich Schreyben und Lesterbuoch des Apts Simon zuo Pegaw* (Eisenberg, 1524), A3r, A4v.

An Anonymous Author on Biblical Authority (1524)

The Christian church judges and acts by the Spirit of God and holds to the holy Word of God and the Gospel. It does not add to it or take away from it, for God does not act against Himself; He commands us not to falsify or diminish or add to His Word. Matt. 15 & 19 & 23 & 24. Deut. 4, Ps. 40 and Baruch 6.

—From Anonymous, *Wider Bruder Cunrat dreiger Augustiner ordens durch das teütschland provincial und diner der ramischen kirchen Ein find Evangelischer warheit* (Colmar: Amandus Karckall, 1524), B4v.

Ursula Weyda on Celibacy (1534)

God made human beings not to main-tain chastity but to increase and multi-ply; Gen. 1[:28]. . . . [O Sir], free yourself [from your vows of celibacy] and turn back again to your right oath and vow previously made to God in baptism, from which you have fallen away [by becoming a monk]. For in baptism we have all vowed to God to believe and to follow His Word; by that, in my view, we have all become "spiritual" or "clergy."

—From Weyda, *Wyder Simon zuo Pegaw*, B3v, C1v.

Anne Askew on the Mass (1545)

Thirdly he asked me, why I said I had rather read five lines in the Bible than hear five masses in the temple. I con-fessed that I said that—not to dispraise either the Epistle or Gospel but because [reading the Bible] greatly edified me and [hearing masses] did not at all. As St. Paul witnesses in 1 Cor. 14[:8] where he says: "If the trumpet gives an uncer-tain sound, who will prepare himself for battle?" . . . Eighth, he asked if I did not think that private masses helped departed souls. I said it was a great idolatry to believe more in them than in the death which Christ died for us.

—From Anne Askew, *The Examinations of Anne Askew*, ed. Elaine V. Beilin (New York: Oxford University Press, 1996), 166–67 (language modernized).

---

substitute anything for Christ. In fact, laity usually did not reject the sacrament or ordinance they often called the Lord's Supper, but they insisted that it be biblical and communal.

Now the chief function of leadership was not intercession but preaching. No one needed an ordained priest in order to confess sins and be right with God, but everyone was eager to have biblically literate preachers. No religious groups—even Anabaptists—gave a formal preaching role to women, but that did not prevent the maid-servants from experiencing the Spirit and speak-ing out (Joel 2:28)! Most laity accepted the idea of appropriate preparation for preachers, whether that was learning scripture and being baptized on confession of faith, or studying the Bible in the light of the Apostles' (or Nicene) Creed and the writings of reformers like Luther, John Calvin, or Caspar Schwenkfeld.

Christ, Faith, and Human Will

With or without a creed, lay theologians insisted on Jesus Christ as the sole Savior and justifica-tion by biblical faith alone. All veneration of the saints or humanly imagined "good works" were rejected; there is no salvation except by faith in Christ alone.

This common agreement, however, could not hide disagreement on the nature of faith and human will. Many laity as well as clergy became convinced that all human beings are powerless to contribute to their own salvation. Faith is trust that God means God's promises of forgiveness in Christ and trust is a sheer gift, not something a human being can do. Others, however, insisted that people have a free choice, if they will use it. These lay theologians tended to read the New

Testament as God's clear law for human salvation. Following that law is obligatory; one to whom God teaches the faith must confess it and practice it—that is justification by faith. Those who keep Jesus' commands are the true church and are saved. Those who claim grace by Roman sacraments, or Protestant "faith alone," but do not demand an informed confession of faith in the Savior Jesus and lives modeled on his clear teaching are not God's church.

It appears that lay theologians of higher socioeconomic rank or greater formal education were more likely to believe in human helplessness. Perhaps this was because they had had more means to test the (in)adequacy of works: masses for the dead, pilgrimages, new altar paintings, rich reliquaries all cost money. They had tried these things and found themselves still uncertain of their salvation. So they sought other means of assurance not subject to human limitations, including their own, and found these in the Pauline texts about human inability and God's grace alone. The lay theologians who believed that human beings can obey God if they truly want to were frequently members of groups with little wealth or formal education. Their confidence in their ability to choose may reflect the influence of the Roman doctrine that everyone must "do what he can," as well as their practical assurance that Christ would not command things his faithful disciples could not do. They certainly believed that the socially privileged would seek excuses to avoid the plain meaning of the text in order to continue their comfortable lives. All laity tended to read the Bible rather literally, but usually the more simple the education, the more literalist the interpretation. There is a certain matter-of-factness in the Anabaptist conviction that Jesus' teachings can and

---

Katharina Schütz Zell on Priesthood of Believers (1534)

[Teach your household] to know that they do not serve human beings but God when they faithfully [in the faith] keep house, obey, cook, wash dishes, wipe up and tend children, and suchlike work which serves human life, and that (while doing this very work) they can also turn toward God with the voice of song. And teach them that in doing this, they please God much better than any priest, monk, or nun in their incomprehensible choir song.
—From Schütz Zell, *Church Mother*, 95.

Katharina Schütz Zell on Christ Alone and Grace Alone (1548 and 1553)

Christ has power to save us from sins, death, and hell, and to give us eternal life. In Him is all salvation, and in no other creature or work in heaven and earth, for no one comes to the Father, or dares to think of coming to Him except through this living Son of God, who should be honored as the Father is. The one who has Him has everything; He is the way, the truth and the life [see John 14:6, 5:23].

That is my glory . . . in God and Christ, not in myself. I glory that God the Father gave me the gift of faith in His Son (which is not given to everyone), solely out of His gracious love, without any ability or merit on my part [see Eph. 2:4-8, 19].
—From Schütz Zell, *Church Mother*, 107, 212.

If you, therefore, desire to enter into the regions of the holy world, and into the inheritance of the saints, gird your loins, and follow after them; search the Scriptures and it shall show you their ways. . . . The angel who spoke to the prophet said; 'There is a city full of all good things; the entrance to it is narrow, as if there were a fire on one side and a deep water on the other; whoever wants to enter that city must first go through that narrow way.' See, my son, that way has no retreats, there are no roundabout or crooked little paths; whoever goes to the left or the right inherits death. See, this is the way which is found by few, and walked by a still much smaller number; for there are some who know well that this is the way to life but it is too severe for them, it pains their flesh.

—From Thieleman van Braght, *The Bloody Theater or Martyrs Mirror of the Defenseless Christians Who Baptized Only Upon Confession of Faith, and Who Suffered and Died for the Testimony of Jesus, Their Saviour, from the Time of Christ to the Year* A.D. *1660*, trans. Joseph F. Sohm (Scottdale, Pa.: Herald Press, 1992), 453–54.

must be followed by any serious Christian and the only bar is human unwillingness to pay the price.

Popular Biblical Interpretation and Lay Theology

Although lay Christians read the Bible without the nuances of a humanist education, there was clearly a range of sophistication among lay readers. At the most popular level, writers and audience continued the traditional connection of daily experience with divine judgment, as the biblical allusions in woodcuts of disasters or miraculous occurrences clearly demonstrate. When using scripture verbally to affirm their faith, laity often linked together loosely paraphrased texts they had absorbed from hearing scripture read or preached. When citing the Bible in polemical contexts, lay writers might quote one text and then give a list of references (probably drawn from the handy proof-text anthologies that were soon circulating or from the works of clerical reformers).

Some lay theologians, however, demonstrate considerable skill in using biblical texts as the grounds of intellectually developed and thoughtful presentations. They knew their Bibles well enough to fit together the specific texts that shaped their ideas into coherent and often very persuasive arguments. Many of these patterns no doubt had their origin in sermons or pamphlets by clergy, but the lay appropriation is rarely wooden. It is sometimes quite creative and usually offers a distinctively lay angle of vision.

Humor and Practicality in Lay Theology

Lay theologians almost always expressed a very practical orientation and a strong sense of humor. Poking fun at immorality was traditional,

Fig. 9.3. A woodcut published in Strasbourg in 1571 by Christian Müller the Younger depicts a catastrophic fire in Gniezno, Poland. On the left a simple shepherd is fear-struck by the appearance of an angel (Acts 2:9) telling him to go into the city and warn them of divine judgment. On the right is the city in flames, a disaster warning them of sin and the need to repent; in the upper right is a vision of the battle of the army of God (white banners with crosses) against the devil's army (black banners) (Rev. 19:11-21). Image from *Deutsche illustrierte Flugblätter*, ed. Harms, Bd. 7, Teil 2, 32–33.

but now similar mocking repartee was common for doctrines. The heresy trial of the Dutch Mennonite martyr Elizabeth in 1549 sparkles with her courage and ability to defend her convictions to hostile men of high social rank who held all the earthly power. Anne Askew, an English gentlewoman burned at the stake a few years earlier (1546), displayed a similar self-possession and humor.

Placing an opponent on the horns of a dilemma born of his own self-contradictory teaching or behavior was a time-honored tactic lay theologians continued to use—for Protestant as well as Roman leaders. In 1557, Katharina Schütz Zell challenged the Lutheran Ludwig Rabus to explain his unauthorized departure from his Strasbourg parish to be head of the church in Ulm. He claimed the high ground of defending the Augsburg Confession (Strasbourg had been forced to return its cathedral to Rome in the Interim), but Roman worship was in Ulm, too. Schütz Zell responded, "If [you say] that the Mass in Ulm is in a corner and cloister, and no one pays attention to it and they hope it will soon go away. . . . O dear sir, I perceive clearly that you think our Lord God is old and no longer sees well, and what happens in a corner does not bother Him: He only looks at the great high temple [cathedral]!"[4]

Lay theologians were always concerned with the practical: teaching and practice must never be

---

An Anabaptist on the Lord's Supper (1549)

Lords: What did the Lord say, when He gave His disciples the Supper? Elizabeth: What did he give them, flesh or bread? Lords: He gave them bread. Elizabeth: Did not the Lord remain sitting there? Who then would eat the flesh of the Lord?

—From Van Braght, *Martyrs Mirror*, 482.

Katharina Schütz Zell on Speaking Out (1524)

If you will not allow yourself to be instructed by the truth, I will patiently suffer injustice with Christ, who teaches me not to resist evil and, when someone strikes me on one cheek. . . . Then I could be excused before God, and also happily, patiently live the Word of God [Matt. 5:11-12a]: "Blessed are you when people . . . lie about you for My name's sake. . . ." Christ also did this when Ananias' servant hit Him in the face. He did not strike back, He did not flee, He did not resist the evil at all, as He had previously taught His disciples. However, He did not keep silent about it as if the servant acted rightly, but He said: "If I have spoken evil, give proof of it, but if not, why do you strike Me?" [John 18:22-23]. For it is sufficient that we Christians suffer injustice; we should not say that injustice is justice. To keep silence is not patience; to suffer is patience. I should tell my innocence to the one who lies about me, and after that if he will not turn back from what he is doing, then I should suffer his injustice. Otherwise by keeping silence I give him grounds to continue in his trumped up lies, and that, in my judgment, is against brotherly love (Lev. 19:18). For I would be unwilling to be left in error and lies without instruction: why should I not also in turn correct the error and lies that my neighbor believes?

—From Schütz Zell, *Church Mother*, 66.

separated. The purpose of theology (talk about God) is to teach Christians to be Christian, which means both believers and doers of God's will. For some people, this meant one-to-one correspondence between Jesus' words and church practice. "Anabaptists" read passages such as Mark 13:13, where Christ says that his followers will be hated by everyone, as evidence that persecution is a necessary sign of the church and anyone who is not persecuted is not godly. For others the connection between teaching and practice was just as essential but might be less literalist. Schütz Zell took worthiness for the Lord's Supper very seriously indeed, but she interpreted "discerning the body" (1 Cor. 11:29) not in the traditional sense of adoring the host but as meaning Christian love for her neighbors, rightly seeing them as Christ's body. In her view she would be unfit for the Supper if she did not trust Christ alone for forgiveness and also love his members.[5]

Salvation and Loving the Neighbor

To say that theology must always be practical is not to say that theology is only about practice. In an age when even hardened sinners counted salvation as the final good, and many people considered it their primary goal in life, to be assured that one held to the right teaching was an obviously practical concern. Uncertainty about salvation had been one of the great anxieties of many late medieval Christians, and a firm positive response to this problem was eminently practical.

Knowing, believing, doing what God requires, right worship, and loving your neighbor are essential. Lay theologians did not appreciate—or treat with much personal interest—the fine distinctions professional theologians were given to making. The two focuses for lay Christians were salvation and "love your neighbor," and they were often willing to tolerate theological variety on what they saw as secondary matters (such as the nature of Christ's presence in the Lord's Supper) in order to preserve brotherly love. However, even loving your neighbors is not sufficient to save you if you are wrong about faith; seeking salvation might require breaking fellowship with family or village or neighbors.

WAYS OF BEING A LAY THEOLOGIAN

But how was the "ordinary Christian" supposed to participate in "lay theology"? Obviously not all could write tracts, or be patrons of authors or preachers. Certainly very few would make the stake their pulpit. Although increasing numbers of laypeople could read and often write in their own vernacular, the great majority were not yet formally literate even in their native language. However, the common culture was still largely shaped by ear and memory; one who might not be able to read fluently could listen to sermons or pamphlets read aloud and sometimes retain what she or he heard in amazing detail. Being a theologian does not require writing your own theology; you must only be willing and able to articulate what you believe, wherever you got it.

Particularly important for the expression of lay theology were memorized prayers and songs, the key sources for what many people knew about God. Learning "by heart" carried no negative connotation of insincerity, and music was popular as entertainment and education. The content of prayers and songs was therefore a critical issue. All reformers, lay as well as clerical, agreed that much popular devotion was unedifying, if not worse. Clergy encouraged believers to learn good (approved) prayers as well as to sing their faith; lay reformers were more likely to concentrate on the latter. Biblical texts and other hymns were set to music; often the tunes were already known or popular, and they were always easy to sing.

Naturally, then, one of the most widespread expressions of lay theology is found in song. In public worship the priesthood of believers was manifested by congregational singing in the vernacular.

Anne Askew
on Women Teaching (1545)

Secondly he said there was a woman who testified that I should read that God was not in temples made with hands. Then I showed him the seventh and seventeenth chapters of Acts of the Apostles, what Stephen and Paul had said there. Whereupon he asked me how I understood those sentences? I answered that I would not throw pearls among swine, for acorns were good enough. . . . Then the bishop's chancellor said I was much to blame for uttering the scriptures. For St. Paul (he said) forbade women to speak or talk of the word of God. I answered him that I knew Paul's meaning as well as he, which is (1 Cor. 14) that a woman ought not to speak in the congregation by way of teaching. And then I asked him, how many women he had seen go into the pulpit and preach? He said he never saw any. Then I said he ought not to find fault with poor women unless they broke the law.

—From Anne Askew,
The Examinations, 166–67.

Instead of the Latin, clerical, male music of the Roman liturgy, laymen and even laywomen were given an active role in prayer and encouraged to use this same "sung theology" in their daily lives. Everyone was urged to read, sing, say their faith. Parents and householders were reminded of their responsibility to learn and sing their faith as they went about their work and also to teach all their dependents. Whether they wrote the songs or (more often) memorized them from hearing texts prepared by others, the musical scriptures, sermons, and catechisms laypeople acquired *became their lay theology.* The evidence is everywhere. Hymns were often the only fixed liturgical forms Anabaptists used, and songs about their martyrs were preserved as witnesses to their faith along with other hymns. French Huguenots and English Puritans were identified by their metrical psalms, which were sung in family gatherings or as lullabies, on battlefields or in prisons, where those awaiting martyrdom proclaimed their faith and lifted up their hearts and voices together.[6] What Christians recited and sang shaped their lives and the way they faced the disaster and death that were always on the horizon.

Instruction took time, but it is clear that "ordinary folk" did learn and appropriate the new religious texts and music. The printer Jean Rivery adapted several of Calvin's prayers to make a pattern for family devotions. The irreverent (like their medieval counterparts) made parodies of religious songs—including some Genevans of their Psalms; misappropriation also demonstrates learning. Schütz Zell listened to the problems of her Strasbourg neighbors and published a collection of hymns to provide them with "sermons in song." She added notes to make the texts even more edifying, and she revised the music to make it as attractive and familiar as possible, so that the mother would want to sing these songs of faith to her crying baby, the maid would do the same as she washed and cleaned, the peasant as he farmed.[7] That way, everyone would know what they believed and be able to talk about God, and every hour of the day that was filled with duties to serve God and neighbor would also ring with the joyous proclamation of faith.

FOR FURTHER READING

Askew, Anne. *The Examinations of Anne Askew.* Edited by Elaine V. Beilin. Women Writers in English 1350–1850. New York: Oxford University Press, 1996.

Ginzburg, Carlo. *The Cheese and the Worms: The Cosmos of a Sixteenth-Century Miller.* Translated by John and Anne Tedeschi. Baltimore: Johns Hopkins University Press, 1980.

Schütz Zell, Katharina. *Church Mother: The Writings of a Protestant Reformer in Sixteenth-Century Germany.* Edited by Elsie McKee. Chicago: University of Chicago Press, 2006.

Van Braght, Thieleman. *The Bloody Theater or Martyrs Mirror of the Defenseless Christians Who Baptized Only Upon Confession of Faith, and Who Suffered and Died for the Testimony of Jesus, Their Saviour, from the Time of Christ to the Year A.D. 1660.* Translated by Joseph F. Sohm. Scottdale, Pa.: Herald Press, 1992.

von Grumbach, Argula. *Argula von Grumbach: A Woman's Voice in the Reformation.* Edited by Peter Matheson. Edinburgh: T & T Clark, 1995.

INSIDERS AND OUTSIDERS

SUSAN R. BOETTCHER

CHAPTER TEN

Conceiving of the history of Christianity as a history of Christians, as Virginia Burrus suggests we do in her introduction to volume 2 of this series, means that we must also consider the boundaries that marked the limits of Christianity. We might accomplish this task simply by asking "Who is not a Christian?" and then making a list of early moderns who found themselves outside the body of Christ. The two primary groups were Jews and Muslims, and as the sixteenth century wore on, although we will not treat them here, the additional category of "heathens," non-Christian peoples with whom Europeans came into contact as they escalated their aggressive conquest of the globe. But in a much earlier era, when the apostle Paul conceived of the body of Christ as one with many members, he referred to the possibility, though rejecting it, that some members were better than others, more prized in Christ than those unfortunate members he described as "feeble" and "uncomely parts" (1 Cor. 12:12-13, King James Version). Despite his rejection of such priorities, and advocacy of an all-encompassing love for one's neighbor in his more famous, subsequent chapter, insider/outsider thinking persisted within Christianity in the form of the conception of heresy.

The margins of the body of Christ were more haphazard than they may seem from our latter-day perspective. In light of the often vague doctrinal atmosphere of the later Middle Ages, thinking about insiders and outsiders is a deceptively simple proposition. The predominant scholarly view of the sixteenth century stresses that the Reformation intensified a process, under way since the later Middle

Ages, of more strictly defining the markers of Christian identity.[1] Thus the Reformation did not create substantially new ideas about the limits of Christianity; it simply intensified sentiments already in place. Although the emergence of Protestantism, in its various forms, did not create a hostile attitude toward non-Christians, the pervasive reevaluation of doctrine and piety focused attention more strongly on individuals and groups seen to deviate from the norm.

The experience of the Anabaptists underlines this point. Though Anabaptists were recognized as Christians, their status as heretics in the eyes of all of the emerging confessions nonetheless pushed them to the religious and political boundaries of emerging "mainstream" Christian society. In some territories, at some times, this marginal status was admittedly less binding than it was at others, a situation no less true for Jews and Turks. Even if it was occasionally difficult to pinpoint the location of these boundaries, however, both insiders and outsiders were very aware of how stringent they were. The process of reevaluation of Christian beliefs and social arrangements led to the creation of notions of identity and defensive boundaries directed both against members of other religions and against other Christians. One obvious way for us to examine this process of pushing some people toward the center and others toward the margins is to consider the usual contemporary views of outsider religions such as Islam and Judaism.

Fig. 10.1. The Little Ship of Christ. "God gave his church, persecuted and expelled, comfort here." Relief over the eastern portal of the Great Church, Emden, in Germany. 1660. See also text at page 254.

The point of stereotypes of outsiders, which were cultivated in a synergy between laypeople and the clergy, was not to understand outsiders on their own terms but rather to tighten up definitions of appropriate Christian belief and practice. As the case of "heretics" shows, however, even marginal groups in church or society could be made to serve the rhetorical purpose of defining the borders of Christianity. Indeed, as different Protestant bodies emerged, each used definitions of the other as heretical in order to bolster its own self-definition.

Aside from such Protestant heretics, we can see this process reflected in the cases of the "feeble" and "less comely parts" of the body of Christ, particularly the poor. Because responsibility for poor relief often continued to be placed with religious authorities in early modern Europe, this interaction frequently has been captured in the records of religious bodies, the subject of the final portion of the essay. Throughout, although it will not be discussed in much detail here, we should also keep in mind that although the purpose of defining a coherent picture of outsiders was important to the formation of confessional Christianity, outsiders typically had views of themselves that did not square exactly with those of insiders.

Before turning to our examination of these four kinds of outsiders, we should pause briefly to consider how we can establish what early modern people knew and believed about the outsiders in their societies. Indeed, the overwhelming majority of sources that report to us about ordinary Christians in this period were created by elites for their own purposes. Historians are often forced to make speculative conclusions about popular attitudes based on the appearance of ordinary individuals in judicial, ecclesiastical, or tax records. Because average people in Reformation Europe did not always read and write, it is sometimes difficult to find evidence that suggests what their beliefs, attitudes, and feelings toward religious outsiders might have been.

It was previously the view that early modern European cultural attitudes were split between "high" and "low" cultural spheres, so that elite culture, while promulgated to the masses, was not representative of popular attitudes. More recent research suggests, however, the presence of shared entertainments and ideals. This common culture suggests that many attitudes, prejudices, and stereotypes were shared and modified by social groups of differing statuses.[2] Thus we can take sermons, books, and woodcuts as evidence of generally shared social attitudes that may have been formulated by elites but had as their presuppositions a broad base of support in their audiences.

ISLAM

We begin with Muslims because they were the most frightening outsiders to the early modern Christian, and because, while every Christian knew something about them, the accuracy of this knowledge in any more than extremely general terms was very limited. The general reputation for Muslim brutality was created in the wake of the invasions of Iberia in the eighth century and subsequent attempts at reconquest, which led to a storm of stories and sagas that processed both the encounter and the resulting trauma left behind in Christian Europe. The Spanish *reconquista* only slowly made inroads into Muslim hegemony. On the Iberian Peninsula, at the military defeat of the last Muslim kingdom in al-Andalus in 1492, Muslims who decided to remain in the now Spanish territories (*mudéjares*) had been granted freedom to practice their religion. This freedom did not last long, however. In 1501, their books were burned, and by 1502, the united crown of Aragon and Castile mandated that they convert or be expelled. Such converts, called *moriscos* by their Christian neighbors, probably practiced only a superficial version of Christianity and maintained their faith and customs privately.

As early as 1508, however, these crypto-Muslims were forbidden to wear traditional dress, including the female veil, and increasingly restrictive legislation followed periodically until 1566, when Philip II took the measure of forcing *moriscos* to surrender their children to Christian families. The resulting revolt in 1568–1570 led to the removal of the *moriscos* from the Granada region, where their proximity to the North African coast had been seen as an invitation to betrayal. Philip III expelled them from Spain permanently after 1609; the number of people uprooted is often estimated at about three hundred thousand. Erasing the alleged surviving pious practices of persisting *moriscos* became the central focus of the Spanish Inquisition after the 1560s, until their expulsion was declared completed in 1614.[3]

The attitude of Spanish Catholics to this minority was highly complex and often ambivalent, not least because of their dominant position in certain industries. In the fourteenth century, particularly, the Spanish and Portuguese crowns had prized Muslims as architects and artisans. By the time of their expulsion, the *moriscos* of Granada seem to have been occupied primarily in day labor and other low-status occupations, but they had preserved their solidarity by living together in particular quarters of Spanish cities. However, because of the long-term presence of Muslims in Spanish territories, local populations were familiar with many customs that marked followers of

Islam, particularly washing and bathing rituals as well as dietary laws and prayer practices.

Even as they withdrew and were expelled from Iberia, however, the advance of Muslims was experienced by Europeans on another front after 1453, when the long-defended city of Constantinople fell to the armies of the Ottoman Empire, releasing a flood of Orthodox Christian refugees toward Western Europe who brought frightening stories and rumors along with them. After the fall of Constantinople, Ottoman advances were regular and alarming. "Turk" was the name assigned by Western Europeans to the soldiers of these advancing armies, although the Ottoman army included members of other nationalities.

After 1453, the armies advanced further eastward. Belgrade was taken in 1521, and significant portions of Hungary fell under Ottoman control after the Battle of Mohacs in 1526. Vienna was besieged in 1529 and Buda captured in 1541. Regular advances, conducted during the Central European growing season, continued until the death of Suleiman the Magnificent on the battlefield near Szigetvar in 1566. Despite the resulting 1568 Peace of Adrianople, which ended armed hostilities for more than a generation, Hapsburg Holy Roman emperors regularly paid tribute to the Turkish ruler, the Sublime Porte, and the Ottomans threatened Vienna as late as 1683.

In this atmosphere, the printing presses of Nuremberg and other German cities generated a regular stream of *Zeitungen* (literally "tidings") or news releases, as we would say today, that reported on events on the battlefields, which were located in growing proximity to Western Europe. They told of brutal armies that abandoned their dead on the field, ignoring the rotting corpses in order to pursue military advantage, and of vicious occupiers who burned the food supplies and eviscerated the children of local communities that refused to cooperate. Despite the sensationalist qualities of these communications, scholars have debated how strongly fear of the Ottomans actually influenced the contemporary situation. The estates of the German Imperial Diet were typically reluctant to tax their membership to aid the emperor for the defense against the Turks, although they always did so in the end. It has been argued, perhaps with some overstatement, that it was this problem that kept the issue of religious reform

on the Diet's agenda for such a long period of time: Protestant powers were able to insist that the Holy Roman emperor take account of
their demands as long as they withheld the monies necessary for the
defense against the Turks.[4]

Political awareness of the Turks among Central Europeans was
conditioned by a fragmentary, apocryphal awareness of the religious
beliefs of Islam. The spiritual transformation that provoked the slogan
sola scriptura (by scripture alone) applied
this standard only piecemeal to the scriptures of other faiths. Notwithstanding
the critical attitude to medieval manuscripts that the Reformation inherited
from humanism, the dominant manuscript tradition of the Koran in Western
Europe was mediated heavily through
twelfth-century Iberian Latin paraphrases
of the Muslim holy book. This material,
the so-called Cluniac corpus, was originally prepared with the goal of mission,
and its compilers disordered the suras, or
sections of the Koran, by rearranging the
material thematically.[5]

The 1543 Latin translation of the
Koran prepared by Theodore Bibliander
was nothing more than an emendation
of these texts. Although Bibliander read
Arabic and used a complete manuscript
Koran to prepare this edition,[6] his language skills were not sufficient to allow

him to notice the many errors in the medieval sources he edited. Even
so, Zurich threatened to suppress the Bibliander translation, since
its patrician city council viewed its content as dangerous, and it was
printed only through the intervention of influential theologians.[7] Aside
from Bibliander, the most widely known information about the Turks
in early modern Europe was Georg of Hungary's "Treatise on the Customs, Way of Life, and Wickedness of the Turks" (*Tractatus de moribus,
conditionibus et nequicia turcorum*) of 1481, allegedly the work of a

Fig. 10.2. Woodcut of an
Ottoman soldier. "I am a
Turk," the rhyme begins,
noting his desire to kill
or enslave Christians
(man, woman and child)
in Croatia, Hungary, and
Austria, or wherever he finds
them. Hans Guldenmundt,
Nuremberg, sixteenth
century.

Georg of Hungary's Treatise on the Turks

The first group are the [Muslim] priests. They are highly esteemed as leaders of the people, as executors and guardians of the Law, as scholars and judges and as directors of the religious institutions, churches and schools of higher learning. They take the view that no one can be saved except by the Law of Mechomet, and seek to convince everyone of this by their teaching. And although they cannot prove it by any argument, authority or example, they use every means imaginable to assert themselves against their opponents. They have strong support among the people, and especially among the princes and officials.

The second group are the so-called Dervishes. They are monks. . . .

The third group are the so-called "czofilar," or Sufi, who devoted themselves to meditation and spiritual exercises. They are highly esteemed as followers of the prophets and the "fathers" who have founded these sects, and claim a higher authority for themselves than the others. They too have no basis at all for their view, but simply say it has been handed down to them from of old. They are of the view, that everyone has to be saved by merit; this merit, which they call "pereketallach," or the God's blessing, suffices for the salvation of souls. Grace and Law are not needed. They show great zeal in their dedication to special prayers and spiritual exercises in the form of vigils and meditations. They never tire of their ever-repeated prayers. . . .

The fourth group is called "horife" in their language, which means heresy. They take the view that everyone is saved by their own particular law, and each people or nation has been given its own law by God by which it must be saved.

—From Georg of Hungary, *Tractatus de moribus conditionibus et nequicia turcorum* (Treatise on the Customs, Lifestyle, and Duplicity of the Turks), ed. Reinhard Klockow, based on the first edition of 1481 (Cologne: Böhlau, 1993), 358–59.

former Turkish captive. The book was freely translated into German and excerpted by Martin Luther and Sebastian Franck.

Georg's book was typical of a series of about twelve quasi-ethnographic texts about the Turks that circulated through most of Western Europe and formed a basic corpus of general knowledge available to readers, much of which was also transmitted to their nonliterate counterparts, often in sermons, but also in songs, poems, news reports, woodcuts, diplomatic documents, and pastoral literature. More than one thousand imprints of *Turcica* (Turkish Customs) appeared in Germany alone during the sixteenth century. (Other influential ethnographies of the early modern period circulated under the names of Hans Schiltberger, Benedetto Ramberti, Antoine Geuffroy, Bartolomej Georgijevic, Luigi Bassano, Giovanantonio Menavino, Theodoros Spanduginos, Pierre Belon, Nicols de Nicolay, and Jacques de Villamont. Some of these authors were diplomats or merchant travelers, others refugees, and still others former captives of the army or slaves in Ottoman areas.)

These books transmitted a great deal of information about Islam to their consumers, although the quality varied. In addition to descriptions of the organization of Muslim

society, they included information about the basic beliefs of the religion, the customs of those who practiced it, and its prophet Muhammad. Interestingly, while the descriptions of religious rituals were
often reasonably accurate, the information about Muhammad was
predominantly scurrilous. His lineage was drawn alternately from
Esau or Ishmael. He is portrayed as a handsome adventurer with a
saucy streak and an impertinent personality with latent self-impor-
tant, even megalomaniac tendencies, who succeeded in bewitching his
wife, Hidigia (Khadija), a sensible woman who was much older and
thus made foolish by his charms.

In this literature, the Koran is said to have been composed after
he fell in with a renegade Aryan monk, Sergius, who helped him
compose the suras. Muhammad suffered from "falling sickness," so in
order to prevent his wife from discovering the truth, he informed her
that these episodes were actually visions of the angel Gabriel. He was
forced to leave Mecca because of his religious ambitions, but he was
followed in his flight to Medina only by his in-laws and a great band
of homeless people and criminals who had nothing better to do. He
eventually took back Mecca not with the aid of faithful followers, but
rather by exploiting the tender mercies of marauding Arab mercenaries. Such was the picture that was painted.

If Europeans were taught that Muhammad was a mountebank
and the Ottoman armies were brutal, Ottoman society was described
in heavily gendered terms with a component of unrestrained lascivi-
ousness thrown in for good measure. According to this literature, after
killing Christian men, Turks raped their women, sometimes even
performing sexual assault on corpses. Another favorite locus of such
accounts was the slave market, where Christian captives were exhibited
like animals for purchase, forced to subject their naked bodies to the
examination of their future Turkish masters. Once purchased, these
slaves were vulnerable to the pornographic gaze and the physical viola-
tion of their new owners. Men were castrated before they were used as
sodomitical objects; Grimm's *Wörterbuch* informs us that Luther was
one of the first German authors to use the new slang "dog-marriage" in
his writings on the Turk to describe deviant sexual practices.

As the sixteenth century wore on, this literature became more
and more extreme in its sexual metaphors, eventually charging that
Muhammad enjoyed using fish as a masturbation aid.[8] The Dutch

ambassador to the Porte, Ogier Ghislain de Busbecq, also discussed the lesbian pleasures of Muslim women, although female same-sex relations were discussed relatively seldom in the *Turcica* literature of this period.[9] While such motifs surely titillated the reader, their ultimate function was to incite audiences to violence or at least active support for resistance against Muslims, who represented a tyrannical authority, as witnessed by the sexual disorder of their society.

Sexual sin pointed as well to another theme: the impending end of time, a situation in which many of the Reformers believed they found themselves. Correspondingly, the Ottoman Empire was identified in all of the relevant religious texts with the small horn of Daniel 7, or alternately with the Antichrist, both heavily laden Christian apocalyptic symbols. Typically, the Ottoman advance was seen as divine punishment for the sins and lax morals of Christian society. At the same time, however, the fact that Christendom suffered the scourge of Turkish brutality was a sign of the divine plan for the future: God would not make his children suffer in this way, authors like Georg suggested, if he did not have their eternal reward in mind as a return for this anguish. Thus the Turks were identified even before the Reformation as divine punishment for Christian unfaithfulness and, correspondingly, the mechanism of divine redemption.

With the exception of individuals living directly in border or battle zones, however, most Christians had virtually no actual experience of Turks. The frightening picture of the Muslim enemy painted in such texts served as an almost infinitely flexible tool for the development of religious identity. The emergence of the Reformation allowed a refinement of the apocalyptic themes in pre-Reformation discourse on the Turks. From the viewpoint of the reformers, the Turkish scourge was the divine punishment not for human sin in general but for the ongoing idolatrous practices embodied in Catholicism. If the advance of the Turks was intensifying in recent years, these authors thought, it was because Protestants continued to tolerate Catholic religious abuses in their midst. Catholic authors writing on the same theme could make the opposite point—and did.

Some information about Ottoman society as presented in this literature was neutral and indeed relatively accurate. It has been argued by Almut Höfert that the ethnographic literature in particular, by portraying a virtuous picture of the Turk, allowed for the emergence of the category "religion" in European discourse, allowing Europeans to think about the possibility of other belief systems.[10] This tendency is easier to see at a later stage; during the Reformation, Islam was primarily categorized and analyzed in terms defined by Christianity.

Such application of the norms of Christianity to an evaluation of Muslim society occasionally produced counterintuitive results. Thus this literature offers some recognition of the "virtuous" aspects of Muslim religious practice, such as memorization of the Koran, the rejection of wine (an especially relevant point in German society, for the Germans reproached themselves for being excessive drinkers), the absence of religious images, and the general disdain for prostitutes. Authors further noted strict punishments for adultery and theft, as well as admirable attitudes about the giving of alms. In particular, Muslim women were characterized as almost peculiarly modest, so that in some households male servants never even saw the faces of their mistresses. But the "virtuous Turk" was an image not intended to praise Muslims but rather to shame Christians for their shortcomings. This classical rhetorical strategy of Western literature—reproaching the self via the virtuous "other"—had been employed at least as early as Tacitus's *Germania*, a text that had experienced a strong revival at the hands of German humanists. If Muslims knew the Koran, why were Christians so ignorant of the Bible? If Turks could live without wine, why were Christians such lushes? If Muslim women were chaste and covered, why did Christian women flaunt their charms for all to see? If Muslims washed themselves five times a day, why were Christians so slovenly?

Such apparent virtues were just the beginning. Indeed, as many authors who wrote "against the Turks" suggested, it was possible to find important elements of Christian teachings in Islam, including monotheism, various testimonies to the divinity of Christ that reflect an orthodox Christology, the virgin birth, Paradise, and the last judgment. Protestant authors in particular occasionally found evidence of arguments for salvation *sola fide* (by faith alone) in the Koran. At the same time, these authors established the central mistakes of Islam: the ultimate denial of Christ's divinity and a superrationalist approach to faith that was destructive to the less intuitively clear dogmas of Christianity.

This contrast between correct and sinful features of Islam allowed the portrayal of the virtuous Turk as an attention-getting reproach to sinful Christian society to reach a high point in the Protestant-Catholic confessional polemic of the mid- to late sixteenth century. Describing the many ways in which Islam corresponded with Christianity and the superior piety of the Turks provided a critical guide to the confessional world as it developed after the Reformation. Whether praising or damning the Turk, the ultimate result was a criticism of the contemporary Christian world.

Just as the virtue of the Turks points out the failings of Christians—as, for example, with the laudable attitude of Islam toward pictures, which highlighted the idolatrous practices of the Old Church—the errors of Christianity were reflected in Islam: discussion of trinitarian errors in the Koran, for example, is easily turned into an attack on the trinitarian errors of the *Schwärmer* (Anabaptists). The result is a worldview that reflects the unstable conglomeration of Central European politics and religion in the sixteenth century, a world in which, from the Protestant standpoint, Catholics were simultaneously brothers and sisters in Christ and sinful, mistaken idolaters, a world in which even idolaters were preferable as brothers in arms in resistance to the inexorable advance of a common enemy.

JEWS

If Turks presented an incomprehensible, foreign "other" to Christian society—and thus could only be depicted in Christian terms—Jews presented a much greater challenge, because they constituted a local foreign body whose origins were intimately related to that of Christianity. In the Christian view, the Gentiles had become the true heirs to the divine promises given to Abraham in Genesis, because the Jews had not recognized Jesus as the embodiment of this promise and of the messianic prophecies of Isaiah and other prophets. Today we call this view "supersessionism," the claim that Christianity had superseded the relationship between God and Israel through its embrace of the messiah Jesus.

Throughout Europe religious art expressed the dominant view of this relationship by contrasting *Ecclesia* (church) and *Synagoga*, with the latter figure blindfolded to symbolize the failure of the Jews to accept the Christian messiah. The Jews not only were part of the tree of salvation that Paul postulated in Romans 11 to explain the failure of Israel to convert en masse to Christianity, but also lived, at least provisionally, in the midst of the body of Christ, with their anticipated full assumption still pending: "And they also, if they abide not still in unbelief, shall be graffed in: for God is able to graff them in again.... And so all Israel shall be saved" (Rom. 11:23, 26, King James Version).

Indeed, the continued presence of Jews as a remnant was arguably essential to Christian views of the end of days, since Rev. 7:4 included a provision that the children of Israel would be sealed under the Lamb of God at such a time. Jewish customs and beliefs were known not only from the circulation of cultural knowledge but also, in some cases, from first-hand experience. Regular association and common heritage were not, however, guarantors of better understanding between Jews and Christians. Nonetheless, the Jew as "other" was even more rhetorically essential to the Reformation than the Turk. The Reformation drew on the way in which the later medieval period manipulated notions of the Jews for its own purposes, but it made them even more important, not only because of the relatively greater integration of Jews than Turks into Christian society but also (eventually) because of the Protestant self-identification with the trials of the biblical people of Israel.

To understand how Protestant identification with the Jews developed, it may be helpful to consider the social background of Jewish

Fig. 10.3. Here we see the Synagogue portrayed as a blindfolded woman, holding the tablets of the Law, her authority shattered by the victorious Christian Gospel. Tobias Stimmer's woodcut of c.1572 is based on a sculpture in Strasbourg Cathedral in which Church and Synagogue are placed side by side.

settlement in Western Europe, a condition marked by repeated persecutions, expulsions, and exiles. The Reformation broke out in the
midst of a wave of Jewish migration from Western to Eastern Europe
that (as in the case of the Muslims) had its hallmark in the expulsions
from Spain of 1492 but did not begin there. Indeed, the Middle Ages,
while relatively peaceful, witnessed attacks on Jews in combination
with the preaching of the First Crusade (1096) and expulsions from
England (1290) and France (1394). Expulsions from Central Europe
were under way after the 1421 massacre of Jews in Vienna; a key event
in this trend was the affair of Simon of Trent, a Christian boy allegedly
tortured and murdered by Jews in 1475.

Still, in Spain an uneasy version of the early arrangement of *con-
vivencia,* or coexistence, prevailed for a long period. This informal
contract was gradually abrogated under increasing political pressure.
Perhaps a hundred thousand Jews converted to Christianity in the
decades around the turn of the fourteenth century, and decrees of
forced conversion (or expulsion) were promulgated in Andalusia
and Aragon in the 1480s. After its establishment in 1481, the Spanish
Inquisition focused heavily on scrutinizing the practices and beliefs of
the descendants of these conversos or "new Christians."

Thus when at least a hundred thousand Jews left Spain in the
expulsions of 1492, it was in the context of a larger process that shifted
the center of the European Jewish population to areas east of the Oder
River by about 1570. Sephardic Jews were migrating by ship from Iberia
to the Netherlands, Hanseatic cities, Italy, North Africa, and Palestine,
but their Ashkenazic cousins were moving more or less simultaneously
overland from former centers of Jewish population in Western Europe
to distant communities in the East, where legal freedom to settle without restriction was greater. The ultimate result of this migration was
the birth of venerable centers of Jewish learning in the East and the
decline into obscurity of the tradition of Central Europe as a home
for outstanding Talmudic scholarship—a tradition that had persisted
during the eleventh to thirteenth centuries in the area between Rhine
and Oder. The picture of Jewish settlement in German-speaking lands
is far from consistent, however; expulsions were often followed by
returns in subsequent years, and we cannot relate either expulsions or
the returns directly to the influence of the Reformation.

Wherever they lived, Jews were forced to negotiate rights of residence with local communities. Sometimes these rights were negotiated directly with a commune; at other times the right of Jews to inhabit an area of a city was mandated by a territorial sovereign or monarch like the Holy Roman emperor, often but not always as a guarantee for past or future moneylending. Jews also frequently served an important financial function in urban areas, with pawn services functioning as an informal banking or credit system for the poor—although it was just as frequent that a decree of expulsion would be formulated as an indignant rejection of this function.

In Central Europe, a growing number of Jews (*Landjuden*) also came to live in tiny numbers (often as few as one or two families) in isolated locations in the country, a trend that saw its beginnings in the sixteenth century. While the complete picture is thus mixed, with periods of increase and decline, it has been pointed out that by the time of the Reformation, very large areas of Germany were already free of Jews. For those who did not experience Jewish life at first hand, however, a body of detailed "ethnographic" literature emerged. This material was intentionally composed in German to facilitate its spread, and until the seventeenth century, it was written virtually exclusively by Jewish converts to Christianity. It described and explained Jewish ritual and religious life to German Gentile readers.[11]

The aim of this literature was to relate the ongoing medieval polemic against the Jews to actual data about them that could either be compared to the reader's own knowledge of the group or serve to orient or augment it. It is not unreasonable to suppose that the noticeably increased level of Jewish migration during the years leading up to the Reformation may have also augmented Christian perceptions of Jews as foreigners and thus enhanced interest in the acquisition of such knowledge. Importantly, however, it added a great deal of detail to the crude picture of the Jews commonly circulating before the Reformation, which was characterized by the dominant motifs of usury, ritual murder ("blood libel"), and host desecration allegations.

Ritual murder charges concerned the belief that Jews murdered young Christian boys to use their blood for religious purposes, including the baking of unleavened bread (*matzah*) for Passover; host desecration refers to the belief that Jews stole consecrated hosts, the bread consecrated in the eucharist, from churches (or caused them to be stolen) in order to torture and draw blood from them. Although these charges originally emerged in twelfth-century England, they quickly made their way to the Continent and enjoyed particular popularity in late fifteenth- to mid-sixteenth-century Germany. A key sign of this popularity is the persistent presence of such images in broadsheets and illustrative woodcuts of the period, which continued to be printed even in Protestant areas. One change in the Reformation was the gradual reduction in actual charges of such crimes, particularly in Protestant areas, not because the authorities and local populations ceased to believe Jews capable of such nefarious deeds, but because the Protestant denial of the doctrine of transubstantiation meant that tortured hosts, even if consecrated, could not actually bleed. Just as in the case of the Turks, discussion of the Jews allowed Protestant writers to use a foreign body to expose and condemn false teaching within the body of Christ.

The absence of actual Jews in many German contexts, particularly outside of imperial cities where their presence was mandated by the emperor, probably facilitated the success of these ethnographies, many of them written by converts. Books such as Johannes Pfefferkorn's *Ich heyß ein buchlein der iuden peicht* (I Am a Little Book about How Jews Confess their Sins; 1508) on Jewish penitential practice and Anthonius Margaritha's *Der gantz Jüdische glaub* (The Whole Jewish Belief; 1530), a compendium of Jewish beliefs, provided neutral descriptions of Jewish ritual but then offered mocking explanations of their meaning that connected seamlessly with medieval polemical literature against the Jews. Margaritha noted, for instance, the Jewish custom of not placing a wedding ring on the bride's third finger, but then insisted that this custom arose from the Jewish desire to avoid the example set by Mary (Jesus' mother), whose wedding ring was said to have been placed on her third finger at her betrothal.[12]

Such depictions updated the content of stereotypes about the Jews without ultimately changing their direction, and given the widespread prevalence of religious attitudes that we would today term superstitious, Christian readers may have found such depictions entirely convincing. Key here, however, is the continued instrumentalization of Judaism in the service of other programs, in this case, that of anti-Jewish polemic. Even those scholars widely seen as defenders of the Jews, like the German humanist Johannes Reuchlin, had to disguise their arguments in the garb of other motives. Reuchlin published several tracts on the virtues of the Hebrew language and the art of the Cabbala. However, when Pfefferkorn proposed that Jewish books be confiscated and burned in order to guard against their danger to Christian society—a proposal that generated an imperial commission to address the question, which ultimately decided in favor of such confiscations—Reuchlin relied on arguments that ultimately served Christianity, such as the position that Hebrew books were necessary for Christian scholars to understand the Old Testament. Such obfuscation appeared to be the only way to oppose the destruction of this literature.[13]

Instrumentalization of minority groups has not been confined to the Reformation period. Non-Jews continued this pattern during the German Enlightenment, treating the problem of Jewish assimilation as a test case for the creation of citizens who would be equal before the law. Government recognition of Judaism as a religion civilly equal to Christianity was offered on the assumption that Jews would conform to larger society. One notes a similar instrumentalization of Jewish aims by Christian groups in our own day in the evangelical lobby's support for the state of Israel, which is based heavily on pointed readings of Old Testament texts offering blessings to those who bless Israel and of New Testament texts that are seen to require the return of the Jews to Israel as a prerequisite for the end of human history. But the Christian instrumentalization of Jews in the Reformation took a particular turn because the idea of supersession made the discussion of both real and imagined Jews and their exile under the prerogatives of God a constant preoccupation of Protestant literature.

In other words, Jews were a constant topic of Protestant discourse because of the particular ways in which reformers used the term "Jew" in their thinking. The early turn of Martin Luther's writing on the Jews suggests that reformist attitudes toward Jews were never simply ones of rejection. Luther showed an open attitude toward Jews in a pamphlet of 1523, criticizing superstitious beliefs about them and persecution directed against them. Admittedly, he primarily made these points with the goal of advancing the idea that Jews would also be positively affected by church reform in that they would be more attracted to a purified Christian church.

Late in his life he wrote pamphlets taking exactly the position he had criticized in 1523, suggesting (perhaps under the influence of an increasingly dark strand in his own thoughts about the impending apocalypse) that since the Jews had not converted when they were treated kindly, they should be coerced to do so in the crudest possible ways: through seizure of their wealth, forced manual labor, destruction of their learning and educational institutions, and, if necessary, forced baptisms. This position did not mitigate his interest in Hebrew literature or insistence that it must be studied, an interest shared not only by the humanists who supported Reuchlin in his verbal scuffle with Pfefferkorn but also by reformers as diverse as Philip Melanchthon, Martin Bucer, Huldrych Zwingli, and John Calvin. Of these, only Melanchthon would have embraced Luther's more radical, later statements. As in the case of the Turks, vicious attitudes toward the Jews were supported by Protestant criticisms of Catholicism, for many preachers charged that Jews were the quintessential representatives of the works-righteousness the Reformation worked so hard to eradicate.

The attitude of simultaneous embrace and rejection was possible because of the self-identification of many Protestant authors with Israel. In other words, the term "Jew" could mean either the Jews of the speaker's contemporary present or "Jews" in the biblical sense— meaning the children of Israel whose peregrinations were narrated in the Old Testament or the body of their descendants who eventually rejected the messiah Jesus in the New Testament. In this second sense of the word, the sense of "Jew" as "member of the community of God," Lutheran pastors who understood the body of Christ as the new Israel often creatively conflated the Israelites of the Bible with members of their own congregations in order to apply the lessons of human sinfulness and divine redemption from the Old Testament to their own parishioners. Somewhat less often, and primarily in texts on the Passion of Jesus, they made the same connection between their members and New Testament Jews.

This rhetorical strategy drew its energy from Old Church typology—the creation of interpretive pairs of metaphors between the Old and New Testaments in order to demonstrate the fulfillment of the divine plan for human history in the life, death, and resurrection of Jesus Christ. But it gained energy in light of the Protestant experience of persecution and its reanimated interest in the Old Testament, particularly among the more radical reforming groups.

Frustration with the Jews may have grown precisely as the self-identification with the Old Testament Israelites intensified—in other words, as reforming groups began to see themselves as the Israelites who had been persecuted throughout history but made the "right choice" and thus were the true Israel—an idea that had been articulated in Old Church culture but never sustained with such energy before. This identification may have made belief in the potential conversion of the Jews to Christianity—the basis upon which the limited toleration of Luther's early writings had been offered—seem to recede, particularly in the light of readings of Matt. 27:25, which appeared to postulate the transmission of an inheritable sin through the assumption of responsibility for the crucifixion of Christ.[14]

This problem is complex because many reformers, most prominently Luther and Melanchthon but also a number of later sixteenth-century Lutheran pastors, indeed rejected such fundamental motifs of the late medieval Western Christian position on Jews like the matter of Jewish guilt for Jesus' death. In any case, understanding the conception of this relationship between the church as the New Israel in the Reformation and biblical conceptions of Israel and the Jews is the most promising and intellectually stimulating area of Reformation research on the Jewish–Christian relationship.

HERETICS AS REFUGEES

As we have seen in the case of the Turks and the Jews, members of other religions were used to define the boundaries of the body of Christ, but the processes of providing an ever more coherent definition of Christian doctrine also meant an increasing tendency to define the acceptable borders of Christianity by reference to the beliefs and actions of deviant Christians. In the later Middle Ages, heresy judgments tended to fall upon either prominent theologians (for example,

Jan Hus of Bohemia, who died on the stake at Constance in 1415) or entire heretical movements openly resistant to the church (for example, the Old Church crusade against Waldensianism). After the end of the fifteenth century, however, the process of looking for and suppressing divergent belief or religious practice made an increasing impact on ordinary people who were fully integrated into society—that is, in situations where they might be assumed to be conforming.

While we tend to associate this process with the establishment of the Spanish Inquisition after 1481, Protestant areas also sponsored religious courts for the disciplining of immoral behavior. It was Reformed areas, however, that were most known for the establishment of "consistories," or religious courts that used a combination of elite surveillance and popular cooperation in order to exercise church discipline, identifying sin in members of the congregation and using different means to encourage congregants to stop sinning and be reconciled to the congregation. Indeed, members of the Reformed confession saw church discipline as the third mark (along with the preaching of the gospel and the correct use of the sacraments) by which the true church could be identified. Ordinances that established such institutions also revealed their purpose: to convert the sinner, avert divine wrath from the congregation, preserve the congregation in healthy doctrine, and (in multiconfessional areas) protect the congregation's reputation as a member of the body of Christ. These ordinances typically established a series of progressive steps for addressing sin within the sacramental body, along the lines of the behavior prescribed in Matt. 18:15-16. Typically, attempts to reconcile individually and admonitions preceded stronger punishments, which could include exclusion from the eucharist or even (rarely) expulsion from the congregation.

The most notorious of the Reformed consistories was that of Geneva, whose almost illegible records have been so ably edited by the team of researchers led by Robert Kingdon.[15] Knowledge of what actually happened in Geneva has proved somewhat anticlimactic. While the elders of the consistory did insist on correct belief and behavior, punishments for minor affairs tended to be lenient. The most common penalties were an order to attend more sermons, commit to memory the new vernacular prayers, or learn to explain different matters of faith. Because Geneva has gained such a reputation for invasive social control, it is easy to forget that Reformed consistories were present throughout Europe. From our modern perspective, it is also easy to forget that local populations often sought out the supervision of consistories, as research on the Bernese countryside (Switzerland) and the multiconfessional towns of East Frisia has shown. In East Frisia, congregants occasionally left Reformed congregations to associate with Mennonites precisely because they found Mennonite church discipline more attractive.

The result of the tightening of religious boundaries in the Reformation was the phenomenon of the religious refugee. The actions of consistories typically led to the flight of individual refugees or tiny, often close-knit groups; large mass migrations were more often created by political decisions to which marginal groups could only respond by flight. Indeed, some historians have seen exile—not only as metaphor, but also as social experience—as the hallmark of Reformed Protestantism.[16]

Most religious refugees were Jews or Protestants fleeing Catholic authorities; the next largest group was comprised of Protestants fleeing other Protestants; the smallest group, which has not been heavily researched, consisted of Catholics who fled Protestant authorities—such as the English recusant priests. We have already noted the expulsion of roughly two hundred thousand Jews from Spain and Portugal after 1492; Protestant sympathizers also were fleeing Iberia in large numbers after the 1520s, when the Inquisition turned its attention to so-called *alumbrados* and other Protestant heretics. After the Anabaptists assumed governance of the city of Münster, would-be saints flocked to the city;

Excerpt from the Registers of the Genevan Consistory, 1542

About Jane, wife of Jehan Corajod, host of the Golden Lion, cobbler:

Answers that she is of this city.... And has not heard the sermons because there is no sermon given, and has not heard Mass and has never been to the sermon since the last Communion was given and has not received the Host.... And knows the prayer, and the confession does not know how to say at all. And prays to God in her heart, because the tongue does not do anything if the heart does not say it. And she prays God always to help her. And she keeps Lent and believes this is well done, because she has lived all her life just as her predecessors taught her. And when she receives Communion she understands that she receives it for the salvation of her soul. The advice of the Consistory: that she not receive the present Communion and that she remain longer in this city than she has done in the past and frequent the sermons and the catechism on Sundays and strive to serve God more fully than she does or has done in the past and make a Christian confession, and that she be given good remonstrances ... and follow the Word of God.... Otherwise the Council will not be content with her.

—*Registers of the Consistory of Geneva in the time of Calvin,* Robert M. Kindgon, gen. ed.; ed. Thomas A. Lambert and Isabella M. Watt; with Jeffrey R. Watt; trans. M. Wallace McDonald (Grand Rapids: Eerdmans, 2000).

when it was retaken by besieging troops, the flow turned in the other direction.

The next large wave of religious migration was triggered in the 1540s by the increasing ability of Hapsburg rulers to insist on Catholic conformity within their territories. The most well-known incident in this wave was the flight of Dutch refugees to England, but it reached its height with the end of the Schmalkaldic War (1547). This war between Charles V and his Lutheran German subjects resulted in the defeat of the Protestants and the temporary ability of the Catholic emperor to enforce a religious settlement within his territories, the Augsburg Interim (1548). The Interim provided for the reintroduction of some Catholic elements of faith and practice into the newly Protestant areas until such time as the Council of Trent could make a definitive statement on matters of controversy. From our perspective a mediating statement, the Interim was regarded by sixteenth-century Protestants as a stunningly evil decree. Pastors in cities who refused to conform to its theological guidelines were driven from their pulpits, and vassals and client rulers of Charles who had tolerated religious diversity in their territories were now forced, under threat of invasion or loss of sovereignty, to expel religious dissidents from their territories.

Many Dutch, French, and German refugees found their way to England after 1548, only to be forced back to the Continent when Mary I, a Catholic and the only child of the union of Henry VIII and the ever-pious Catherine of Aragon, came to the throne upon the death of her Protestant brother, Edward VI, whose reign had been particularly hospitable to refugee theologians. As the turmoil of the confessional period mounted, so did the groups and numbers of refugees: Italian heretics fleeing the Italian cities as these became more aggressive about enforcing their theological standards, Dutch fleeing the persecutions of the Dutch revolt after 1570, Bohemian Catholics fleeing after the advance of Protestantism there in the 1580s, Bohemian Protestants fleeing after the re-advance of Catholicism in the early seventeenth century, Huguenots fleeing France during the chaos of the religious wars, and so on. Some of these people made their way as far as Central America in order to maintain their convictions, but the same ships that carried Jews and Protestant dissidents also carried the apparatus of the Inquisition, which was established in New Spain.

Sometimes such refugees were lucky and were able to find permanent homes where they were able to cultivate their faith without challenge: such was the case in the city of Wesel, where a massive influx of
Calvinist refugees changed the religious convictions of the governing
patriciate completely in less than two generations. But more often
their fate was a much darker one: both conversos and *moriscos* who
successfully fled Iberia often found a rather tepid reception among
coreligionists in their new homes, who were suspicious that their faith
or customs had been contaminated by their immersion in Christian
society.

One brief example from East Frisia may suffice to show the most
disturbing element of the wave of refugees: their frequent inability to
find permanent homes once they had made their ideas suspicious by
an initial flight. The Polish nobleman and Reformed theologian John
a Lasco went over to the Reformation in the 1540s, an event marked
by his decision to marry, made during his sojourn in Louvain. When
persecution of heretics emerged, he traveled east to East Frisia, where
he found employment as the territorial church superintendent and
pastor to the newly formed Reformed Church in Emden. After the
promulgation of the Interim, a Lasco decided to migrate to England,
where he was associated with the so-called Strangers Church, a church
organized separately from the Church of the England, although tolerated by the English government, set up to accommodate the streams
of Calvinist refugees who were reaching England.

When Mary ascended the throne, a Lasco and his congregation
were forced to flee back to the Continent. They attempted to leave
ship in Denmark, but the refusal of the Danish king to allow them to
disembark meant that they were forced to stay on board in the middle
of the winter in rough seas. Eventually, after unsuccessful attempts to
land in Rostock, Wismar, Lübeck, and Hamburg, they were allowed to
land at Emden. They immortalized their thanks for the refuge offered
them there in a portal depicting the "little ship of Christ." But even as
most of his congregants thankfully settled in the East Frisian harbor
city, a Lasco could not stay; driven away by a controversy over the catechism he formulated, he joined the German refugee church at Frankfurt as its superintendent, where he did not stay long, either. Like
many a migrating Jewish family, a Lasco ended his days in Poland.[17]

THE POOR

We end our account of "outsiders" with the poor, who are arguably not outsiders—after all, for most of the early modern period, the resident working poor of the cities lived cheek by jowl with their more comfortable counterparts.[18] But insofar as early modern Christianity was established in the context of particular social situations, the tendency of all societies to define insiders and outsiders was also expressed in the arrangements of Christianity. The vast majority of inhabitants wanted to belong, to be insiders. The great feast and festivals, the annual citizenship ceremonies in cities, and even religious rituals like the eucharist, for example, drew people of different social stations together, celebrated common values and norms, and symbolized the organic relationship between Christians that was supposed to be reflected in the events of everyday life. But the tense political and social atmosphere of the Reformation fostered an uneasy awareness that these were far from normal times. Ceremonies and cultural rituals such as Carnival revealed people's fears that the world was really "upside down" and might be skidding toward disaster. Accordingly, people's dreams and nightmares tended to fix not only upon obvious outsiders to the body of Christ like Turks and Jews or even irritants to it like refugees, but also upon individuals and groups on the outskirts of society: wandering players and itinerant preachers, mercenaries and brigands, peripatetic students and mendicant friars, prostitutes and peddlers.

Certainly, by today's standards, most Christians of the Reformation could probably be categorized as poor. Evidence suggests, however, that the numbers of the poor were increasing steadily in the sixteenth century; working-class Europeans were caught in the "scissors" of falling real wages and a slight but regular inflation that appears to have characterized the entire sixteenth century, which is sometimes said to have been exacerbated by Spain's introduction of American silver into the European money supply. Wages in some European cities were so low that day laborers were allowed to go home at midday to deliver their wages so that food might be purchased for their families' evening meals. Depending on the area, in most of Europe between 20 and 60 percent of some communities fell into the categories of the regularly employed working poor, seasonal laborers with livelihoods at risk during the cold months of the year, together with the unfortunates at the bottom of the pile such as the elderly, beggars, people with disabilities, and vagabonds.

Moreover, in the medieval period, the poor had been considered an essential component of the church—both the voluntarily and the involuntarily poor. While the foundation for an ideal of poverty was laid in the Christian Gospels, repeated movements toward a more radical ideal of voluntary poverty were also a standard pattern in Christian history at the latest from the beginning of the monastic orders. Later, in the thirteenth century and afterwards, figures like Francis of Assisi founded new orders in which ideals of poverty were primary elements. And the fifteenth century was characterized by "observantine," or reforming, movements in many of the older orders, such as the Dominican and Augustinian orders, that responded to the increased prosperity of monastic communities by espousing a program of renewed rigor in their poverty. It was exactly the tradition of the Reformed Augustinians that was to attract Martin Luther to the cloister.

Fig. 10.4. Even for the affluent and well-protected travel in the early modern period was a hazardous business, but for the families of the poor, especially in inclement weather, it was sheer misery. Note the mother's bare feet in this 1520 drawing. Lucas van Leyden (1494–1533), *Tyl Eulenspiegel*, 1520.

But even the random, unorganized poor played a prominent role in late medieval religious ideals, since caring for the poor, either through spontaneous charity or organized endowments, was viewed as a good work. Donors and recipients of charity could thus (at least ideally) be linked in a soteriological bond in which the donor performed a good work and the recipient prayed for the donor's soul.

This relationship accounts, perhaps, for what both contemporaries and scholars have seen as a somewhat ad hoc quality to charity before the Reformation—for its point was not only or primarily the alleviation of poverty. The act of charity had an ideal value apart from its effects or effectiveness. Charity as an aspect of lay piety before the Reformation can perhaps be most closely seen in the activities of confraternities—associations of laymen, typically by guilds within a particular city, that organized charity both for suffering members of the guild and for the needy within their city.

Somewhat stereotypically, it had been thought that the Reformation had effected the most important changes in European poor relief, a position most closely articulated in the writings of the German sociologist Max Weber. Research in the 1980s and 1990s, however, has shown that the Old Church's arrangements were under attack before the Reformation, although the Reformation added a pointed quality to such criticisms. In the rhetoric of many Reformers, investment in other kinds of good works—particularly religious artwork and altarpieces, images of the saints that often included donations for clothing, candles and oil lamps, chantries, and monastic endowments generally—consumed funds that would more appropriately be used to feed and clothe the poor directly. In this context, like Turks, Jews, and heretics, the poor served a rhetorical role in the Reformation as the justification for the dissolution of the venerable charitable endowments of the Middle Ages in their many forms. Certainly, much of the proceeds from the dissolution of these institutions was indeed directed toward poor relief, but at the same time, as even reforming preachers in Germany noted, attacking a bastion of the powerful Old Church allowed opportunities for cities and individuals to enrich themselves at the Church's expense.

The rhetoric about such changes, particularly in the Holy Roman Empire, appears to have been much greater than its actual effects. The attempt to provide more effective poor relief preceded the Reformation; civic administration of poor relief resources was also seen as an element of the commune's obligation to enforce public order. The process was accelerated in Protestant territories by a general employment of new (or recycled) notions of Christian government. The creation of a "common chest" that combined all resources for charity into a single fund usually administered by a secular or civic administration was a key element of the Reformation's approach to the poor. But this development did not mean that individual donations or administrations ceased.

Both Catholic and Protestant communities encouraged increasing examination of the poor in order to see whether they were "deserving," but Protestant governments were more likely to initiate labor programs. The resulting abandonment of the association between poverty and Christianity in both confessions meant that charity began to be used as a tool to create lines between insiders and outsiders: according to the justness of need, membership in a specific community, or morality of the recipient. Particularly in multiconfessional areas, it could become a tool for enforcing confessional unity, in that church communities responsible for providing charity to their own members were reluctant to distribute it to dissidents. Here, the poor were forced to negotiate the boundaries between communal welfare, religious support, and acts of private charity. In the Netherlands and northern Germany the creation of a Reformed diaconate led to the explicit introduction of confessional concerns into the distribution of charity. Occasionally, poor families ran athwart of this problem: in Emden, at least one case is known where charity was provided for the mother and children of a Reformed family but not to the father, who was unwilling to support his family and apparently unable to seek religious reconciliation with the congregation.[20]

CONCLUSION

Processes of centralization and accompanying marginalization are always at work in the dynamics of particular groups, but it is perhaps at moments of religious crisis like the Reformation that such processes become most obvious to observers. The process of creating outsiders did not, as we have seen, require accurate knowledge of the people so treated; it generally manifested a particular power structure that made some individuals more vulnerable than others and created a series of stereotypes that could be attached to those people to justify their marginalization. When groups like Turks, Jews, refugees, and the poor were discussed within Christian society, in an age before religious toleration and value-neutral social welfare, their images were instrumentalized for the purpose of tightening the borders of Christianity itself. This manipulation of their images for other purposes is characteristic of the ways in which all religious minorities—Christian or not—were popularly depicted.

FOR FURTHER READING

Bell, Dean Phillip, and Stephen G. Burnett, eds. *Jews, Judaism, and the Reformation in Sixteenth-Century Germany* (Leiden: Brill, 2006).

Boettcher, Susan R. "German Orientalism in the Age of Confessional Consolidation: Jacob Andreae's Thirteen Sermons on the Turk, 1568," in *Comparative Studies of South Asia, Africa, and the Middle East* 24 (2004): 101–15.

Martin, John Jeffries. *Venice's Hidden Enemies: Italian Heretics in a Renaissance City* (Berkeley: University of California Press, 1993).

Perry, Mary Elizabeth. *The Handless Maid: Moriscos and the Politics of Religion in Early Modern Spain* (Princeton: Princeton University Press, 2005).

Safley, Thomas Max, ed. *The Reformation of Charity: The Secular and the Religious in Early Modern Poor Relief* (Leiden: Brill, 2003).

THE LANGUAGE
OF THE COMMON FOLK

PETER MATHESON

CHAPTER ELEVEN

"What wonderful German!"[1] Whose German is being referred to? Believe it or not, Utz Rychsner, a weaver in the heady days of the early Reformation in Augsburg, is talking about the language of Jesus of Nazareth! He expresses in this vivid way his conviction that Christ lived, worked, and spoke the language of ordinary people like Rychsner himself and that Jesus still addresses folk today in language they can understand. In the imaginary dialogue between a weaver and a priest, composed by Rychsner in 1523, Christ is said to speak in plain German, his message is crystal clear, and to hear it all we need to do is read the Gospels, since printing has made them easily accessible for laypeople. Extracts from the Gospels do in fact pepper the fiery pamphlets Rychsner wrote, summoning his "sisters and brothers" in Augsburg to speak out, to commend the faith to others, and to have no scruples about criticizing the priest-ridden church of their time.

Rychsner had studied scripture carefully, read many of Martin Luther's writings, and thought carefully about the arguments of his opponents. He is not one of the famous pamphleteers of the Reformation, his influence being very much limited to Augsburg, and his thought has limited depth and range. Yet the very ordinariness of his language and the simplicity of his faith make him a good representative of what tens of thousands of ordinary people were thinking and feeling in the early 1520s.

Jesus' ministry, Rychsner believed, was to humble folk, though the "bigwigs" in church and state might have forgotten this. God's language, the language of the prophets and Jesus, was not some elevated, elitist discourse. He talked in the same way as ordinary people talked. Rychsner lashed out at the arrogance, delusions, and greed of the church hierarchy, these "wretched bloodhounds." He is aware that by using such language, "one might be accused of whipping up insurrection, although these are the very words of God."[2] Rychsner's writings swing between elation and outrage and encourage action. He writes because he has to. He writes to fire people up, to inform them, but also to motivate them, to effect change. He mirrors the restlessness of his time. He was, after all, writing on the eve of the Peasants' War, the greatest social conflagration in Europe before the French Revolution. Sebastian Lotzer, another advocate of lay articulacy, was soon to draft the *Twelve Articles*, the most widespread statement of the insurgents' concerns during the Peasants' War of 1524–1525. This was politically incorrect language with a vengeance!

ORDINARY FOLK "WISE UP"

Here, then, is a new phenomenon. Ordinary people, including the much derided peasants, are coming out into the open, "becoming visible" or, to use another expression common at the time, "wising up." Countless pamphlets had called upon them to "wake out of their sleep," to let their light shine forth. They might not be priests or monks; they might know no Latin. They might have to work day and night, but Jesus, their Savior, had been a layman, too, a carpenter. The spiritual leaders of the time had branded Jesus himself as ignorant, after all. So the time had come for the people to speak from the rooftops. So ran the new song: the dance of the poor and downtrodden could begin.

Laypeople were indeed finding their own voice, helped by the newfangled printing press, which churned out cheap, accessible pamphlets for artisans and peasants, mothers and fathers, for the young and the not so young. They were not just readers of these pamphlets, either. Laywomen and artisans figured among the authors as well as brilliant publicists such as Luther. The language they used was drawn from their daily lives: rough, earthy, direct, graphic, colorful, and angry at times—but lyrical, too. As they saw the morning star of the

gospel shining in the sky, "women and cobblers spread the divine word" and leapt for joy.[3]

The symbolic world of religion and that of language have always been inseparable, so it is no surprise that many of the fundamental shifts in the use of language in our period are intimately related to the various Reformations: humanist, Catholic, Lutheran, Radical, and Reformed. Christian humanists such as Erasmus, writing from the beginning of the sixteenth century, encouraged lay literacy and education, including that of women. The humanists were often to be found haunting the trendy printing presses. Luther himself was evangelical about education, enthusiastic about vernacular as well as classical languages, and beat the drum, like so many of the reformers, for directness and simplicity of discourse. He was acutely aware of the need for German psalms and hymns in worship. The groundswell of anticlericalism and the dynamics of apocalyptic thought, the pervasive sense that the end was at hand, challenged traditional and Latinist patterns of discourse, whether in liturgy, Bible, devotional books, teaching, or preaching. The old linguistic world was turned upside down. In addition to the undermining of the lay/clerical divide, the newfound vigor and range of vernacular languages coincided with an emergent nationalism, a relocation of cultural energies into national or regional identity. Henry VIII's proclamation of England as an "empire," and his support for an English-language version of the Bible, are a good

Fig. 11.1. Printing depicted as a bakery. Albrecht Dürer (1471–1528), *Missive Bakery*, 1511.

example of this mélange of concerns. It demonstrated new attitudes to the papacy, but it also strummed the lyre of national pride.

A NEW LANGUAGE

The primary focus in this chapter will be the changing language of lay spirituality, of worship and personal devotion, as seen, for example, in the little primers or catechisms that taught children and "simple folk" the basics of the faith: the Creed, the Lord's Prayer, the Ten Commandments. The bulk of the illustrative material will be taken from the early years of the Lutheran Reformation in Germany. We will be arguing that the Reformation represented a remarkably swift and fundamental transformation in people's imaginative worlds and that this remarkable replacement of one set of mental images by another was made possible in part by the emergence of a new vocabulary, a new language. This was woven out of the narratives and metaphors of scripture, on the one hand, and the voice of the "common people," on the other.

The interweaving of scriptural stories, songs and poems, prophecies, parables, and letters with the oral and literary discourse of laymen and laywomen was itself an extraordinary phenomenon. The "language of Canaan" became the language of day-to-day life, and vice versa. As the civic chronicles of the early Reformation period testify, the main carriers of this new way of talking were the little books or pamphlets that flooded the market, together with the sermons of the reforming preachers. The personality cult of the miracle-working saint was replaced almost overnight by that of iconic leaders in Wittenberg or Strasbourg or Zurich, whose message was brokered to the locals by urban or rural "opinion makers," the city clerks or village headmen, teachers, preachers, and traveling students. (Note the complex filtering process; romantic conceptions about the unmediated emergence of the voice of the "common folk," or of charismatic leaders, are not helpful.)

Much has been written about the communication revolution of the early Reformation period. Certainly the printing press can be likened in its impact to the computer revolution of our own day, but printing itself has to be set within a much more comprehensive cultural upheaval. Just as important as books and pamphlets were sermons, endless little groups discussing the latest sensation, public disputations, and the vivid images of the popular artist and the heart-throb of music. We must never underestimate, either, the lightning speed and effectiveness of rumor at this time.

As significant as the new technology was the linguistic explosion: translations from Hebrew and Greek and Latin opened up new worlds for scholar and layperson alike, while the dizzying rise of the vernacu-lar languages meant that written and oral language reinforced one another in homes and mills and streets and inns as well as churches. A contemporary of Rychsner in Augsburg, the painter Jörg Breu, reminds us, too, of the key role of visual language and symbolism.[4] It was harnessed by ordinary folk to promote their cause and placard their self-understandings. Art for its own sake, after all, is a very mod-ern conception. In this period, art was as much a tool as language. The images of art were part of the texture of worship, of feast and festival, of education and nurture, of war and diplomacy, of codes of honor and the gradations of hierarchy. The iconoclasm of the period, whose zeal and fury drove people to smash images, deface paintings, lop off saints' breasts, and poke out their eyes, is an indirect attestation to its seductive charm and power. It was complemented, moreover, by what we can call the iconopoeic energies of the reformist movement, its iconic creativity, its minting and reception of new images.

Thousands of pamphlets were penned in an attempt to meet the demand for a straight, clear, lively, homely language suitable for uncomplicated, *ainfeltigen* (literally onefold) people. The very idea of bothering to reach such simple souls with literature was itself shatter-ingly new, an extension of the evangelical enthusiasm of the preacher, balladeer, or singer. The insistence on simplicity, clarity, and—by implication—authenticity was so often repeated that it attained a formulaic quality. Again and again pamphlets offered a "full report" on crucial events, or a "thorough explanation of evangelical teaching," emphasizing the desire to inform "every pious Christian." This gave laypeople the chance to read up on matters that concerned them in a familiar language and digest them at leisure, in their own time and space. Their concern was seldom for the minutiae of doctrine, but rather for direct access through scripture to the central themes of faith. The new understanding of baptism, whether in its Lutheran form for children or its Anabaptist form for adults, hammered home the right and duty of *ordinary* believers to be articulate about their faith.

LAY EMPOWERMENT

This doctrine of the priesthood of all believers meant that heads of families had a particular responsibility for religious formation in the home, one centered on catechism or scripture. The baptismal "oath" laid the privilege and burden of "confessing" the faith on every single Christian. The foundation for this simplification and laicization of faith and piety was the stellar authority of scripture, which appeared to offer laypeople a way to be less dependent on the religious professionals. The latter's reliance on scholastic philosophy and canon law could be completely sidestepped and indeed discredited as the mere fantasies of human reason, the "stuff of dreams and the work of the devil." Scripture, on the other hand, was seen as clear and unambiguous:

> They teach us endless lies
> Dreamed up from their own minds
> Their heart knows no real ties
> To God's Word they are blind.
> One chooses this, another that,
> Arguing with one another, tit for tat
> While they vaunt themselves as saints.[5]

With its accessibility and affordability (a pamphlet could be bought for the cost of a chicken) the printing press created an unprecedented intimacy between scholars on the one hand and local readers on the other. The revered Dr. Luther was at the same time their friend Martin, who chatted to them whenever they picked up his latest writing. "What's all the rage at Augsburg these days? What do they think of Luther? Does his teaching still rule the roost?" the priest asks the weaver in Rychsner's dialogue. "More than ever" was the answer.[6]

This sense of "being in touch" was reinforced by the writing's being hot off the press. The very name given the pamphlets, *Flugschriften,*

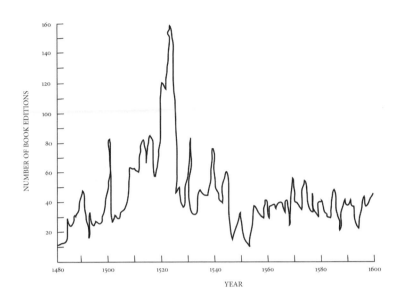

Fig. 11.2. Graph showing frequency of pamphlet printing in the Reformation era. From Miriam Usher Chrisman, *Lay Culture, Learned Culture: Books and Social Change in Strasbourg, 1480–1599* (New Haven: Yale University Press, 1982), 287. Adapted by permission.

or flying writings, hints at the speed with which news, ideas, controversies spread. The Frankfurt book fair and small armies of book peddlers ensured that news from distant centers such as Wittenberg and Zurich spread in all directions at breakneck speed. The general lack of copyright meant that local printers could and did pirate successful editions from elsewhere within weeks. Old political boundaries became irrelevant, especially in the early years of the Reformation, when censorship authorities, Catholic and Protestant, had yet to get their act together. Bishops and universities charged with exercising control by the papacy were often somnolent. So those who had been the last to know anything in the past could now be "connected" by a set of interlocking networks. Through their pastor or teacher or lay leader even remote communities could feel they were in touch with the new buzzwords of a Luther or colleagues such as Karlstadt, with his particular interest in informing and activating lay Christians.

The profit motive of the printers linked hands with the crusading concerns of the reformers and the appetite of the readers to encourage an accessible style and language. Tracts and pamphlets often took the form of dramatized conversations, as in Rychsner's dialogue. Other pamphlets bore traces of their origins as letters to close friends, sermons to fired-up congregations, or records of tense controversies. A pamphlet might take the form of an information

pack, with background information about the particular issue that
had provoked it, reports on the event itself, and the subsequent
outcome. The strong pedagogical concern of the authors, generally
yoked to a passionate message, put a premium on lucid, nontechnical
language, rather like the cheap popular editions produced for workers' and trade-union groups in the twentieth century. The woodcuts
and broadsheets that accompanied the pamphlets reinforced the
message and slotted it into a visual landscape, reducing complex
issues to cartoon-style simplicity and vividness, shoehorning new
ideas into the readers' imaginations.

We should hesitate, then, to describe such writings as "propaganda,"
although the term is still frequently used in the secondary literature
about this period. Nevertheless, "propaganda" is a pejorative label, and
it make little sense to regard the pastors, preachers, lay confessors, and
letter writers who were the authors as "propagandists." Rather, their
language was prophetic or pastoral, torn from their own hearts, not
conscious manipulation. This is as much true of Luther's "rhetoric of
the heart" as of the plain discourse favored by the Reformed and Puritan traditions. Indeed, one could argue that by breaking down difficult
issues of theology or church controversy into simple language, these
popular writings empowered laypeople, enabling them to articulate
their own concerns and to challenge previous interpretations. To have
the "right words," after all, is the first step to gaining control over one's
own faith and life. There is a crucial distinction between the brain-
washing of propaganda and offering laypeople tools to read scripture
for themselves. Moreover, abundant evidence shows that readers tai-
lored what they read to their own particular needs.

On the other hand, as the various Reformations hardened into
confessional form, it certainly is the case that the language of tracts
and catechisms and the use of visual media became increasingly stan-
dardized and "top-down." As the interests of the secular and ecclesiastical establishments came to predominate by the middle decades of
the sixteenth century, the propagandist element was to become much
more prominent. The processes of confessionalization, which included
the growing professionalization of the clergy, and the imposition of
uniform confessions of faith and orders of worship and church polity represented countervailing tendencies to the democratization of

religious language. Lay preachers and women writers were shouldered out very quickly, not to reappear in any numbers until eighteenth- and nineteenth-century Pietism and Methodism. The sacral language of Latin may have been demoted, but in Lutheran worship Latin had a place until the nineteenth century, and it long remained central to theological scholarship and teaching. Protestantism's insistence on the preacher's competence in Hebrew and Greek and Catholicism's gradual introduction of regular seminary education for priests after the Council of Trent also had a tendency to separate the pastors linguistically and culturally from their flocks.

RESOURCES FOR LAYPEOPLE MULTIPLY

Initially, however, the availability of vernacular Bibles, hymns, catechisms, devotional tracts, liturgies, pamphlets, and broadsheets created a multiplicity of resources for a great variety of audiences. Civic chroniclers mention in one breath the "common folk," the "little" books they read, and the common (vernacular) language they used. As the printing presses flexed their muscles, a "fourth estate" was born, and something very akin to modern public opinion emerged.

Closely related to this was the genial skills of Luther, the Swiss reformer Huldrych Zwingli, the Englishman William Tyndale, and others as translators of the Bible. Vernacular Bibles had been around before, but they were clumsy, wooden, uninspiring works. It is embarrassing to compare them with the reformers' translations. It was not only that the latter went back to the original Greek and Hebrew. They breathed the whole world of the Psalms and prophetic writings, the Gospel parables and narratives. Humanists like John Colet had paved the way by recognizing that the letters of Paul were written by a real historical person to specific, living communities. What the reformers rediscovered, then, was the popular, indeed populist nature of the Bible. The "wild animal" of passionate biblical rhetoric was released from its ecclesiastical domestication.

Language, after all, is not just about naming things. It is the way in which we reach out beyond ourselves. A real translation conveys this dynamic process, especially as reformers followed Erasmus in emphasizing that in the Incarnation God "accommodates" God's own self to human understanding. Biblical scholarship and theology minted a new vocabulary and syntax very different from that of the bishop's court, the university, and the monastery. Faith and piety were now, in the eyes of radicals such as Thomas Müntzer, open to the scrutiny of the elect throughout the world, and so he waved good-bye to privileged hole-and-corner institutions with their own in-house jargon. Luther's *Appeal to the German Nobility* had talked of the need to collapse the legal ramparts around ecclesiastical authority and privilege. But the challenge to the linguistic fences around the gospel may have been still more significant.

THEOLOGY GOES PUBLIC

The audience for theology, then, was widening. The original audience for Luther's defense of his writings might have been the university context of Wittenberg or Leipzig, or the Imperial Parliament or Diet at Worms in 1521, where the Holy Roman emperor was flanked by the nobility, the clerical hierarchy, and the wealthy burgesses from the towns. When Luther's arguments were catapulted into print, however, the ordinary reader in town or village could eavesdrop on them. Significantly, the abortive challenge of the Bavarian noblewoman Argula von Grumbach to the Ingolstadt university in 1523, summoning the theologians to a public debate in German, became a sensational success when her published appeal to them went into fourteen editions within two months.[7] Denied an audience with the theologians, she created her own far larger audience by the use of print.

For the new audience a new form of discourse was required. It was no accident, therefore, that those reaching out often used the conversational, colloquy form, in which old and new worlds of discourse were seen to meet head-on, friars and learned clergy being outwitted by simple cobblers, spoon makers, or village leaders. On the woodcut at the front of his *Entertaining Conversation*, the weaver Rychsner and a priest face up to one another and exchange questions and answers as equals. We need to remember that it was normal at this time for books and pamphlets to be read aloud in the homes and inns where people gathered. Thus these little pamphlets, so often generated by a specific event, in turn generated countless other mini-events with far-flung local audiences, who would have tossed in their own caustic comments. In this way oral and literary discourse constantly reinforced one another. The fictional colloquies, moreover, were often complemented by actual civic disputations, where representatives of the old Church traded arguments with the new evangelical preachers, under the wary eyes of the magistrates. This is very public theology indeed, with discussion being held in German and scripture used as the plumb line for truth and error.

The origins of the whole Reformation have often been traced back to Luther's perhaps apocryphal nailing of his Ninety-Five Theses against indulgences to the door of the Castle Church in Wittenberg. More important than any such symbolic act is that he tossed out philosophical language in favor of biblical and pastoral. The Latin theses, originally conceived for a scholarly disputation among professional theologians, were then translated into German and rapidly broadcast in print, together with explanatory material. This is a good illustration of the widening ripples of attention, as scholars broke out of the halls of learning and "took to the road," adapting their language as they did so to their new readers. The language of lay authors, moreover, reflected their very different field of experience. Argula von Grumbach's writings could only have been written by a woman. She trawled scripture for insights and biblical models that spoke to her as layperson and woman. Popular pamphlets, colloquies, and disputations could be seen, therefore as exciting new vehicles that took the sacred language of theology into the public square, the epicenter of secular life.

This multiplicity of new audiences meant the invasion of new spaces. Small discussion groups sprang up everywhere. Some, like the Staupitz circle in Nuremberg, were famous. Most were just gatherings of the interested and the curious. Theology simultaneously became more intimate and more public. In the privacy of a student's lodging, around the kitchen table, or in the back room of an inn, ideas could be explored without the presence of the traditional gatekeepers. Clergy and religious in fact often did participate, but not to dominate. Humanists had already fostered the discussion of biblical and ethical questions among friends in their "sodalities," informal groups of friends. Their poetic and literary approach to scripture, the *via rhetorica* as they called it, had already generated a very different language from the philosophical one of the university theologians. Now a much wider group of laypeople from both town and countryside began to make the Bible their own.

HOW LAYPEOPLE READ SCRIPTURE

We have become habituated to the idea of the centrality of scripture to Protestantism, but the phenomenon is a strange one. There could scarcely have been anything more alien and remote from the life of early modern Europe than the thought and experience of ancient Israel and the primitive church. Yet this very strangeness proved attractive, posing a challenging alternative to the church and society of the time. The interpretive skills of the reformers enabled the horizons of the prophets and apostles to be fused with those of contemporaries. Its narratives and central symbols found expression in language that spoke to the yearnings and perceptions of ordinary people.

We are only just beginning to understand how laypeople read their Bibles at this time. We know they often interiorized it, learning great tracts of it off by heart. Selections of key passages circulated. Sebastian Lotzer, for example, began to collect sayings from scripture that related to contested issues and published them in what amounted to a little biblical concordance. He noted the practical point that now the Bible books were divided up into chapters, it would be much easier for laypeople to locate the references.[8] For the wandering, persecuted Anabaptist groups, similar groupings of biblical texts were available and were of crucial value in providing these largely artisan or peasant groups with stepping stones through scripture.

Laypeople did not read scripture academically or analytically but as the very voice of God, as the well from which they would draw salvation. They found their own way to move from text to text, to form their own "compass" within scripture. This enabled them to ignore some parts and give priority to others, to cherish those metaphors of freedom, or light, or the "new song" that activated whole clusters of memories, feelings, images, and contexts for them.

The scriptures, then, were read and reread, underlined, digested, memorized, "studied," as many laypeople liked to put it, but in their own space and in their own language. Laypeople wrote to one another about their queries and their findings; they exchanged pamphlets that had helped them with their friends. This immersion in scripture equipped them with questions and perspectives, and above all a new vocabulary, a whole treasury of stories, proverbs, images, models, and arguments that they could deploy when they listened to sermons and discussions. The Zurich "Prophecy," with its articulated progression from Hebrew and Greek exegesis to Latin and finally to a vernacular exegesis of scripture is another fascinating experiment in bridging, linguistically, "high" and "low" culture, clerical and lay theology. "I need to say to you how I understand the Gospel in my simple way," says Rychsner to the priest. "I, too, can ask questions; I can hear answers," says Argula von Grumbach, a mere laywoman, to the Ingolstadt theologians.[9] Women, one need scarcely add, had hitherto been regarded as having no business in church pulpits or university podiums!

Lay Christians such as Sebastian Lotzer and Argula von Grumbach, therefore, threw down the gauntlet to the "professional" theologians. No one group, they believed, and certainly not the wealthy and the powerful, had a monopoly on the language of God, the prophets, the evangelists, and the apostles. Their ideal was a partnership between pious, learned preachers and a thoughtful laity who, if possible, would buy their own New Testament so that they could follow up on the sermon at home.

Given the low literacy rates, however, even in the cities, most laypeople had to rely on their memories or on friends reading scripture aloud for them. Above all, they had to rely on the biblical sermon. Again, it is hard for us to recapture the attractiveness of the sermon for contemporaries or to hear it as they did. An analogy may be the huge popularity of poetry under totalitarian regimes. The preacher was valued primarily for his role in "breaking open" scripture, the true food for the soul, so that, as many stressed, the Word of God would flourish especially among ordinary people. Anabaptists systematically used little collections of key texts to assist their interpretation of scripture. But in mainline Protestantism too, the laity sought to exercise their ministry by speaking in their own characteristic accents.

Rychsner, for example, uses drastic, down-to-earth language in his critique of church taxes such as tithes: if the cow's milk dries up, the clergy grab the sheep's wool; if that fails, they pull the skin right back over the sheep's ears.[10]

THE CATECHISM

Catechisms, often described as the Bibles of the poor, were the basic teaching tool of all the churches, being cordially embraced by Catholic reformers as well. They operated primarily by the memorization of the most basic affirmations of faith: the Lord's Prayer, the Creed, the Ten Commandments. To some extent they can be viewed as tools of top-down confessionalization, the provision of stock answers to all life's problems. There is considerable evidence of the unpopularity of sleepy Sunday afternoon catechism sessions in rural areas.

If we adopt a nonelitist point of view, however, catechisms can also be seen as an educational breakthrough. Their "echo" technique, in which the answer was partly contained in the question, provided a welcome nudge to the learner. Their use of direct and simple language need not exclude profundity. One suspects that many who today speak so dismissively about the catechisms have never paid close attention to their language, which often exhibits a direct, biblical, and personal thrust. The concern to reach ordinary people in terms they understood should not be underestimated. The use of memorization enabled the young, illiterate, or semi-literate to interiorize the faith and to acquire a framework for their lives, which stretched back to Adam and forward to the conclusion of all things at the last judgment. Catechisms varied considerably in their sophistication; they sometimes included hymns to sing or questions for discussion or even information, say, about the origins of biblical words.

Luther's Larger Catechism 1529: You Shall Not Kill

So we must make absolutely clear to the simplest folk what the key issue is when it forbids killing: First of all, it means not harming anyone physically or otherwise. Not letting your tongue wag, either, to plan or suggest this; moreover, not to use or agree to use anything that will insult anyone, and finally not to harbor in your heart hostility to anyone or wish them ill because of anger or hate. Your body and soul are to be innocent, then, in regard to everyone, but especially those who wish or do you ill.

—From *Luthers Werke: Kritische Gesamtausgabe [Schriften]* (Weimar: H. Böhlau, 1883–1993), 31/1.159; my translation.

Much depended, of course, on the skill with which the catechism was taught. A great deal more research is needed on the way in which catechizing enriched the biblical and religious vocabulary of ordinary people. The same is true of religious drama, with which the Jesuits were to have particular success but which took off in German and Dutch Protestantism as well.[11] It has even been argued that the growing popularity of secular theater in Protestant countries—one thinks of Shakespeare himself—may be attributed to the loss of the variety and wealth of traditional Catholic ceremonies.

THE BIBLE AS A BLUEPRINT FOR CHANGE

Reform concerns and initiatives, of course, extended far beyond what we would regard today as religious or church matters. Candle makers' guilds, learned sodalities, little groups of earnest believers, women spinning or washing clothes together—all tossed ideas around about everything from the reliability of the new preacher to poor relief, taxation, and the lack of good sanitation. They often turned to the Bible to express their hopes and frustrations and to find models for a better church and society. The local community or congregation, its nose rubbed each day in the realities of domestic, civic, and agrarian problems and tensions, found itself as much a part of a web of learning as the school or college. Its village spokesmen, city clerks, guild masters, and parents were not interested in speculative theology. They wanted an expression of the faith that made sense of the ups and downs of daily life.

So it is no surprise that the language of a lay pamphleteer such as Rychsner is vivid, personal, and biblical. He does not attempt an abstract defense of Christian egalitarianism. Instead he speaks of the common descent of all, rich and poor, from Adam and Eve, and of our oneness in Christ. We are all, he argued, God's children, all brothers and sisters, born of one earth, one God, and one Spirit. The "painted" clergy (by which he meant that they looked good only on the surface) claim to be better than us, and think they alone are the church. Jesus, however, has taught us to call no one "Master." God looks as favorably on peasants and beggars as on the great prelates. He points to pious women such as Susanna, a favorite subject for depiction on stained glass or in paintings, who defied the elders of her time. Or to Balaam's ass, another favorite, who was so much more open to the Word of God than his embarrassed master. Tradition, on the other hand, was given scant weight. Rychsner was critical of the traditional proof texts used to justify the seven sacraments. "Dear sir, there is no way you can sift oral confession from them." If we were to follow custom and regard marriage as a sacrament, the Jews, heathens, and Turks would also have to be credited with celebrating a sacrament.

Every layperson, therefore, has the God-given right and duty to criticize abuses wherever they exist. Jesus led the way by driving the money changers out of the temple. Rychsner scoured scripture for heroes and villains. On virtually every page of his writings we find references to ancient Israel or to the New Testament church. He looked to Jeremiah and Ezekiel for inspiration, and like them he was enraged by the liars and false shepherds of his time. He saw equivalent figures to the high priests Annas and Caiaphas, or cruel rulers like Herod and Pilate, emerging in his own day. He imagined with grim satisfaction the multitude of millstones that would be required to drown contemporaries who seduced the innocent with their superstitious illusions and devilish ideas. He was particularly outraged, like so many pamphleteers, by those who dared to imprison, exile, and execute the preachers of the gospel. References to "flogging," "flaying," "beheading," "burning alive" recur constantly in his pamphlets and in those of his time. No words spoke so loudly as the body language of martyrdom, which sparked off Luther's first hymn and had a preeminent place in Anabaptist hymnology. The reemergence of persecution recalled the great days of the early church.

Rychsner's language was full of little stories and homespun logic. The popes' actions demonstrated that what drove them was not love for Christ or his sheep but their greedy pursuit of wealth, honor, and power. The reader is shaken and aroused by his incandescent rage at such "robbery." Indulgences and masses for the dead were denounced as a financial stunt; folk could see that even the clergy did not believe in them. They just felt that if the pope were shearing the flock, they might as well flay it! The clergy had lied so often that if they were for once to speak the truth, no one would believe them! Their credibility was shot. The mediatory power of the priest was "a bad joke." The peasants knew the priests were lying and couldn't take them seriously. The language he uses about such "masters," whom he describes as godly scoundrels, messengers of the devil, amassers of rich benefices, simoniacs who bought their way into church office, and then lived happily with their whores, degenerates at times into moralistic abuse. It has, however, the authentic ring of passion of those who feel "ripped off." Its excesses and extremes mirror what was perceived as a church and society utterly intolerable to God.

The language could be crude or anti-Semitic. The Sacrament of Extreme Unction was just smearing oil on the dying. All the edicts of the councils and the popes should be put into a sack and thrown away. Judas only sold Christ once; the priests do it every day. Jesus kissed the disciples' feet; in contrast, the pope expects his feet to be kissed. Irony jostles with sarcasm and derision. A vivid wintry image has horses, bells jingling on their harnesses, pulling a sledge through the snow. They remind him of clergy dressed in the cap and bells of a fool. A Jewish school would welcome a pig sooner than priests would welcome scripture. In a near-blasphemous reference to the crucifixion, Rychsner has the priests crying out to their "God," the pope: "Eloi, Eloi, why have you forsaken me?"

This truly ferocious anticlericalism is framed by apocalyptic concepts and language. The "man of sin" threatens to defile the holy of

Fig. 11.3. Albrecht Dürer's (1471–1528) famous series "Horsemen of the Apocalypse" (1497–1498) predates the Lutheran Reformation and catches the awed sense of people at the beginning of the sixteenth century that a vast cosmic struggle between good and evil was in train, that it would have awesome consequences, and that neither men nor women, neither clerics nor laity, would be immune from it.

Fig. 11.4. This is perhaps the most famous and influential depiction of Luther as the Wittenberg nightingale, "who is now heard everywhere," hailing the dawn, and with it a new age of peace and harmony. Note the sun on the left, with Christ as the Resurrection lamb below it, and the moon on the right. Luke 19 is quoted at the bottom: "Should these be silent, the very stones will cry out." The 1523 poem of Hans Sachs, the Nuremberg cobbler, which accompanies it, begins with a stirring "Wacht auf!" (Wake up!).

holies. Scripture is caught up in a deadly battle with pagan traditions, the "mouth of truth" with the "mouth of lies," Christ with Antichrist. Indeed, everything is so topsy-turvy, Rychsner complains, that one becomes completely dizzy. The honor due to God alone is given to idiotic saints or to ridiculous processions and practices, while the gospel is denounced as heretical.

It is not all criticism and abuse. The straightforwardness and transparency of scripture is stressed again and again; it runs pure and clear like freshwater. Rychsner is a passionate advocate of a "better way," a cleansed church and a reformed society. "Those who love the Lord love what the Lord loves." The pamphleteer's "dear brothers and sisters," the lay Christians, are called upon to preach the gospel, to feed the hungry, to clothe the naked, to watch over the sick and those in prison. The spirit of truth will lead them into all truth, for they are a chosen people, a royal priesthood: "Therefore, dear brothers and sisters in Christ, let us pray to God by night and by day for grace, for strength of faith, love and hope in God our Savior, for he has promised us in John 16 that we will receive whatever we ask."[12]

We have focused on the simple language of a single particular writer. But it illustrates how the issues raised in one pamphlet seem to have flown from one end of the country to the other. Rychsner's forthright advocacy of the right and duty of laypeople to highlight abuses in church and state is echoed in similar pamphlets in the same year by the much more famous author Hans Sachs in Nuremberg, by

Argula von Grumbach in the little Franconian town of Dietfurt, and by Martin Bucer in Strasbourg, to mention only a few. The coincidence of themes may be partly because everyone was eagerly reading the latest pamphlets. Sebastian Lotzer, Eberlin von Günzburg, and Balthasar Hubmaier, for example, all hailed Argula von Grumbach's intervention against the Ingolstadt theologians as a remarkable sign of the times, showing that God was acting in quite a new way. But it was partly also that the issues were much the same everywhere, and their simultaneous expression was more a matter of spontaneous combustion than of any specific influence.

Although we no longer make the mistake of attributing everything in the Reformation to Luther, it would be equal folly to deny the centrality of his role in coining a new language of faith. Luther's *Appeal to the German Nobility* of 1520, with its new vision of the church, provided the basis for much of Rychsner's writing, though Rychsner applied it to a much more egalitarian agenda. Argula von Grumbach's defiant tribute to Luther's gifts as a translator of scripture could be replicated a thousand times. Many of the broadsheets— vivid depictions, for example, of Luther leading those who "lay in darkness" into the light—wove together visual and poetic imagery in a memorable if highly simplified manner, so that by 1524 Luther had attained almost mythical status. One moment he might appear as the Wittenberg nightingale, singing beautifully to the glory of the gospel, the next as the club-wielding German equivalent of Hercules. A typical satirical poem or squib from Speyers in 1524 wedded derision of the pope, his cardinals, and his pet theologian John Eck, with a heart-rending cry to Luther for help from Christ's faithful, who lay imprisoned in Egyptian darkness, like the people of Israel before Moses freed them:

> O Martin, free us from our fate
> Have mercy on our wretched state
> For we have long been bound in chains
> In darkness, turned quite blind
> By human teaching, rule and code
> No longer knowing God,
> No longer, either, Jesus Christ
> Though he alone the savior is
> Who meets our greatest need.[13]

THE "NEW SONG" OF THE GOSPEL

We turn now from church practice and theology to worship. Perhaps the most elemental mode of access to people's hearts, worship was transformed by the introduction of congregational psalms and hymns. In recent decades we have rightly been reminded of the lively participation of the laity in pre-Reformation worship. This should not detract, however, from a recognition of the extraordinary popularity of the move toward vernacular worship in the Reformation period.

One notable feature of this was the Lutheran chorale, with its insertion of vernacular language and popular melodies into the very heart of worship. Luther himself liked to characterize Christ as the "new song" of the Gospel. Singing, of course, is a medium in which body, mind, and soul are all caught up, one that bonds singers together in a profound way. We are beginning to appreciate the intimate links between preaching, the vernacular Bible, and participatory hymn-singing in the early Reformation. Printing, singing, and preaching are often mentioned in one breath by the reformers. Beginning in 1524, Lutheran songbooks and song sheets began to pour out; and the latter were even more important for the ordinary layperson. In Nuremberg alone nearly three hundred songbooks or song sheets appeared between 1525 and 1570.

The transformation of worship was, however, a very gradual one, as initially the four- or five-part vernacular hymns were designed for choral singing. Moreover, most congregational members could not read, so they took time to learn the new lyrics by heart, though they generally knew the melodies already. They were predictably slow, therefore, at exploiting the full range of new songs from Luther, Paul Speratus, Hans Sachs, and others. Luther's skill, however, at combining traditional melodies with new hymns or translations of Latin ones ensured that the Reformation eventually sang its way into people's hearts. He was particularly conscious of the importance of music for young people and for the great mass of the illiterate. Nor was he alone. There was a host of other superb hymn writers. Hymns were of particular importance for the Anabaptists. One hardly needs to emphasize the importance of the rhythmic beat and haunting tunes of the metrical psalms in the Calvinist tradition, whether sung provocatively at street corners as a form of civil disobedience or given voice within French Huguenot "temples" or Scottish kirks and homes.

WORSHIP IN THE COMMON TONGUE

Worship comprised more than hymns, however. The new vernacular services as a whole were immensely popular even in rural areas. We know that people flocked in 1523–1524 from adjoining villages to the new vernacular services in Thomas Müntzer's little Saxon town, Allstedt, for example. Defending his pioneering German Mass, Müntzer insisted that God's revelation had to be made accessible and transparent to rough, ordinary people. He believed that those wise in the ways of this world can always find a thousand clever reasons to evade the truth. The Hebrew and New Testament Scriptures testify, however, that it is precisely to the poor, the humble, to women and old people that God prefers to speak. So it was vital, in Müntzer's view, that the prayers, hymns, readings, and liturgy of the sacraments should not be in Latin but in a language ordinary people can understand.

His basic assumption is that all the elect need to be addressed by God. Worship is not some piece of hocus-pocus, a magical act channeled through the priest. It is a participatory act of the whole congregation. The role of the preacher is to cry out in the wilderness of people's hearts. The whole community are concelebrants in consecrating the bread and the wine. Likewise, all take part in the declaration of absolution from sin. There is a sense here of biblical language not as a mere talisman but as a trigger for the working of the Spirit in the abyss of the heart. This interiorization of faith is expressed in a vocabulary that is mystical as well as biblical. In Luther, scripture had become populist; in Müntzer, mysticism, too, became populist.

Müntzer's insistence on the necessity for translation, the "carrying over" of words from one cultural world to another, reminds us that translation provoked much reflection in the Reformation period. On the fringes but nonetheless significant, there was the Renaissance quest for "the perfect language" and a growing awareness of a new world beyond the seas. Thus a consciousness of the multiplicity and relativity of language began to develop. Müntzer was aware that Latin might have been appropriate at an earlier stage of Germany's history but that Germans should now have the scriptures in their own language. No one language should be privileged above another.[14] Luther, always a brilliant wordsmith, was aware of the need to observe how ordinary people use words in the home, the marketplace, and at work and to adjust religious language accordingly. Discipleship was worked out, after all, not in some ethereal spiritual world but within the vocation of day-to-day living.

We need to reflect more on the linguistic collisions in this period, the explosions of knowledge of classical and biblical languages paralleling the giant strides made by vernacular languages. Such "commuting" between languages always introduces creative clashes of metaphorical and syntactical worlds, fresh ways of framing reality. The way in which the Hebrew language stimulated Luther's whole understanding of grace and covenant is a case in point. At the end of the sixteenth century, Peter Albinus, at the Saxon court, believed that the discovery of new lands and languages flashed out an eschatological signal. Since all languages retain something of the imprint of God's mind, according to Albinus, recovering the languages freed us from corruption and restored the Pentecostal vigor of the primitive church.[15]

EARTHINESS AND IMMEDIACY

Both Luther and Müntzer were, of course, university-trained intellectuals. It is illuminating, however, to see how a laywoman such as Argula von Grumbach rediscovered for herself and others the directness of biblical language. She felt, as she often said, that she spoke "with" Deborah or Jeremiah or Paul. It was as if they were her contemporaries. Where God was concerned, the networks of communication transcended centuries, indeed millennia. Reading her writings, one finds it impossible to miss the conviction that the prophets or evangelists or apostles communicated with her directly as she, in turn, hoped to communicate to her listeners and readers. One is struck in her writings and those of countless contemporaries by a pervasive sense of immediacy.

If it is true, as this chapter has been arguing, that the Reformations struck root because they gave ordinary people their voice, it will be no surprise that humor often played a part. The astonishing productivity and popularity of the Nuremberg cobbler Hans Sachs makes him one of the best exponents of folk culture. His poems were often sung at home or in the tavern, or used in conjunction with visual art on broadsheets, enhancing their attractiveness to an illiterate or semi-literate audience. They could be learned by heart, and the images with which they were associated made them doubly memorable. His language was that of the home and the workplace, while his thought combined much common sense with deep moral indignation at any abuse of privilege and wealth. The rather scurrilous anticlericalism that runs through much of it is modified by a warm humanity.

Take his poem "The Simple Monk." An abbot in conflict with a local knight had sent learned scholars and zealous ascetics from his monastery to protest at the confiscation of his livestock. In desperation he finally sent a simple monk, instructing him not to reject any food offered, thinking he would probably be given something inedible such as fox meat. But the knight set before him game birds of all sorts, which the simple monk gobbled up "like a butcher's dog." When challenged that this was surely against his order's rule, he reported the abbot's instructions. The knight saw the funny side and was so taken by the naïveté of the monk that he returned the cattle to the abbey. Hans Sachs draws the moral:

> Note that a harsh or subtle mind
> Has scant effect in our present time,
> While simple friendship, kindness, fun
> Appeal much more to an honest man.
> Grim vengeance then
> Can give way to peace;
> So resort to whatever skill you please
> If it brings all enmity to cease.[16]

Finally, we should note that the massive circulation and pervasive use of Bible translations, catechisms, and hymns had an unexpected outcome. It furthered the standardization of vernacular languages while simultaneously deepening and broadening their linguistic range.

Dialects by no means disappeared, and indeed frequently publishers modified spelling, punctuation, and syntax to suit their own regional markets. Others, however, were like Froschauer, who apologized to his local readers that in his German version of Oecolampadius's *On the Sacrament of Thanksgiving* he had not "used our language at Zurich but printed it in the common language of those from other areas so that they too could understand it and so it would be useful to many."[17] Thus the influence of Luther's Bible and the King James Bible on the evolution of modern German and English is incalculable.

Nothing in history is ever simple. We have to guard against exaggerations. Vernacular Bibles, sermons, prayer books, and hymns had been around for centuries. England, with its acute suspicion of vernacular versions of the Bible, was something of an exception, and even there, devotional works in English abounded. The anti-classicizing, anti-elitist stream of Christian tradition had never dried up. Throughout the medieval period people were reminded that God spoke through eccentric prophets, crude fishermen, desert saints, and humble martyrs as well as through the Latinist codes of theologians. Vernacular discourse had been the métier of the preaching friars and laywomen's groups such as the Beguins. Rychsner himself refers warmly to famous civic preachers such as Geiler von Kaisersberg in Strasbourg. People in town and country had always gathered around the preaching cross or the pulpit, not least during Lent, to hear sermons addressed to them in their own language. And who could forget the popularity of the cycles of mystery plays, the songs of the pilgrims, and the romances woven around the Crusades? Unforgettable, too, was the vernacular language of stained glass or the carved figures of Mary and the child, the apostles, and the martyrs. All of these were of the people and for the people.

Nonetheless, the sixteenth century did represent a watershed. Preaching shifted its focus from "emblems" or illustrations and entertaining stories to the central biblical themes. For writers such as Rychsner, this meant above all the free forgiveness of sin through the rose-red blood of the Savior. Popular art, ballads, plays, pamphlets, hymns and sermons, and private study of the Psalms and the Gospels were woven together to form, as in Reformation Augsburg, a vivid, varied, but coherent tapestry. The language of faith was drawn from the life and work of ordinary people.

Language is power. The nineteenth-century philosophers of language used to talk of language as an inexplicable miracle springing from the heart of a nation. We have learned to be deeply suspicious of such romantic nationalism. Yet within the body of the Christian church such "miracles" of linguistic energy and creativity have occurred again and again, not least in apostolic and patristic times.[18] The Reformation undoubtedly saw another such outpouring. The lasting contribution of this period may well be the liberation of biblical language, some exquisitely beautiful liturgy, and the burgeoning of hymnody and psalmody. The time of Shakespeare and the exuberant Rabelais was also that of Luther, of the King James version, the Calvinist Psalms, Cranmer's glorious *Book of Common Prayer*, the wonderful poetry and prose of the Spanish mystics. We feast on them still.

FOR FURTHER READING

Boyle, Marjorie O'Rourke. *Erasmus on Language and Method in Theology.* Erasmus Studies 2. Toronto: University of Toronto Press, 1977.

Brandt, Deborah. *Literacy as Involvement: The Acts of Writers, Readers, and Texts.* Carbondale: Southern Illinois University Press, 1990.

Boureau, Alain, et al. *The Culture of Print: Power and the Uses of Print in Early Modern Europe.* Edited by Roger Chartier. Translated by Lydia G. Cochrane. Cambridge, U.K.: Polity, 1989.

Chrisman, Miriam Usher. *Lay Culture, Learned Culture: Books and Social Change in Strasbourg, 1480–1599.* New Haven: Yale University Press, 1982.

Matheson, Peter. *The Rhetoric of the Reformation.* Edinburgh: T & T Clark, 1998.

Morrall, Andrew. *Jörg Breu the Elder: Art, Culture and Belief in Reformation Augsburg.* Histories of Vision. Aldershot, U.K.: Ashgate, 2002.

Paxman, David B. *Voyage into Language: Space and the Linguistic Encounter, 1500–1800.* Aldershot, U.K.: Ashgate, 2003.

Perelman, Chaim, and Lucy Olbrechts-Tyteca. *The New Rhetoric: A Treatise on Argumentation.* Translated by John Wilkinson and Purcell Weaver. Notre Dame, Ind.: University of Notre Dame Press, 1969.

Scribner, R. W. *For the Sake of Simple Folk: Popular Propaganda for the German Reformation.* Cambridge Studies in Oral and Literate Culture 2. Cambridge: Cambridge University Press, 1981.

NOTES

Introduction. Reforming from Below

1. *The Collected Works of Thomas Müntzer*, ed. and trans. Peter Matheson (Edinburgh: T & T Clark, 1988), 335.

2. *Erasmus*, ed. Richard L. DeMolen (London: Edward Arnold, 1973), 134.

3. *The Essential Carlstad*, trans. and ed. E. J. Furcha (Waterloo, Ont.: Herald, 1995), 104, 116.; see also *Anticlericalism in Late Medieval and Early Modern Europe*, ed. Peter A. Dykema and Heiko A. Oberman, Studies in Medieval and Reformation Thought, vol. 51 (Leiden: Brill, 1993).

4. See also the interesting article by the Marxist historian Adolf Laube, "Social Arguments in Early Reformation Pamphlets and Their Significance for the German Peasants' War," *Social History* 12 (1987): 361–78.

5. See Thomas A. Brady, *Ruling Class, Regime and Reformation at Strasbourg, 1520–1555* (Leiden: Brill, 1978), 294; Miriam Usher Chrisman, *Conflicting Visions of Reform: German Lay Propaganda Pamphlets, 1519–1530* (Atlantic Highland, N.J.: Humanities, 1996).

6. Carlo Ginzburg, *The Cheese and the Worms: The Cosmos of a Sixteenth-Century Miller,* trans. John and Anne Tedeschi (London: Routledge & Kegan Paul, 1980).

7. *Argula von Grumbach: A Woman's Voice in the Reformation*, ed. Peter Matheson (Edinburgh: T & T Clark, 1995), 89f.

8. J. H. Hexter, *Reappraisals in History* (Chicago: Chicago University Press, 1979), 266; see also Brad Gregory, *Salvation at Stake: Christian Martyrdom in Early Modern Europe* (Cambridge: Harvard University Press, 1989).

9. *Die Chroniken der deutschen Städte*, vol. 25 (Leipzig: Hirzel, 1896), 208, my translation.

10. Robert W. Scribner, "Is There a Social History of the Reformation?" *Social History* 4 (1976): 499.

Chapter One. The Piety of Townspeople and City Folk

1. *Passevent parisien respondant à Pasquin Romain* (Paris: Isidore Liseux, 1875 [1556]), 26–27.

2. Archives Municipales, Aimargues, GG 57, folios 66–77v, 86v–87.

3. Archives d'État de Genève, Registres du Conseil, 40, folio 222, August 24, 1545.

4. Quoted in *Confessions and Catechisms of the Reformation*, ed. Mark Noll (Grand Rapids: Baker Book House, 1991), 61.

5. Quoted in *Calvinism in Europe, 1540–1610: A Collection of Documents*, ed. Alastair Duke, Gillian Lewis, and Andrew Pettegree (Manchester: Manchester University Press), 54.

6. *Institutes* 3.20.5 and 3.20.33, from John Calvin, *Institutes of the Christian Religion*, ed. John T. McNeill (Philadelphia: Westminster, 1960), 2:854–55, 896–97.

7. Quoted in Arnold Hunt, "The Lord's Supper in Early Modern England," *Past and Present* 161 (November 1998): 82.

8. Archives Municipales, Nîmes, RR 60, folios 55, 60v, 67v, 95v, 147.

9. On this point, Calvin quoted Paul, "Rebuke them in the presence of all, so that the rest may stand in fear"(1 Tim. 5:20), in *Institute* 4.12.3, from Calvin, *Institutes*, 2:1231.

Chapter Two. Rural and Village Piety

1. Keith P. Luria, *Territories of Grace: Cultural Change in the Seventeenth-Century Diocese of Grenoble* (Berkeley: University of California Press, 1991), 32–34.

2. For discussions of the first view, see Gerald Strauss, *Luther's House of Learning: Indoctrination of the Young in the German Reformation* (Baltimore: Johns Hopkins University Press, 1978), and C. Scott Dixon, *The Reformation and Rural Society: The Parishes of Brandenburg-Ansbach-Kulmbach, 1528–1603* (Cambridge: Cambridge University Press, 1996), 147–57. On confessionalization, see Marc R. Forster, *Catholic Revival in the Age of the Baroque: Religious Identity in Southwest Germany, 1550–1750* (Cambridge: Cambridge University Press, 2001), 13–16.

3. Forster, *Catholic Revival*, 86–90, 119; Keith P. Luria, *Sacred Boundaries: Religious Coexistence and Conflict in Early-Modern France* (Washington, D.C.: Catholic University of America Press, 2005).

4. Jean-Michel Sallmann, *Naples et ses saints à l'âge baroque* (Paris: Presses Universitaires de France, 1994), 124, 131, 160–65, 178–93; Sara T. Nalle, *God in La Mancha: Religious Reform and the People of Cuenca, 1500–1650* (Baltimore: Johns Hopkins University Press, 1992), 156; Luria, *Territories of Grace*, 155; Philip M. Soergel, *Wondrous in His Saints: Counter-Reformation Propaganda in Bavaria* (Berkeley: University of California Press, 1993), 164–65; Marc R. Forster, *The Counter-Reformation in the Villages: Religion and Reform in the Bishopric of Speyer, 1560–1720* (Ithaca, N.Y.: Cornell University Press, 1992), 224; William A. Christian Jr., *Apparitions in Late Medieval and Renaissance Spain* (Princeton: Princeton University Press, 1981), 111–12.

5. Louis Châtellier, *The Religion of the Poor: Rural Missions and the Formation of Modern Catholicism, c. 1500–c. 1800*, trans. Brian Pearce (Cambridge: Cambridge University Press, 1997), 149, 161.

6. Nalle, *God in La Mancha*, 175; Luria, *Territories of Grace*, 126–27, 130 n. 86, 160; Sallmann, *Naples et ses saints*, 78–79.

7. Forster, *Catholic Revival*, 112–13.

8. William A. Christian Jr., *Local Religion in Sixteenth-Century Spain* (Princeton: Princeton University Press, 1981), 134–41.

9. Luria, *Territories of Grace*, 122–23.

10. Soergel, *Wondrous in His Saints*, 159–62.

11. Dixon, *The Reformation and Rural Society*.

12. John Bossy, *Christianity in the West, 1400–1700* (Oxford: Oxford University Press, 1985), 57–75.

13. David Gentilcore, *From Bishop to Witch: The System of the Sacred in Early Modern Terra d'Otranto* (Manchester: Manchester University Press, 1992), 82–83, 97–100; Forster, *Catholic Revival*, 127–29.

14. Forster, *Catholic Revival*, 127.

15. Ibid., 142; Gentilcore, *From Bishop to Witch*, 72, 98.

16. Luria, *Territories of Grace*, 182–202.

17. Jean-Claude Schmitt, "Apostolat mendiant et société: Une confrérie dominicaine à la veille de la réforme," *Annales: Économies, Sociéties, Civilisations* 1 (January–February 1971): 83–104.

Chapter Three. A People's Reformation?

1. *Basilikon Doron*, 1599, in *The Political Works of James I*, ed. C. H. McIlwain (Cambridge: Harvard University Press, 1918), 23–24.

2. Margo Todd, *The Culture of Protestantism in Early Modern Scotland* (New Haven: Yale University Press, 2002), 149.

3. John Aubrey, *The Remaines of Gentilisme*, ed. James Britten (London, 1881); David D. Hall, *Worlds of Wonder, Days of Judgment: Popular Belief in Early New England* (Cambridge: Harvard University Press, 1990 [1989]).

4. Margaret Sanderson, "Catholic Recusancy in Scotland in the Sixteenth Century," *The Innes Review* 21 (1970): 87–107; J. Kirk, "The Kirk and the Highlands at the Reformation," *Northern Scotland* 7 (1986): 1–22.

5. Samantha Meigs, *The Reformations in Ireland: Tradition and Confessionalism, 1400–1690*. Early Modern History (New York: St. Martin's, 1997), 73–74.

6. Diarmaid MacCulloch, *The Reformation* (New York: Viking, 2004), 387.

Chapter Four. Entering the World

1. A full version of this chapter appears in David Cressy, *Birth, Marriage, and Death: Ritual, Religion, and the Life-Cycle in Tudor and Stuart England* (New York: Oxford University Press, 1997), 15–34. Used by permission.

2. Patricia Crawford, "The Construction and Experience of Maternity in Seventeenth-Century England," in *Women as Mothers in Pre-Industrial England*, ed. Valerie Fides (London: Routledge, 1990), 3–38; Linda Pollock, "Embarking on a Rough Passage: The Experience of Pregnancy in Early Modern Society," in Fides, *Women as Mothers*,

39–67; Adrian Wilson, "The Ceremony of Childbirth and Its Interpretation," in *Fides, Women as Mothers*, 68–107; Adrian Wilson, "Participant or Patient? Seventeenth-Century Childbirth from the Mother's Point of View," in *Patients and Practitioners: Lay Perceptions of Medicine in Pre-Industrial Society*, ed. Roy Porter (Cambridge: Cambridge University Press, 1986), 129–44; Audrey Eccles, *Obstetrics and Gynaecology in Tudor and Stuart England* (Kent, Ohio: Kent State University Press, 1982).

3. Christopher Hooke, *The Child-birth or Womans Lecture* (1590; *Short-Title Catalogue [1475–1640]*, ed. A. W. Pollard and G. R. Redgrave [London: Bibliographical Society][hereafter *STC*] 13702), sigs. B₃v, Dv.

4. Richard Adams, "How May Child-Bearing Women Be Most Encouraged?" in *A Continuation of Morning-Exercise Questions and Cases of Conscience*, ed. Samuel Annesley (London: Joshua Dunton, 1683), 662.

5. Richard Hooker, "Of the Laws of Ecclesiastical Politie," in *The Works of That Learned and Judicious Divine, Mr. Richard Hooker* (1723), 268, 209; Robert Hill, *The Pathway to Prayer and Pietie* (1610; *STC* 13473), 415; Hooke, *The Child-birth*, sig. B2v; William Hinde, *A Faithful Remonstrance of the Holy Life and Happy Death of John Bruen of Bruen-Stapleford* (1641), 3.

6. Elizabeth Joceline, *The Mothers Legacie, to Her Unborne Childe* (1624; *STC* 14624), 1; Elizabeth Clinton, *The Countesse of Lincolnes Nurserie* (1622, *STC*, 5432), 19, 20; Ernest Axon, ed., *Oliver Heywood's Life of John Angier of Denton* (Manchester: Chetham Society, 1937), 124; Alice Thornton, *The Autobiography of Mrs. Alice Thornton* (Durham, U.K.: Surtees Society, 1875), 84; E. S. de Beer, ed., *The Diary of John Evelyn*, 6 vols. (Oxford: Oxford University Press, 1955), iii, 368.

7. Hooke, *The Child-birth*, sigs. B2v-B3; Crawford, "The Construction and Experience of Maternity," 19; *A Thanksgiving for the Queenes Maiesties Safe Deliverance* (1605; *STC* 16535), sig. A2v (the phrase "fruitful vine" derives from Judges 9:9 and 13); Jane Sharp, *The Midwives Book: Or the Whole Art of Midwifery Discovered* (1671), 18, 33; *The Problemes of Aristotle* (1597; *STC* 764); Alan Macfarlane, *The Family Life of Ralph Josselin: A Seventeenth-Century Clergyman: An Essay in Historical Anthropology* (Cambridge: Cambridge University Press, 1970), 83; Jacques Gélis, *History of Childbirth: Fertility, Pregnancy, and Birth in Early Modern Europe*, trans. Rosemary Morris (Boston: Northeastern University Press, 1991), 36; Gail Kern Paster, *The Body Embarrassed: Drama and the Disciplines of Shame in Early Modern England* (Ithaca, N.Y.: Cornell University Press, 1993), 166–84.

8. William Keatinge Clay, ed., *Liturgical Services: Liturgies and Occasional Forms of Prayer Set Forth in the Reign of Queen Elizabeth* (Cambridge: Cambridge University Press, 1847), 217, 199; *Articles Whereupon It Was Agreed by the Archbishoppes and Bishoppes of Both Provinces and the Whole Cleargie* (1571; *STC* 10036a), no. 9.

9. John Milton, Sonnet 19, in *The Poetical Works of John Milton*, ed. H. C. Beeching (Oxford: Oxford University Press, 1900), 86; Daniel Featley, *Ancilla Pietatis: or, The Hand-Maid to Private Devotion* (1626; *STC* 10725), 498; Daniel Featley, *Clavis Mystica: A Key Opening Divers Difficult and Mysterious Texts of Holy Scripture* (1636; *STC* 10730), 207; Sampson Price, *The Two Twins of Birth and Death* (1624; *STC* 20334); 8–14; Folger Shakespeare Library, Ms. V.a. 436, "Nehemiah Wallington, Writing Book 1654," 1.

10. John Donne, *Sermons*, ed. George R. Potter and Evelyn M. Simpson, 10 vols. (Berkeley: University of California Press, 1953–1962), 5:171–72. Within this one paragraph Donne cites Job 14:4; Pss. 5:6; 51:5; Prov. 30:12; and Eph. 2:3. According to Donne, baptism did not completely eradicate the stains of original sin (2:166).

11. John Day, *Day's Festivals or, Twelve of His Sermons* (Oxford, 1615; *STC* 6426), 236–37; John White, *The First Century of Scandalous, Malignant Priests* (1643), 50; Harold Smith, *The Ecclesiastical History of Essex under the Long Parliament and Commonwealth* (Colchester, 1932), 111, 171.

12. Charles Severn, ed., *Diary of the Rev. John Ward . . . 1648 to 1679* (1839), 102; R. S. Latham and W. Matthews, eds., *The Diary of Samuel Pepys*, 9 vols. (Berkeley: University of California Press, 1970–1976), 3:91.

13. Beryl Rowland, *Medieval Woman's Guide to Health: The First English Gynecological Handbook* (Kent, Ohio: Kent State University Press, 1981), 31; David Cressy, "De la Fiction dans les Archives? Ou le Monstre de 1569," *Annales École des Hautes Études en Sciences Sociales* 48 (1993): 1314.

14. Pollock, "Embarking on a Rough Passage," 52; John Parkinson, *Paradisi In Sole, Paradisus Terrestris: A Garden of All Sorts of Pleasant Flowers* (1629; *STC* 19300), 40, 199, 274; John Gerarde, *The Herbal or General Historie of Plantes* (1636; *STC* 11752); Leonard Sowerby, *The Ladies Dispensatory* (1652); John Manningham, *The Diary of John Manningham of the Middle Temple, 1602–1603*, ed. Robert Parker Sorlein (Hanover, N.H.: University Press of New England, 1976), 82; John Pechey, *Some Observations Made upon the Maldiva Nut: Shewing Its Admirable Virtue in Giving an Easie, Safe and Speedy Delivery to Women in Child-bed* (1694).

15. Keith Thomas, *Religion and the Decline of Magic: Studies in Popular Beliefs in Sixteenth- and Seventeenth-Century England* (New York: Oxford University Press, 1997 [1971]), 28, 31, 34, 73; James Gairdner, ed., *Letters and Papers, Foreign and Domestic, of the Reign of Henry VIII*, x (1887), 138-43; Walter Howard Frere, ed., *Visitation Articles and Injunctions of the Period of the Reformation*, 3 vols. (London: Longmans, Green, 1910), 2:59; Percival Price, *Bells and Man* (New York: Oxford University Press, 1983), 111; Gélis, *History of Childbirth*, 69–75, 116–18; Rowland, *Medieval Woman's Guide to Health*, 33.

16. *The Sarum Missal in English*, trans. Frederick E. Warren, 2 vols. (London: Mowbray, 1913), 2:161–64; John Bale, *A Declaration of Edmonde Bonners Articles concerning the Cleargye of London Diocese* (1561; *STC* 1289); fo. 61; Gélis, *History of Childbirth*, 69; Thornton, *Autobiography*, 145; de Beer, *Diary of John Evelyn*, 4:150, v. 190.

17. John Gerard, *The Autobiography of an Elizabethan* (London: Longmans, Green, 1951), 20; *Visitation Articles and Injunctions*, 2:59; *The Injunctions and Other Ecclesiastical Proceedings of Richard Barnes, Bishop of Durham, from 1577 to 1587* (Durham, U.K.: Surtees Society, 1850), 18; John Strype, *Annals of the Reformation*, 3 vols. (Oxford: Oxford University Press, 1824), 1:243; *The Book of Oaths* (1689), 162. Margo Todd is studying the "lost sacrament" of unction among the seventeenth-century Protestant ministry.

18. John Rylands Library, Manchester, Ms. 524, "The Acts and Speeches of Richard Greenham," fo. 35v.

19. Crawford, "The Construction and Experience of Maternity," 22; Sharp, *Midwives Book,* 182–83; Nicholas Culpeper, *A Directory for Midwives* (1651), 150–53; William Sermon, *The Ladies Companion, Or, the English Midwife* (1671), 96; Rowland, *Medieval Woman's Guide to Health,* 33–34; Thomas, *Decline of Magic,* 189–90.

20. Hill, *Pathway to Prayer and Pietie,* 411–13, qu. 411; Samuel Hieron, *A Helpe unto Devotion* (1612; *STC* 13407), 270–81; Featley, *Ancilla Pietatis: or, The Hand-Maid to Private Devotion,* 492–514, qu. 492.

21. *John Cosin: A Collection of Private Devotions,* ed. P. G. Stanwood (Oxford: Oxford University Press, 1967)287–88; Samuel Rowlands, "Godly Prayers," in *Heavens Glory, Seeke It* (1628; *STC* 21383), 228–31; George Wither, *Halelviah* (Manchester: 1641), 76–78; John Oliver, *A Present for Teeming Women: Or, Scripture-Directions for Women with Child, How to Prepare for the Hour of Travel* (1663), title page, sigs. A2, A3. Another edition, titled *A Present to Be Given to Teeming Women: By Their Husbands or Friends,* was published in 1669.

22. Pollock, "Embarking on a Rough Passage," 48; British Library, Egerton Ms. 607, "Devotional Pieces by Elizabeth Countess of Bridgewater," fos. 22v, 27, 31.

23. New College, Oxford, Ms. 9502, "Robert Woodforde's Diary."

24. *The Diary of Ralph Josselin 1616–1683,* ed. Alan Macfarlane (London: Oxford University Press, 1976), 50, 325, 403, 415; Macfarlane, *Family Life of Ralph Josselin,* 84.

25. *The Diary of the Rev. Henry Newcome, from September 30, 1661, to September 29, 1663,* ed. Thomas Heywood (Manchester: Chetham Society, 1849), 30; *The Autobiography of Henry Newcome, M.A.,* ed. Richard Parkinson (Manchester: Chetham Society, 1852), 303; *The Rev. Oliver Heywood, B.A. 1630–1702: His Autobiography, Diaries, Anecdote and Event Books,* ed. J. Horsfall Turner, 4 vols. (Brighouse, 1882–1885), 2:63, 73, 101, 222; 3:155.

26. *Prayers Appointed to be vsed in the Church at Morning and Evening Prayer by every Minister, For the Queenes safe deliverance* (1605; *STC* 16534), sigs. A2, A3v; *Thanksgiving for the Queenes Maiesties safe deliverance* (1605; *STC* 16535); *A Thanksgiuing and Prayer for the safe Child-bearing of the Queenes Maiestie* (1629, 1631; *STC* 16548.3, *STC* 16549.5). H. R. Wilton Hall, *Records of the Old Archdeaconry of St. Albans: A Calendar of Papers A.D. 1575 to A.D. 1637* (St. Albans, 1908), 127, records the distribution and reading of these prayers.

27. Hooke, *The Child-birth or Womans Lecture,* sig. D; *Prayers and Thanksgiving to Bee Used by All the Kings Maiesties Loving Subjects for the Happy Deliverance of His Maiestie, the Queene, Prince, and States of Parliament, from the Most Traiterous and Bloody Intended Massacre by Gunpowder, the Fift of November, 1605* (1605; *STC* 16494). For the cultural politics of these anniversaries, see David Cressy, *Bonfires and Bells: National Memory and the Protestant Calendar in Elizabethan and Stuart England* (Berkeley: University of California Press, 1989).

28. *A Continuation of Morning-Exercise Questions,* 662.

29. Henry Barrow, *Writings, 1587–1590,* ed. Leland H. Carlson (London: Allen & Unwin, 1962), 463; William Gouge, *Of Domesticall Duties,* 3rd ed. (1634; *STC* 12121), 405.

30. "The Diary of Richard Rogers," in *Two Elizabethan Puritan Diaries,* ed. M. M. Knappen (Gloucester, Mass.: P. Smith, 1966 [1933]), 73–74, 76.

31. *Diary of Ralph Josselin,* 50, 325, 415, 502; Macfarlane, *Family Life of Ralph Josselin,* 82–85.

32. Matthew Storey, ed., *Two East Anglian Diaries, 1641–1729: Isaac Archer and William Coe* (Woodbridge, Suffolk: Boydell, 1994), 125, 139.

33. *The Journal of Nicholas Assheton,* ed. F. R. Raines (Manchester: Chetham Society, 1848), 81; *Oliver Heywood's Life of John Angier,* 124–26.

34. *Diary of John Evelyn,* iv. 150.

35. Joceline, *Mothers Legacie, to Her Vnborne Childe,* sig. A5. "The Approbation" was written by Thomas Goad, rector of Hadleigh, Suffolk. Mrs. Joceline's story was retold in *A Continuation of Morning-Exercise Questions,* 654, and in N. H., *The Ladies Dictionary* (1694), 143. *The Mothers Legacy* was reprinted in 1625, 1635, 1684, and in its centenary year 1724.

36. Jacques Guillemeau, *Child-Birth, or The Happy Deliverie of Women* (1612; *STC* 12496), 86.

37. Roger Schofield, "Did the Mothers Really Die? Three Centuries of Maternal Mortality in The World We Have Lost," in *The World We Have Gained: Histories of Population and Social Structure,* ed. Lloyd Bonfield, Richard M. Smith, and Keith Wrightson (Oxford: Blackwell, 1986), 231–60; see Antonia Fraser, *The Weaker Vessel* (New York: Knopf, 1984), 59–80; Irvine Loudon, *Death in Childbirth: An International Study of Maternal Care and Maternal Mortality 1800–1950* (Oxford: Clarendon, 1992), 158–62; Adrian Wilson, "The Perils of Early Modern Procreation: Childbirth with or without Fear?" *British Journal for Eighteenth-Century Studies* 16 (1993): 1–19.

38. Cambridge University Library, Additional Ms. 8499. All quotations from Archer's diary can be found in *Two East Anglian Diaries,* 117–71.

Chapter Five. Baptism and Childhood

1. *Registres du Consistoire de Genève* (Registers of the Genevan Consistory), 3, f. 73, May 19, 1547.

2. *Registres du Consistoire de Genève,* 15, f. 152, August 17, 1559.

3. Philippe Ariès, *Centuries of Childhood: A Social History of Family Life,* trans. Robert Baldick (New York: Vintage, 1962); Lawrence Stone, *The Family, Sex and Marriage in England 1500–1800* (London: Weidenfeld and Nicolson, 1977); Edward Shorter, *The Making of the Modern Family* (New York: Basic Books, 1975); Nicholas Orme, *Medieval Children* (New Haven: Yale University Press, 2001); Shulamith Shahar, *Childhood in the Middle Ages,* trans. Chaya Galai (London: Routledge, 1992); Linda Pollock, *Forgotten Children: Parent–Child Relations from 1500 to 1900* (Cambridge: Cambridge University Press, 1983).

4 Linda Pollock, "Parent–Child Relations," in *The History of the European Family,* ed. David I. Kertzer and Marzio Barbagli, vol. 1: *Family Life in Early Modern Times 1500–1789* (New Haven: Yale University Press, 2001), 196; Pier Paolo Viazzo, "Mortality, Fertility and Family," trans. Caroline Beamish, in *Family Life in Early Modern Times,* ed. Kertzer and Barbagli, 164–69.

5. Karen E. Spierling, *Infant Baptism in Reformation Geneva: The Shaping of a Community 1536–1564* (Aldershot, U.K.: Ashgate, 2005), 42–50.

6. Spierling, *Infant Baptism*, 61–104, 170–76; Susan C. Karant-Nunn, *The Reformation of Ritual: An Interpretation of Early Modern Germany* (London: Routledge, 1997), 50–61.

7. *Registres du Consistoire de Genève*, 6, f. 29, April 30, 1551.

8. Orme, *Medieval Children*, 200–205; Gerald Strauss, *Luther's House of Learning: Indoctrination of the Young in Reformation Germany* (Baltimore: Johns Hopkins University Press, 1978), 157–58; Margo Todd, *The Culture of Protestantism in Early Modern Scotland* (New Haven: Yale University Press, 2002), 74.

9. Catechism quoted in Strauss, *Luther's House*, 164. Jean Louis Flandrin, *Families in Former Times: Kinship, Household and Sexuality*, trans. Richard Southern (Cambridge: Cambridge University Press, 1979), 110–11.

10. *Les Sources du droit du Canton de Genève*, vol. 2, ed. Émile Rivoire and Victor van Berchem (Arau: H. R. Sauerländer, 1933), 526 (March 1, 1549); *Registres du Consistoire de Genève*, 10, f. 9v, March 21, 1555; 15, f. 132, July 20, 1559; Spierling, *Infant Baptism*, 198–205; Raymond A. Mentzer, "*Disciplina nervus ecclesiae:* The Calvinist Reform of Morals at Nîmes," *Sixteenth Century Journal* 18, no. 1 (Spring 1987): 106; Todd, *Culture of Protestantism*, 42.

11. Quoted in Strauss, *Luther's House*, 198.

12. *Registres du Conseil de Genève* (Registers of the Genevan City Council), 30, f. 159, January 29, 1537; William G. Naphy, "The Reformation and the Evolution of Geneva's Schools," in *Reformations Old and New: Essays on the Socio-Economic Impact of Religious Change, c. 1470–1630*, ed. Beat Kümin (Aldershot, U.K.: Ashgate, 1996), 183–94.

13. Merry E. Wiesner, *Women and Gender in Early Modern Europe*, 2nd ed. (Cambridge: Cambridge University Press, 2000), 145–50.

14. Menno Simons, "The Nurture of Children" quoted in Keith Graber Miller, "Complex Innocence, Obligatory Nurturance, and Parental Vigilance: 'The Child' in the Work of Menno Simons" in *The Child in Christian Thought*, ed. Marcia J. Bunge (Grand Rapids: Eerdmans, 2001), 213; Steven Ozment, *When Fathers Ruled: Family Life in Reformation Europe* (Cambridge: Harvard University Press, 1983), 144–50; Joel F. Harrington, "Bad Parents, the State, and the Early Modern Civilizing Process," *German History* 16, no. 1 (1998): 16–28.

15. Shahar, *Childhood*, 143; see also Orme, *Medieval Children*, 98–100.

16. *Registres du Consistoire de Genève*, 17, f. 65v., April 25, 1560; Todd, *Culture of Protestantism*, 302.

17. *Registres du Consistoire de Genève*, 20, f. 12v, March 11, 1563.

18. Robert Jütte, *Poverty and Deviance in Early Modern Europe* (Cambridge: Cambridge University Press, 1994), 100–142; Timothy G. Fehler, *Poor Relief and Protestantism: The Evolution of Social Welfare in Sixteenth-Century Emden*, St. Andrews Studies in Reformation History (Aldershot, U.K.: Ashgate, 1999), 62–70, 154–218.

19. Todd, *Culture of Protestantism*, 311.

20. Fehler, *Evolution of Social Welfare*, 91–93, 195–98; Todd, *Culture of Protestantism*, 310–11; Joel Harrington, "Escape from the Great Confinement: The Genealogy of a German Workhouse," *Journal of Modern History* 71, no. 2 (June 1999): 308–45.

21. Martin Dinges, "Huguenot Poor Relief and Health Care in the Sixteenth and Seventeenth Centuries," in *Society and Culture in the Huguenot World 1559–1685*, ed. Raymond A. Mentzer and Andrew Spicer (Cambridge: Cambridge University Press, 2002), 157–59.

22. George von Grumbach to his parents; 5 June 1525. Bavarian Central State Archives; Personenselekt Cat. 110: f. 11.

Chapter Six. Women and Men, Together and Apart

1. 1569 church ordinance from Wolfenbüttel, quoted in Susan C. Karant-Nunn, *The Reformation of Ritual: An Interpretation of Early Modern Germany* (London: Routledge, 1997), 80.

2. *Twelve Articles of the Peasants*, quoted in Peter Blickle, *Communal Reformation: The Quest for Salvation in Sixteenth-Century Germany*, trans. Thomas A. Brady Jr. and H. C. Erik Mielfot (Atlantic Highlands, N.J.: Humanities, 1992), 21.

3. Swiss democracy, so praised in the stories about William Tell, continued that gender division until very recently, for Switzerland was the last country in Europe in which women were given the right to vote. They won suffrage only in 1971, after eighty-two referenda, and they still cannot vote in certain local elections today.

4. "Common woman"—*gemeine Frau* in German—was the standard phrase for a woman who sold sex for money, what we would now call a prostitute. (The word "prostitute" was not used until the nineteenth century.) She was termed "common" not because she was lower-class or ordinary, but because her sexual activities were shared in common by many men rather than being available only to her husband.

5. Translated and quoted in John H. Bratt, "The Role and Status of Women in the Writings of John Calvin," in Peter de Klerk, ed., *Renaissance, Reformation, Resurgence* (Grand Rapids: Calvin Theological Seminary, 1976), 9.

6. A saying attributed to the Ursulines, quoted and translated in Elizabeth Rapley, *The Dévotes: Women and Church in Seventeenth-Century France* (Montreal: McGill-Queen's University Press, 1990), 29.

7. Strasbourg, Archives municipales, Akten der XXI, 1631, fol. 40, my translation.

8. Jewish women in early modern Europe continued to observe the Levitical prescriptions as much as they could; Jewish quarters in many cities had special baths for women's purification rituals after menstruation and childbirth.

9. Quoted in David Cressy, *Birth, Marriage and Death: Ritual, Religion, and the Life Cycle in Tudor and Stuart England* (Oxford: Oxford University Press, 1997), 227.

10. Injunctions of the bishops of Salisbury, Gloucester, and York, cited in Cressy, *Birth*, 118.

11. Adolph Franz, ed., *Das Rituale des Bishofs Heinrich I. von Breslau* (Freiburg: Herder, 1912), 23.

12. Translated and quoted in Karant-Nunn, *Reformation*, 20.

13. The Church of England, *The Two Books of Homilies* (Oxford, 1859), 505.

14. Franz V. Spechtler and Rudolf Uminsky, eds., *Die Salzburger Landesordnung von 1526* (Göppingen: Kimmerle, 1981), 119, my translation.

15. Johannes Geiler von Kaisersberg, *Die aeltesten Schriften* (Freiberg in Breisgau: Herder, 1877), 73, my translation.

Chapter Seven. Leaving the World

1. Philippe Ariès, *The Hour of Our Death*, trans. Helen Weaver (London: Penguin Books, 1981), 189—an example from late medieval Paris.

2. Ronald Finucane, "Sacred Corpse, Profane Carrion: Social Ideals and Death Rituals in the Later Middle Ages," in *Mirrors of Mortality: Studies in the Social History of Death*, ed. Joachim Whaley (London: Europa, 1981), 42.

3. Ralph Houlbrooke, *Death, Religion and the Family in England, 1480–1750* (Oxford: Clarendon, 1998), 153.

4. Germain Marc'hadour, "Introduction," in Thomas More, *The Supplication of Souls*, ed. Frank Manley et al., Yale Edition of the Works of St. Thomas More (New Haven: Yale University Press 1990), xciii; Craig M. Koslofsky, *The Reformation of the Dead: Death and Ritual in Early Modern Germany, 1450–1700* (New York: St Martin's, 2000), 26.

5. A. N. Galpern, "The Legacy of Late Medieval Religion in Sixteenth-Century Champagne," in *The Pursuit of Holiness in Late Medieval and Renaissance Religion*, ed. C. Trinkaus and H. O. Oberman (Leiden: Brill, 1974), 149.

6. Joyce Youings, *The Dissolution of the Monasteries*, Historical Problems: Studies and Documents 14 (London: Allen & Unwin, 1971), 140.

7. Peter Marshall, *Beliefs and the Dead in Reformation England* (Oxford: Oxford University Press, 2002), 26.

8. Ibid., 53–56; Steven E. Ozment, *The Reformation in the Cities: The Appeal of Protestantism to Sixteenth-Century Germany and Switzerland* (New Haven: Yale University Press, 1975), 71, 111–16.

9. Koslofsky, *Reformation of the Dead*, 40–78; Susan Karant-Nunn, *The Reformation of Ritual: An Interpretation of Early Modern Germany* (London: Routledge, 1997), 178–79; Andrew Spicer, "'Defyle Not Christ's Kirk with Your Carrion': Burial and the Development of Burial Aisles in Post-Reformation Scotland," in *The Place of the Dead: Death and Remembrance in Late Medieval and Early Modern Europe*, ed. Bruce Gordon and Peter Marshall (Cambridge: Cambridge University Press, 2000), 149–69.

10. Patrick Collinson, "England," in *The Reformation in National Context*, ed. Bob Scribner, Roy Porter, and Mikúlash Teich (Cambridge: Cambridge University Press, 1994), 88.

11. Andrew Spicer, "'Rest of their Bones': Fear of Death and Reformed Burial Practices," in *Fear in Early Modern Society*, ed. William Naphy and Penny Roberts (Manchester: Manchester University Press, 1997), 168, 176; Euan Cameron, *The European Reformation* (Oxford: Oxford University Press, 1991), 233; Marshall, *Beliefs and the Dead*, 206, ch. 4; Anthony Fletcher and Diarmaid MacCulloch, *Tudor Rebellions*, 5th ed. (Harlow: Pearson Education, 2004), 152; Karant-Nunn, *Reformation of Ritual*, 185; Jürgen Beyer, "A Lübeck Prophet in Local and Lutheran Context," in *Popular Religion in Germany and Central Europe, 1400–1800*, ed. Bob Scribner and Trevor Johnson (New York: St. Martin's, 1996), 166–82.

12. Peter Marshall, "Angels around the Deathbed: Variations on a Theme in the English Art of Dying," in *Angels in the Early Modern World*, ed. Peter Marshall and Alexandra Walsham (Cambridge: Cambridge University Press, 2006).

13. Houlbrooke, *Death, Religion and the Family*, 165–70; Karant-Nunn, *Reformation of Ritual*, 145–52; Jay Goodale, "The Clergyman between the Cultures of State and Parish: Contestation and Compromise in Reformation Saxony," in *The Protestant Clergy of Early Modern Europe*, ed. Scott Dixon and Luise Schorn-Schütte (New York: Palgrave Macmillian, 2003), 106.

14. Marshall, *Beliefs and the Dead*, ch. 5; Bruce Gordon, "Malevolent Ghosts and Ministering Angels: Apparitions and Pastoral Care in the Swiss Reformation," in Gordon and Marshall, *Place of the Dead*, 104.

15. Clare Gittings, *Death, Burial and the Individual in Early Modern England* (London: Croom Helm, 1984), 60–65; Spicer, "Rest of their Bones," 175, 177; Penny Roberts, "Contesting Sacred Space: Burial Disputes in Sixteenth-Century France," in Gordon and Marshall, *Place of the Dead*; John Bossy, *The English Catholic Community 1570–1850* (London: Darton, Longman and Todd, 1975), 140–43; David Dymond, "God's Disputed Acre," *Journal of Ecclesiastical History* 50, no. 3 (1999): 464–97.

16. Patrick Collinson, "'A Magazine of Religious Patterns': An Erasmian Topic Transposed in English Protestantism," in Patrick Collinson, *Godly People: Essays on English Protestantism and Puritanism* (London: Hambledon, 1983); Koslofsky, *Reformation of the Dead*, 82, 107–14.

17. Bob Scribner, "Introduction," in Scribner and Johnson, *Popular Religion*, 10.

Chapter Eight. The Dream of a Just Society

1. Adolf Laube, "Radicalism as a Research Problem in Early Reformation," in *Radical Tendencies in the Reformation: Divergent Perspectives*, ed. Hans J. Hillerbrand (Kirksville, Mo.: Sixteenth Century Journal, 1988), 9–23.

2. Heiko A. Oberman, "The Gospel of Social Unrest," in *The German Peasant War of 1525: New Viewpoints*, ed. Bob Scribner and Gerhard Benecke (London: Allen & Unwin, 1979), 39–51.

3. Heinz Schilling, "Confessional Europe," in *Handbook of European History, 1400–1600*, ed. Thomas A. Brady Jr., Heiko A. Oberman, and James D. Tracy (Leiden: Brill 1995), 2:641–81.

4. W. Ian P. Hazlett, "Settlements: The British Isles," in Brady, Oberman, and Tracy, *Handbook of European History, 1400–1600*, 2:480: "They embodied the Kirk's aspirations rather than achieved reality. Yet their educational, social welfare, and disciplinary policies appealed to ordinary people."

5. Günther Franz, *Der deutsche Bauernkrieg* (Darmstadt: Wissenschaftliche Buchgesellschaft, 1977), 62–79; Tom Scott, *Freiburg and the Breisgau: Town–Country Relations in the Age of Reformation and Peasants' War* (Oxford: Clarendon, 1986), 173–89, where the Fritz conspiracies are presented as indubitable matters of fact.

6. Oberman, "Gospel of Social Unrest," 40.

7. Miriam Usher Chrisman, *Conflicting Visions of Reform: German Lay Propaganda Pamphlets, 1519–1530* (Atlantic Highlands, N.J.: Humanities, 1996), 65–89.

8. Ulrich Bubenheimer, *Thomas Müntzer: Herkunft und Bildung* (Leiden: Brill 1989).

9. See *The German Peasants' War: A History in Documents*, trans. and ed. Tom Scott and Bob Scribner (Atlantic Highlands, N.J.: Humanities, 1991), 19–28.

10. Adolf Laube, "Lotzer, Sebastian," and "Schappeler, Christoph," in *The Oxford Encyclopedia of the Reformation*, ed. Hans J. Hillerbrand (New York: Oxford University Press, 1996), 2:454–55, 4:1. Laube prefers Lotzer as single author of the *Twelve Articles*: "Whether Schappeler had directly participated in the formulation of the Twelve Articles—the most widely circulated program of the German Peasants' War—is controversial. In all probability the wording is solely that of Sebastian Lotzer."

11. Text in Peter Blickle, *The Revolution of 1525: The German Peasants' War from a New Perspective*, trans. Thomas A. Brady Jr. and H. C. Erik Midelfort (Baltimore: Johns Hopkins University Press, 1981), 195–201.

12. Text in Scott and Scribner, *German Peasants' War*, 130–32.

13. Peter Blickle, "Republiktheorie aus revolutionärer Erfahrung (1525)," in *Verborgene republikanische Traditionen* (Tübingen: Bibliotheca Academica, 1998), 195–210.

14. Abbreviated text in Scott and Scribner, *German Peasants' War*, 269–76.

15. Oberman, "Gospel of Social Unrest," 48.

16. Hans-Jürgen Goertz, *Thomas Müntzer: Apocalyptic Mystic and Revolutionary* (Edinburgh: T & T Clark, 1993), 173–207: R. Emmet McLaughlin, "Apocalypticism and Thomas Müntzer," *Archive for Reformation History* 95 (2004): 98–131.

17. Werner O. Packull, "The Image of the Common Man in the Early Pamphlets of the Reformation (1520–1525)," *Historical Reflections* 12 (1985): 253–77.

18. Blickle, *Revolution of 1525*, 185.

19. James M. Stayer, "The Passing of the Radical Moment in the Radical Reformation," *Mennonite Quarterly Review* 71 (1997): 147–52.

20. Franz Lau, "Der Bauernkrieg und das angebliche Ende der lutherischen Reformation als spontaner Volksbewegung," *Luther-Jahrbuch* 26 (1959): 109–34.

21. Bruce Gordon, *The Swiss Reformation* (Manchester: Manchester University Press, 2002), 146–90, 283–316; see also Amy Nelson Burnett, "Basel and the Wittenberg Concord," *Archive for Reformation History* 96 (2005): 33–56.

22. Thanks are due to Tom Scott for his invaluable advice in the composition of this chapter.

Chapter Nine. The Emergence of Lay Theologies

1. Ursula Weyda, *Wyder das unchristlich Schreyben und Lesterbuoch des Apts Simon zuo Pegaw* (Eisenberg, 1524), C3v.

2. See Carlo Ginzburg, *The Cheese and the Worms: The Cosmos of a Sixteenth-Century Miller*, trans. John and Anne Tedeschi (Baltimore: Johns Hopkins University Press, 1980); Anselm Schubert, *Augustin Bader, das Schwert des Messias: Reformation, Täufertum und Kabbalah* (Habilitationsschrift, Georg-August-Universität Göttingen, 2006).

3. Camilla Russell, *Giulia Gonzaga and Religious Controversies in Sixteenth-Century Italy* (Turnhout, Belgium: Brepols, 2006), 99.

4. Elsie Anne McKee, *Katharina Schütz Zell*, vol. 2: *The Writings: A Critical Edition* (Leiden: Brill, 1999), 194.

5. Thieleman Van Braght, *The Bloody Theater or Martyrs Mirror of the Defenseless Christians Who Baptized Only upon Confession of Faith, and Who Suffered and Died for the Testimony of Jesus, Their Saviour, from the Time of Christ to the Year A.D. 1660,* trans. Joseph F. Sohm (Scottdale, Pa.: Herald Press, 1992), 436, gives a good example of Mark 13:13 in the letter of Walter of Stoelwijk. See also Katharina Schütz Zell, *Church Mother: The Writings of a Protestant Reformer in Sixteenth-Century Germany* (Chicago: University of Chicago Press, 2006), 166–67.

6. Brad S. Gregory, *Salvation at Stake: Christian Martyrdom in Early Modern Europe* (Cambridge: Harvard University Press, 1999), 197 et passim; 441 n. 6 lists bibliography on Anabaptist hymnody. See also Barbara Diefendorf, "The Huguenot Psalter and the Faith of French Protestants in the Sixteenth Century," in *Culture and Identity in Early Modern Europe (1500–1800): Essays in Honor of Natalie Zemon Davis,* ed. Barbara Diefendorf and Carla Hesse (Ann Arbor: University of Michigan Press, 1993), 41–63; Horton Davies, *Worship and Theology in England: I. From Cranmer to Hooker, 1534–1603* (Princeton: Princeton University Press, 1970), 384–91, and *II. From Andrewes to Baxter and Fox, 1603–1690* (Princeton: Princeton University Press, 1975), 268–81.

7. Elsie Anne McKee, *John Calvin: Writings on Pastoral Piety* (Mahwah, N.J.: Paulist, 2001), 217–19, for Rivery; Thomas A. Lambert, "Preaching, Praying and Policing the Reform in Sixteenth Century Geneva" (Ph.D. dissertation, University of Wisconsin, Madison, 1998), 342–43, for parodies; Schütz Zell, *Church Mother,* 92–96.

Chapter Ten. Insiders and Outsiders

1. Susan R. Boettcher, "Confessionalization: Reformation, Religion, Absolutism, and Modernity," *History Compass* 2:1 (2004).

2. See, for example, Tessa Watt, *Cheap Print and Popular Piety 1550–1640* (Cambridge: Cambridge University Press, 1991).

3. For some examples of "morisco" encounters with the Inquisition, see Lu Ann Homza, *The Spanish Inquisition, 1478–1614: An Anthology of Sources* (Indianapolis: Hackett, 2006).

4. Stephen A. Fischer-Galati, *Ottoman Imperialism and German Protestantism, 1521–1555* (Cambridge: Harvard University Press, 1959); For a parallel perspective on how the question of dealing militarily with "outsiders" affected relationships between "insiders," see Sigrun Haude, *In the Shadow of "Savage Wolves": Anabaptist Münster and the German Reformation during the 1530s* (Boston: Humanities Press, 2000).

5. On the accuracy of the Cluniac Corpus, see Thomas E. Burman, "Tafsir and Translation: Traditional Arabic Qur'an Exegesis and the Latin Qur'ans of Robert Ketton and Mark of Toledo," *Speculum* 73 (1998), 703–32.

6. UB (University Library) Basel Ms. A III 19.

7. Harry Clark, "The Publication of the Koran in Latin: A Reformation Dilemma," *Sixteenth Century Journal* 15 (1984), 3–12.

8. Silke Falkner, "Having It Off with Fishes, Camels, and Lads: Sodomitic Pleasures in German-Language Turcica," *Journal of the History of Sexuality* 13 (2004), 401–27.

9. Edward Seymour Forster, trans., *The Turkish Letters of Ogier Ghiselin de Busbecq* (Baton Rouge: Louisiana State University Press, 2005).

10. Almut Höfert, *Den Feind beschreiben: "Türkengefähr" und europäisches Wissen über das Osmanische Reich, 1450–1600* (Frankfurt/Main: Campus Verlag, 2003).

11. Yaacov Deutsch, "Polemical Ethnographies: Descriptions of Yom Kippur in the Writings of Christian Hebraists And Jewish Converts to Christianity in Early Modern Europe," in *Hebraica Veritas,* Allison P. Coudert and Jeffrey S. Shoulson, eds. (Philadelphia: University of Pennsylvania Press, 2004).

12. Erika Rummel, *The Case Against Johannes Reuchlin: Religious and Social Controversy in Sixteenth-Century Germany* (Toronto: University of Toronto Press, 2002).

13. Susan R. Boettcher, "Preliminary Considerations on the Rhetorical Construction of Jews in Lutheran Preaching at Mid-Sixteenth Century," *Bundeseinheit und Gottesvolk. Reformierter Protestantismus und Judentum im Europa des 16. und 17. Jahrhunderts.* Achim Detmers, ed. (Wuppertal: Foedus, 2005), 105–36.

14. Robert Kingdon, ed., *Registres du Consistoire de Geneve au temps de Calvin* (Geneva: Droz, 1996f).

15. Heiko A. Oberman, *The Reformation. Roots and Ramifications* (Edinburgh: T & T Clark,1994) esp. 217–20.

16. Henning P. Jürgens, *Johannes a Lasco in Ostfriesland. Der Werdegang eines europaischen Reformators* (Tübingen: Mohr Siebeck, 2002).

17. This is the conclusion of Philip Benedict, *Rouen during the Wars of Religion* (Cambridge: Cambridge University Press, 1981). An excellent book on late medieval and Reformation conceptions of poverty, from which much of the following material is drawn, is Lee Palmer Wandel, *Always Among Us: Images of the Poor in Zwingli's Zurich* (Cambridge: Cambridge University Press, 1991).

18. A useful overview of poor relief arrangements in specific European contexts from which much of this overview is drawn is Thomas Max Safley, ed., *The Reformation of Charity: The Secular and the Religious in Early Modern Poor Relief* (Leiden: Brill, 2003).

19. Timothy G. Fehler drew my attention to this case; see also his book, *Poor Relief and Protestantism: The Evolution of Social Welfare in Sixteenth-Century Emden* (Aldershot: Ashgate, 1999). Similar instances of connecting church discipline with poor relief in Emden after the mid-1570s are found in Heinz Schilling, ed., *Die Kirchenratsprotokollen der Gemeinde Emden,* 2 vols. (Cologne: Böhlau, 1989).

Chapter Eleven. The Language of the Common Folk

1. "Wie kündth ers doch teutscher geredt habenn?" Utz Rychsner *Ain hüpsch Gesprechbiechlin,* H.-J.Köhler, *Flugschriften des 16 Jahrhunderts* 9/36 (Augsburg: Heinrich Steiner, 1524), Ciii; hereafter *Gesprechbiechlin.*

2. *Ain schöne Unterweysung* Köhler 737/1881 (Augsburg: Heinrich Steiner 1524), Bv; hereafter *Unterweysung.*

3. Thomas Stör, *Von dem Christlichen Weingarten*, Köhler: Fiche 99/261 (Zwickau: Jörg Gastel, 1524), Ai.

4. Andrew Morrall, *Jörg Breu the Elder: Art, Culture and Belief in Reformation Augsburg* (Aldershot, U.K.: Ashgate, 2002).

5. Martin Luther, "Ach Gott, vom Himmel sieh darein," in Markus Jenny, *Luthers Geistliche Lieder und Kirchengesänge*, Archiv zur Weimarer Ausgabe der Werke Martin Luthers, vol. 4 (Cologne, Vienna: Böhlau Verlag, 1524), 177, my translation.

6. *Gesprechbiechlin*, Ai.

7. Peter Matheson, *Argula von Grumbach: A Woman's Voice in the Reformation* (Edinburgh: T & T Clark, 1995), 56–95.

8. *Ein fast tröstlich, christelich, unüberwindlich Beschirmbüchlin*, Köhler, 1306–7/3382 (Augsburg: Melchior Ramminger, 1524), Aii.

9. *Gesprechbiechlin*, Aiiv; Matheson, *Argula von Grumbach*, 89.

10. *Gesprechbiechlin*, Aiiv.

11. Gary K. Waite, *Reformers on Stage: Popular Drama and Religious Propaganda in the Low Countries, 1515–1556* (Toronto: University of Toronto Press, 2000).

12. *Unterweysung*, Aiii, Aii, Aiiv, Biiiv; *Gesprechbiechlin*, Biii; *Unterweysung*, Aiiiv Aiiiiiv, Diii, Aiiiiv, Biiv, Di; *Gesprechbiechlin*, Bi, Aiii; *Unterweysung*, Civ, Cii; *Gesprechbiechlin*, Ciii, Ciiiiv, Ciiii, Cii,; *Unterweysung*, Eiii, Di, Eiv, Biiiv; *Gesprechbiechlin*, Eiv; *Unterweysung*, Biiv, Ci; *Gesprechbiechlin*, Aii; *Unterweysung*, Div, Biiiiv, Diiiv.

13. Otto Clemen, "Ein Spottgedicht aus Speier von 1524," Archiv für Reformationsgeschichte 5 (1906): 78, my translation.

14. *The Collected Works of Thomas Müntzer*, ed. and trans. Peter Matheson (Edinburgh: T & T Clark, 1988), 162–82.

15. See David B. Paxman, *Voyage into Language: Space and the Linguistic Encounter, 1500–1800*. (Aldershot, U.K.: Ashgate, 2003), especially 23, 98.

16. *Sämtliche Fabeln und Schwänke von Hans Sachs*, vol. 5, ed. Edmund Goetze and Carl Drescher (Halle: Max Niemeyer, 1904), 21, my translation.

17. Arno Schirokauer, "Der Anteil des Buchdrucks an der Bildung des Gemeindeutschen," *Deutsche Vierteljahresschrift für Literaturwissenschaft und Geistesgeschichte* 25 (1951): 343, quoted in Frederic Hartweg, "Buchdruck und Druckersprachen," in *Flugschriften als Massenmedium der Reformationszeit*, ed. H.-J. Köhler (Stuttgart: Ernst Klett, 1981), 50, my translation.

18. Peter Matheson, *The Rhetoric of the Reformation* (Edinburgh: T & T Clark, 1998), and *The Imaginative World of the Reformation* (Minneapolis: Fortress Press, 2002).

INDEX